KAMPUCHEA

Marxist Regimes Series

Series editor: Bogdan Szajkowski,
Department of Sociology, University College,
Cardiff

Afghanistan Bhabani Sen Gupta
Angola Keith Somerville
Ethiopia Peter Schwab
Ghana Donald I. Ray
Grenada Tony Thorndike
Guyana Colin Baber and Henry B. Jeffrey
Hungary Hans-Georg Heinrich
Kampuchea Michael Vickery
Marxist Local Governments in Western Europe and Japan ed. Bogdan Szajkowski
Romania Michael Shafir
Soviet Union Ronald J. Hill

Further Titles

Albania
Benin and The Congo
Bulgaria
Cape Verde, São Tomé and Príncipe
China
Cuba
Czechoslovakia
German Democratic Republic
Guinea-Bissau
Democratic People's Republic of Korea
Laos
Madagascar
Mongolia
Mozambique
Nicaragua
Poland
Surinam
Vietnam
People's Democratic Republic of Yemen
Yugoslavia
Zimbabwe
Marxist State Governments in India
The Diversification of Communism
Comparative Analysis
Cumulative Index

KAMPUCHEA

Politics, Economics and Society

Michael Vickery

Frances Pinter (Publishers), London
Lynne Rienner Publishers, Inc., Boulder

First published in Great Britain in 1986 by
Frances Pinter (Publishers) Limited
25 Floral Street, London WC2E 9DS

First published in the United States of America by
Lynne Rienner Publications Inc.
948 North Street
Boulder, Colorado 80302

Printed in Great Britain

British Library Cataloguing in Publication Data

Vickery, Michael
Kampuchea: politics, economics and society.—
(Marxist regimes series)
1. Cambodia—Social traditions—1975-
I. Title II. Series
959.6'04 HN700.3.A8
ISBN 0-86187-422-6
ISBN 0-86187-423-4 (Pbk)

Library of Congress Cataloging in Publication Data

Vickery, Michael.
Kampuchea: politics, economics and society.
(Marxist regimes series)
Bibliography: p.
1. Cambodia—Politics and government—1975—
2. Cambodia—Economic conditions. 3. Cambodia—
Social conditions. I. Title. II. Series.
JQ932.V53 1986 959.6'04 86-479
ISBN 0-931477-73-5
ISBN 0-931477-74-3 (pbk.)

Typeset by Joshua Associates Limited, Oxford
Printed by SRP Ltd, Exeter

Editors Preface

For many years now Kampuchea (also known as Cambodia) has been a battle zone for local as well as superpower interests. The consequences of these ongoing rivalries have had a devastating effect on the Khmer people, their ancient civilization and culture. In recent times Kampuchea has seen more dramatic changes than most countries in the region. The country even has the doubtful distinction of being the only one where the Marxist regime (that of Pol Pot) was overthrown by another Marxist government with the help of a Marxist neighbour (Vietnam). This book describes and analyses the present as well as the past in this small and backward country with its peasant economy, and suggests the type of lessons that might be learnt from the Kampuchean experience by other smaller states in the developing regions of the world.

The example and experience of Kampuchea is particularly interesting to the study of Marxist regimes, which has commonly been simply equated with the study of communist political systems. For many years it was not difficult to distinguish the eight regimes in Eastern Europe and four in Asia which resoundingly claimed adherence to the tenets of Marxism and more particularly to their Soviet interpretation—Marxism–Leninism. These regimes, variously called 'People's Republic', 'People's Democratic Republic', or 'Democratic Republic', claimed to have derived their inspiration from the Soviet Union to which, indeed, in the overwhelming number of cases they owed their establishment.

To many scholars and analysts these regimes represented a multiplication of and geographical extension of the 'Soviet model' and consequently of the Soviet sphere of influence. Although there were clearly substantial similarities between the Soviet Union and the people's democracies, especially in the initial phases of their development, these were often overstressed at the expense of noticing the differences between these political systems.

It took a few years for scholars to realize that generalizing the particular, i.e. applying the Soviet experience to other states ruled by elites which claimed to be guided by 'scientific socialism', was not good enough. The relative simplicity of the assumption of a cohesive communist bloc was questioned after the expulsion of Yugoslavia from the Communist Information Bureau in 1948 and in particular after the workers' riots in Poznań in 1956 and the Hungarian revolution of the same year. By the mid-1960s, the totalitarian model of communist politics, which until then had been very much in force, began to crumble. As some of these regimes articulated demands for a distinctive path of socialist development, many specialists studying these systems began to notice that the cohesiveness of the communist bloc was less apparent than had been claimed before.

Also by the mid-1960s, in the newly independent African states 'democratic' multi-party states were turning into one-party states or military dictatorships, thus questioning the inherent superiority of liberal democracy, capitalism and the values that went with it. Scholars now began to ponder on the simple contrast between multi-party democracy and a one-party totalitarian rule that had satisfied an earlier generation.

More importantly, however, by the beginning of that decade Cuba had a revolution without Soviet help, a revolution which subsequently became to many political elites in the Third World not only an inspiration but a clear military, political and ideological example to follow. Apart from its romantic appeal, to many nationalist movements the Cuban revolution also demonstrated a novel way of conducting and winning a nationalist, anti-imperialist war and accepting Marxism as the state ideology without a vanguard communist party. The Cuban precedent was subsequently followed in one respect or another by scores of regimes in the Third World who used the adoption of 'scientific socialism' tied to the tradition of Marxist thought as a form of mobilization, legitimation or association with the prestigious symbols and powerful high-status regimes such as the Soviet Union, China, Cuba and Vietnam.

Despite all these changes the study of Marxist regimes remains in its infancy and continues to be hampered by constant and not always pertinent comparison with the Soviet Union, thus somewhat blurring the important underlying common theme—the 'scientific theory' of the laws of development of human society and human history. This doctrine is claimed by the leadership of these regimes to consist of the discovery of objective causal relationships; it is used to analyse the contradictions which arise between goals and actuality in the pursuit of a common destiny. Thus the political elites of these countries have been and continue to be influenced in both their ideology and their political practice by Marxism more than any other current of social thought and political practice.

The growth in the number and global significance, as well as the ideological political and economic impact, of Marxist regimes has presented scholars and students with an increasing challenge. In meeting this challenge, social scientists on both sides of the political divide have put forward a dazzling profusion of terms, models, programmes and varieties of interpretation. It is against the background of this profusion that the present comprehensive series on Marxist regimes is offered.

This collection of monographs is envisaged as a series of multi-disciplinary textbooks on the governments, politics, economics and society of these countries. Each of the monographs was prepared by a specialist on the country concerned. Thus, over fifty scholars from all over the world have contributed monographs which were based on first-hand knowledge. The geographical diversity of the authors, combined with the fact that as a group they represent many disciplines of social science, gives their individual analyses and the series as a whole an additional dimension.

Each of the scholars who contributed to this series was asked to analyse such topics as the political culture, the governmental structure, the ruling party, other mass organizations, party-state relations, the policy process, the economy, domestic and foreign relations together with any features peculiar to the country under discussion.

This series does not aim at assigning authenticity or authority to any single one of the political systems included in it. It shows that depending on a variety of historical, cultural, ethnic and political factors, the pursuit of goals derived from the tenets of Marxism has produced different political forms at different times and in different places. It also illustrates the rich diversity among these societies, where attempts to achieve a synthesis between goals derived from Marxism on the one hand, and national realities on the other, have often meant distinctive approaches and solutions to the problems of social, political and economic development.

University College
Cardiff

Bogdan Szajkowski

Contents

Acknowledgements

Facilities for writing this book were provided by the Centre for Asian Studies and the Thai Ceramics Archaeological Project, University of Adelaide.

Within the People's Republic of Kampuchea arrangements for travel and research were made by the Press Section, Ministry of Foreign Affairs, and the guide assigned to me for my visit in November 1984, Miss Chea Chan Nakry, was particularly helpful. I would also like to thank the various PRK officials who gave time to answer my questions about their departments.

In Phnom Penh, Fred and Minh Kauffman of the Mennonite Central Committee provided hospitality and photocopying facilities; and Jake Buhler of the same organization has also been very helpful.

During the 1984 trip, Otome Hutheesing collaborated in the collection of data, and she has aided me in the preparation of the text.

David Chandler, Noam Chomsky, Stephen Heder, Serge Thion and, in particular, Ben Kiernan have provided me with information from their own research or published material of which I had not been aware; and Ben Kiernan corrected several errors in the first draft of Chapter 3. None of them, of course, is responsible for any errors which may remain.

List of Tables

Preface

The Name of the Country

The name 'Kampuchea', or *kambuja* in conformity with traditional orthography, first appears in Cambodia in tenth-century inscriptions to refer to the people, the *kambu-ja*, 'born of Kambu'—a figure of Indian mythology. Eventually, via the expression *kambuja-desa*, 'Kambuja-country', or 'country of those born of Kambu', the term came to mean the country itself; and in early modern times it passed into European languages as Camboxa (Portuguese), Cambodge (French), and Cambodia (English). Since at least the sixteenth-century 'Kampuchea' has been part of the country's official name in Khmer, except under Lon Nol who preferred 'Khmer' (Khmer Republic), another native ethnic term of perhaps greater antiquity than 'Kampuchea'. The term 'Khmer' is still current and appropriate as an ethnonym or language name, both within Cambodia and in foreign languages.

The name 'Cambodia' then, like 'Italy', 'Spain', and 'Turkey', is a well-established English equivalent of the native name, and I prefer to use it when writing in English, except when emphasizing proper titles, such as People's Republic of Kampuchea (PRK) and Democratic Kampuchea (DK).

Sources and Their Use

This book is based as far as possible on material from within Cambodia—written material provided by the government; the local press; my own observations, including interviews and informal conversations with Cambodian officials and people met in casual encounters; and information provided by foreign aid personnel working there. This has been supplemented by the work of other scholars and by reports in the international press.

I have also occasionally made use of information from refugees on the Thai border, or published accounts of other writers based on such material. As I have demonstrated elsewhere (Vickery 1984), however, such information may be very useful only if the source can be interviewed independently and analytically. The raw statements of refugees about PRK wrongdoing and Vietnamese iniquities are too frequently exaggerated or patently false.

The political and international situation of the PRK makes research difficult, much more difficult than in most of the European Marxist states.

The PRK, after replacing a regime almost universally recognized as loathsome, has found itself subjected to more, and increasing, sustained political and military opposition fuelled by prestigious foreign support than the regime that it replaced. The foreign support has come from China, the ASEAN states and the United States, and with respect to the last represents continuing destructive interest by that power in Cambodia for the past ten years.

Cambodia is thus at war, with normal wartime restrictions on travel and research, particularly by foreigners. Since 1979 I have made two visits—for three weeks in August-September 1981 and for five weeks from the end of October through November 1984. The last visit I was told by both PRK officials and by foreigners working in Cambodia, was unusually long. It is nevertheless not long enough to investigate everything that should go into a book like this one. Normal descriptive documentation of state organization, and normal statistical documentation in available published form do not yet exist in the PRK. All such information must be obtained through interviews with people who are usually overworked. Moreover, even though I emphasized that I did not insist on meeting cabinet ministers, that I would be satisifed with anyone who could provide the information I required, in most cases it was only a minister who was willing to talk about the work of a ministry. For the formal acquisition of information, one must reach the top to get anything at all. Thus, much detailed information on organization, and most statistical information I wanted, was placed on my agenda for a meeting with the Planning Ministry, which in the end never took place because of other commitments by its officials during the period of my visa.

I consider that these difficulties arise from the country's objective situation, and are not due to ill will or a desire to disguise the true picture. Given Cambodia's experiences with the West, in particular with the United States, Cambodia has been quite generous in according travel and research facilities to Americans.

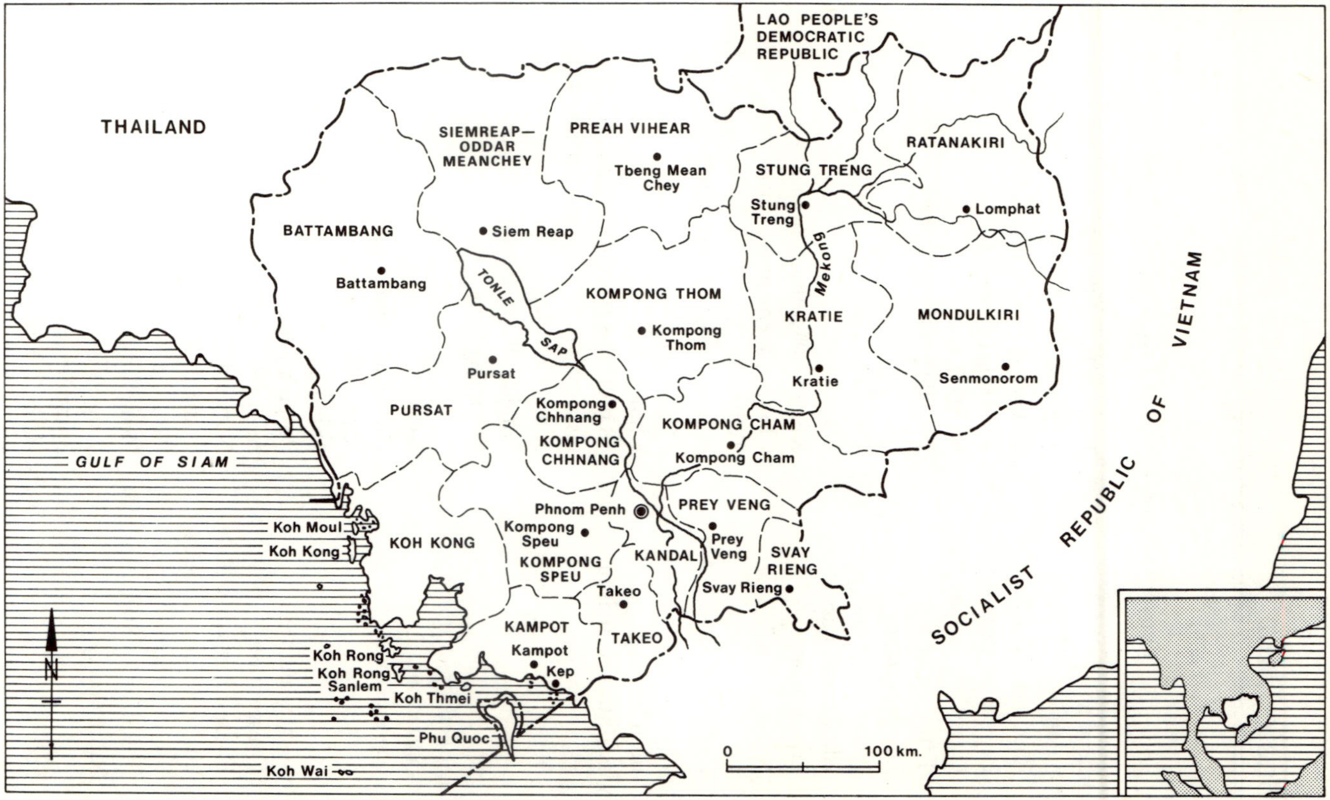
THAILAND
LAO PEOPLE'S DEMOCRATIC REPUBLIC
SOCIALIST REPUBLIC OF VIETNAM
GULF OF SIAM
BATTAMBANG
Battambang
SIEMREAP—ODDAR MEANCHEY
Siem Reap
PREAH VIHEAR
Tbeng Mean Chey
STUNG TRENG
Stung Treng
RATANAKIRI
Lomphat
MONDULKIRI
Senmonorom
KRATIE
Kratie
Mekong
TONLE SAP
KOMPONG THOM
Kompong Thom
PURSAT
Pursat
Kompong Chhnang
KOMPONG CHHNANG
KOMPONG CHAM
Kompong Cham
Phnom Penh
PREY VENG
Prey Veng
SVAY RIENG
Svay Rieng
KANDAL
Kompong Speu
KOMPONG SPEU
KOH KONG
Takeo
TAKEO
KAMPOT
Kampot
Kep
Koh Moul
Koh Kong
Koh Rong
Koh Rong Sanlem
Koh Thmei
Phu Quoc
Koh Wai
N
0
100 km.

Basic Data

Only PRK, post-1979 data have been considered

Official name	People's Republic of Kampuchea
Population	7.2 million (1984)
Population density	100 per sq. km. in heartland
Population growth (% p.a.)	2.5–3,000 (1979–85)
Urban population (%)	6.95 (1985)
Total labour force	145,000 (state employees)
Life expectancy	n/a
Infant death rate (per 1,000)	150–200
Child death rate	n/a
Ethnic groups	Khmer, 90%; ethnic minorities include Chinese, Vietnamese, Cham, Brao, Tampuon, Pear, Kachak, Stieng, Lao, Thai
Capital	Phnom Penh, 500,000 (1985)
Land area	181,000 sq. km.
Official language	Khmer
Administrative divisions	18 provinces (*khet*), divided into 122 districts (*srok*), 1,325 sub-districts (*khum*), and 9,386 villages (*phum*), plus two municipalities—Phnom Penh and Kompong Som
Membership of international organizations	None
Foreign relations	Diplomatic and consular relations with 27 states; representatives of 10 countries residing in Phnom Penh (November 1984)
Political structure	People's Republic
Constitution	As of July 1981
Highest legislative body	National Assembly of 117 members
Highest executive body	Council of State
Prime Minister	Hun Sen (since January 1985)
President (of State Council)	Heng Samrin
Ruling party	People's Revolutionary Party of Kampuchea
Secretary General of the Party	Heng Samrin (since December 1981)

Party Membership	10,000 est.
Growth indicators	n/a
National income	n/a
Food production per capita	n/a
Exports	$4–5 million (1983)
Imports	$200 million (1983)
Exports as % of GNP	n/a
Main exports	Rubber, beans, timber, kapok, tobacco
Main imports (% n/a)	Food, consumer goods, fuel, raw materials, equipment
Destination of exports (%)	Socialist countries 95. Non-socialist countries 5
Main trading partners	Vietnam, Soviet Union, Eastern Europe
Foreign debt	n/a
Foreign aid	$150 million p.a., est.
Food self-sufficiency	Est. 310,000 ton deficit (1985)
Foreign investment	n/a, probably none
Armed forces	30,000 est.
Education and health	
School system	10 years (7–17)
Primary school enrolment	1,689,690 (1983–4)
Secondary school enrolment	6,969 (1983–4)
Higher education	Faculty of Medicine, Denistry and Pharmacy; Kampuchea-Soviet Higher Technical Institute; Language School; teacher training institutions
Adult literacy	n/a
Population per hospital bed	n/a
Population per physician	n/a
Economy	
GNP	n/a
State budget	n/a
Defence expenditure as % of state budget	n/a
Main crops	Rice, rubber, beans, kapok, tobacco
Land tenure	State ownership with family allotments of 1,500 sq. m.
Main religions	Buddhism (90%+), Islam, folk religion

Population Forecasting

The following data are projections produced by Poptran, University College Cardiff Population Centre, from United Nations Assessment Data published in 1980, and are reproduced here to provide some basis of comparison with other countries covered by the Marxist Regimes Series.

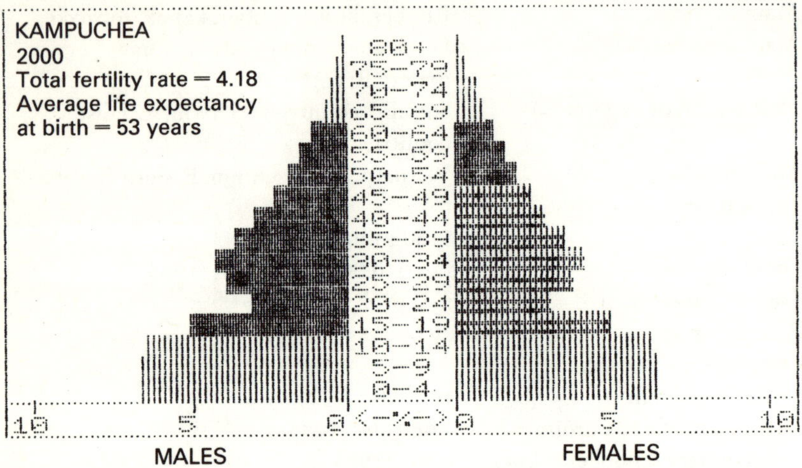

Projected Data for Kampuchea 2000

Total population ('000)	10,610
Males ('000)	5,315
Females ('000)	5,295
Total fertility rate	4.10
Life expectancy (male)	51.9 years
Life expectancy (female)	55.0 years
Crude birth rate	30.7
Crude death rate	12.8
Annual growth rate	1.79%
Under 15s	38.49%
Over 65s	3.62%
Woman aged 15–49	24.27%
Doubling time	39 years
Population density	59 per sq. km.
Urban population	23.7%

Abbreviations

DK	Democratic Kampuchea
DRV	Democratic Republic of Vietnam
ICP	Indo-China Communist Party
KPRC	Kampuchean People's Revolutionary Council
KPRP	Khmer People's Revolutionary Party (founded 1951)
NLF	National Liberation Front
PRC	People's Revolutionary Committee
PRK	People's Republic of Kampuchea
PRPK	People's Revolutionary Party of Kampuchea (1981–)
RGNUC	Royal Government of National Union of Cambodia
Sangkum	Sangkum Reastr Niyum (Popular Socialist Community), Sihanouk's political movement from 1955 to 1970
SRV	Socialist Republic of Vietnam
SWB	*Summary of World Broadcasts*
UIF	United Issarak Front

Glossary of Khmer terms

cau sanghat	ward chief
corvée	a tax
dong	unit of Vietnamese currency
Khet	province
khmer loeu	upland Khmer
kret-chbap	Decree-Law
krom pracheachon	citizen's group
krom samakki	Solidarity Groups
protean	president
riel	unit of Cambodian currency
sangharaja	'Sangha King', title of the head of the Buddhist Monkhood before 1975
sanghat	ward
srok	district (sub-division of a province)
wat	Buddhist temple

Part 1
History, Political Traditions and Social Structure

1 Geographical Setting

Cambodia is situated in South-East Asia between 10° and 15° degrees latitude and between 102° and 108° longitude. Its area is 181,000 square kilometres; and it is bounded on the east and south-east by Vietnam, on the west by Thailand, and in the north by Thailand and Laos. Along the south and south-west, Cambodia faces the Gulf of Thailand.

The climate is monsoon tropical, with a rainy season lasting from April to September in the central agricultural area, where most of the population live. The rest of the year is relatively dry. Mean temperatures vary from 21° to 35° C.

The country consists mainly of low plains cut by many rivers, most of which flow into the Mekong or the Tonle Sap, the inland sea in the country's centre, which joins the Mekong at Phnom Penh. There are low mountain ranges along the northern border with Thailand and in the south-west, and the north-east is a forested plateau of higher altitude than the central plain. An important geographical peculiarity of the country is that during the Mekong flood season between June and October the overflow from the Mekong causes the Tonle Sap to reverse its course and the Tonle Sap expands to several times its normal area, silting and fertilizing the rice plains and providing a large supply of fresh-water fish. The high-water point is around 1 October, and from mid-October the Mekong begins to recede and the Tonle Sap resumes its normal flow. All important water courses within Cambodia's modern boundaries feed into the Mekong-Tonle Sap system. Along the south-west coast a few rivers flow seaward, but they do not provide outlets for the country's central agricultural area where population centres have developed.

Although this unified water-course system has always been an integrative factor, especially prior to the construction of modern roads, the ultimate channels into which everything flows are the Mekong and Bassac which reach the sea across what is now southern Vietnam. There is no other good southern route to the sea out of central Cambodia. The economy of all of southern and eastern Cambodia, if it is not to be autarkic, depends on control of the mouths of those two rivers. Seen in another way, whoever controls the area around the river mouths can exert strong pressure on Cambodia south of the Tonle Sap.

In the north-west the rivers also flow into the Tonle Sap, but that area is close, just across a narrow watershed, to other rivers flowing into the Gulf of Thailand, and very near to one good, short overland portage to such an alternative river system via the Wattana Gap. There is thus an objective geographical potential for Cambodia's north-west to become orientated towards the West, if political conditions, for instance, should render the eastward orientation precarious. Cambodia thus has an inherent geographical-economic tendency towards fissiparity, which has in fact been manifest in many instances throughout its history.

The natural wealth of the country lies chiefly in agriculture, forest products and fishing. Over 80 per cent of the population live in the central plain where rice is the most important product. Here also lie the rich fishing grounds of the Tonle Sap inland sea and connecting rivers. The production of industrial raw materials such as rubber and cotton was important before the 1970–5 war and these are slowly being redeveloped. Much of the west and north-east consists of forested hills containing valuable timber. Industrial-quality mineral deposits have not been discovered, although iron exists and has traditionally been exploited by local craftsmen.[1]

The Population

A rather high degree of ethnic homogeneity prevails, with the majority Khmer (including related Mon-Khmer groups) accounting for 90–95 per cent of the population. The most important minority are the Islamic, Malayo-Polynesian speaking Cham, who are believed to number about 185,000 in the PRK today.[2] Several smaller ethnic groups linguistically related to the Khmer, and in some cases to the Cham, inhabit outlying areas, in particular the north-eastern hills, but also the far west, northern Kompong Thom Province, and one very small group near the south coast in Kampot Province.[3] Before 1970 Chinese and Vietnamese each accounted for 6–7 per cent of the population, but virtually all Vietnamese were expelled or killed in 1970–9, and are now slowly drifting back in numbers currently estimated at 2-300,000. Chinese numbers have also diminished, first because as urban dwellers they were susceptible to the rigours of 1975–9, and because a disproportionate number have chosen to emigrate since 1979.[4]

Cambodian demography in general, and in particular the total population figure, has occasioned considerable controversy since 1979. At one extreme, 3 million, or nearly half the 1975 population, are said to have died in 1975–9; and in fact that figure is official doctrine in the PRK. On the other hand, current estimates of PRK population, both by Cambodian government organs and by international agencies are in the order of 7.2 million, and there are half a million more outside that estimate, on the Thai border or abroad. This suggests that the death toll over normal was well under one million. PRK officials wish to have it both ways—3 million dead *and* over 7 million now alive—somthing demographically implausible, if not impossible.[5]

There is little doubt that the estimated present total is fairly accurate, as accurate as the pre-war population figures. Even if a census as such has not been taken, each administrative entity maintains running totals of its populations which are forwarded and totalled at the next higher level.[6]

2 Historical Background

The Cambodians, or Khmer, unlike their neighbours the Thai and the Vietnamese, have inhabited their present homeland since the beginning of recorded history in the second and third centuries AD. Between the ninth and the fourteenth centuries their state, known conventionally as the Angkor Empire, encompassed present-day Cambodia and parts of Thailand, Laos and Vietnam. During the fourteenth and fifteenth centuries the political and economic centre shifted from Angkor, north of the Tonle Sap inland sea, to the Phnom Penh region, and Cambodia, like its neighbours, became orientated towards the international maritime trade route. By the eighteenth century the competition from rival polities, Ayutthaya in the west and Champa, then Vietnam, in the east, had prevailed, and by the mid-nineteenth century Cambodia had become a semi-independent state subordinate to its neighbours (see Coedès 1968; Briggs, 1951; Vickery, 1977; Chandler, 1983a).

French interest in Cambodia began at that time, and the first French conquests in southern Vietnam in 1859–61 were followed by a protectorate treaty with Cambodia in 1863. French authority rested lightly on Cambodia under this treaty, and provided King Norodom with the needed protection against both the Thai and local dissidents (Chandler, 1983a, pp. 139–41).

In June 1884 another treaty, intended to modernize Cambodian administration and put French officials at the heart of the system, was imposed on King Norodom against his wishes. In reaction, serious rebellions broke out in several parts of Cambodia, and they threatened both the new French regime and its Cambodian royal clients. From early 1885 fighting lasted a year and a half, several thousand French and allied Vietnamese troops were tied down, and the rebels only laid down their arms when King Norodom was allowed to proclaim that the French would continue to respect Cambodian customs and laws—that is, the pre-treaty system. Although the treaty was ratified in 1886, most of its provisions did not come into effect until twenty years later, after King Norodom's death (Chandler, 1983a, pp. 144–5).

Thereafter, until the independence struggles following the Second World War, no revolt of such magnitude threatened the authorities, and the Cambodian population acquired its reputation for cheerful passivity. Signs of discontent were there, but they never resulted in broadly-based action.

The low level of active mass opposition was not due to any particular benevolence of the regime. Cambodians paid the highest taxes in Indo-China, supporting not only the French colonial budget but also the parallel Cambodian administration which the French were protecting, and whose royal and aristocratic elites still demanded traditional privileges and dues, even if many of their *de jure* rights had been shorn after 1884. The French demand for exports depressed living standards (Chandler, 1983a, p. 156) and on some construction projects death tolls among the corvée labour-force rivalled the human destruction of the 1975–9 revolution (Vickery, 1984, p. 15, Chap. 1, n. 42).

Neither was there an elite or intellectual opposition to French domination equivalent to the nationalist movements in Vietnam, perhaps simply because the protectorate *did* offer some protection for the status of traditional elites, while the few new men who rose through the very limited educational system were accommodated in prestigious posts.

The most famous elite protest after the nineteenth-century rebellions was that of Prince Yukanthor, eldest son of King Norodom and heir presumptive, in 1901 (Hess, 1901). But Yukanthor was calling, not for the overthrow of the protectorate, but for more protection for the traditional aristocracy whose positions were being undermined by talented upstarts in the French service.

The heyday of the upstarts was the reign of Sisowath (1904–27), a collaborator of the French since the 1870s, and whom the French had often used as a threat against his recalcitrant brother Norodom, and that of Sisowath's son Monivong (1927–41). With kings who no longer opposed the French, traditional-style rebellions abated, or turned into banditry pure and simple, and as Cambodia 'became a relatively efficient revenue-production machine' (Chandler, 1983a, p. 148), a number of enterprising men saw the advantage of aiding the French in the collection of produce, and a whole new class of French-orientated officialdom was formed, some of them descendants of old courtier families, others of lower-class origin who saw the advantage of learning French language and methods at a time when the royalty and aristocray still looked down on all that was foreign.

The most famous of the 'new men', and the one who most attracted Yukanthor's ire, was Palace Minister Thiounn, who started out as a secretary to French officials in the 1880s, by the early twentieth century had risen to be Minister of the Palace and virtual Prime Minister, and who did not retire until 1941.[1] He was the epitome of the colonial subject who quickly saw how to turn the new regime to an advantage which would not have been open to his class under the traditional monarchy. Although such men seemed 'revolutionary' to princes like Yukanthor, they did not seek to overturn the social system, but only to secure places for themselves at the top. Accepted for their ability by the French in a way that they would not have been accepted previously, they served the new regime energetically while, incidentally, amassing considerable personal wealth.[2] Many of them established new 'aristocratic' families, which are still prominent today. Thiounn's grandsons, for example, among the first Cambodians to have full university education in France, are among the Democratic Kampuchea (Pol Pot) leadership (Vickery, 1984, Chap. 5, n. 8; Kiernan, 1984, pp. 30–2).

Although the Thiounns were among the first, and the most notorious, the Cambodian administrative structure which continued to grow throughout the twentieth century alongside and subordinate to the French came to be staffed by a new elite descending partly from former aristocracy, but to a large extent from men who owed their new fortunes to the French Protectorate. Right across the political spectrum of the 1960s and 1970s, from Lon Nol to Son Sann, and including Sihanouk courtiers like Nhiek Tioulong, the modern Cambodian political elite descended from, and often were themselves, French colonial functionaries. In the provinces they carried on from countless generations of similar men, sometimes their own ancestors, but they also took over positions at the centre which had once been princely prerogatives. While the ministries throughout the 1930s contained many princes, their absence after 1945 was conspicuous, and royalty, outside the palace, either lived aimlessly on inherited wealth or worked in subordinate administrative jobs. Princes at the top, like Sirik Matak, were a rarity after the early 1950s, and it is no doubt significant that he was from a minor branch of royalty (Yukanthor, 1955, pp. 248–58).

Thus Cambodia, despite neglect and exploitation, was peaceful; at least there was no attempt to overturn the system or expel the French. There was endemic banditry, often as destructive for the communities involved as revolution, but it was without political content and was not a major threat to the Protectorate. Only two significant episodes of political opposition stand out in the early twentieth century, the 1916 Affair and the assassination of *Résident* Bardez in 1925, and they are more remarkable for what they were not than for what they were.

Both these events were intimately related to economic exploitation in the form of excessive taxation. In the early months of 1916 numerous peasant delegations from the eastern provinces—in total perhaps as many as 100,000 people—travelled to Phnom Penh to present petitions to the King complaining of high taxes. They were peaceful, and they dispersed when exhorted to return home by the King, who promised to alleviate their problems. The demonstrations were not particularly anti-French, and had no effect on the way the French ran the country. What surprised the authorities was the rapidity and efficiency with which they were organized—unexpected in the supposedly lazy and individualistic Cambodians (Chandler, 1984, pp. 153–4; Osborne, 1978, p. 242). That unexpected organizational ability no doubt presaged events of the 1950s and 1970s, equally surprising to those who found themselves opposed by the later peasant movements.

The second noteworthy political event of the time, the Bardez Affair, was the only murder of a French official on duty to occur in the twentieth century. Ferdinand Bardez, an effective tax collector who was then *résident* in Kompong Chhnang, was killed, together with his Cambodian interpreter and a militiaman, while trying to collect taxes in an outlying village. A crowd of several hundred began to march on the provincial seat to demand remission of taxes, but dispersed before reaching their destination, and the episode did not lead to further political ferment (Chandler, 1983a).[3]

Another phenomenon of the 1920s, which was non-violent and not overtly political, but which had political implications worth attention at the present time, was the interest of numbers of ordinary Cambodians in the Vietnamese Cao Dai religion. Around 1927, again in a time of severe economic difficulties, thousands of Cambodian peasants began making pilgrimages to worship and participate in ceremonies at the Cao Dai headquarters near Tayninh, unconcerned that Cao Dai was the faith of their 'hereditary enemy', the Vietnamese. In the words of one historian, this may have 'reflected the reaction of a disoriented peasantry ready to turn to the newly offered salvation that they believed would involve the regeneration of the Cambodian state (Osborne, 1978, p. 242; Vickery, 1984, pp. 12, 180). At the very least it should put one on guard against any facile dogma about Cambodian-Vietnamese incompatibility.

3 Modern Political History: The Development of Marxist Groups

Before the Second World War

Only in the late 1930s was a modern nationalist movement formed, interestingly under the leadership of Khmers from the 'lost' Cambodian provinces of Kampuchea Krom, 'lower Cambodia', in southern Vietnam (Cochin-China) who were perhaps less in awe of traditional Cambodian symbols of authority such as the King. They were joined by descendants of the new men who had incurred Yukanthor's ire;[1] and the new Cambodian nationalists, with the Khmer-language newspaper *Nagaravatta* as their mouthpiece, although exceedingly moderate, were a threat to the French with their demand for independence, and to the Cambodian royalty, with their ideas for social and economic modernization—perhaps even a closet republicanism.

Under the leadership of San Ngoc Thanh and Pach Chhoeun, Vietnam Khmers who were respectively adviser and editor of *Nagaravatta*, this loosely organized group conducted their propaganda efforts from 1936 to 1942. The war brought little change within Cambodia, since Franco-Japanese agreement maintained the colonial administration in Indo-China while giving the Japanese the facilities they desired. Eventually, clandestine anti-French propaganda conducted among monks and Cambodian soldiers in the colonial service resulted in arrests; and in July 1942 a mass demonstration protesting the arrest of monks engaged in this nationalist propaganda work was broken up by the police and several leaders were arrested (Kiernan, 1984, pp. 40–60). Son Ngoc Thanh escaped to Japan, others were imprisoned in Pulou Condore, and *Nagaravatta* was closed.

On 9 March 1945 the Japanese interned the French and offered independence to the three Indo-China states. King Sihanouk took up the offer, abrogated all treaties with the French, promulgated a new Basic Law, and formed a government of traditionalists who had already made administrative careers under the French. In May, Son Ngoc Thanh was brought back from Japan and was soon appointed Minister of Foreign Affairs, then, after a group of his young followers invaded the palace on 9 August, Sihanouk was forced to make Thanh Prime Minister.[2]

The Thanh government showed their intention to make the most of such independence as had been granted; and some of Thanh's pronouncements, long forgotten, are worth reviewing at the present time. Already, as Foreign Minister, Thanh took control of all domestic propaganda, and his ministry announced the following propaganda programme in July:

1. support the Great Asian War, which is the emancipation of the peoples of this part of the world;
2. only complete victory will guarantee independence;
3. reawaken the historical grandeur of 'Kampuchea' (in French text);
4. create a national army;
5. achieve the union of all peoples in Cambodia, especially the Annamites and the Khmer;
6. concentration of all economic activities.

In connection with (4), it was announced that the Japanese were forming a troop of 'Cambodian Volunteers', the Captain of which was Thiounn Muong, who had just returned from a 'long exile because of his activities in favour of racial solidarity', presumably between Vietnamese and Khmer.

There seems also to have been considerable ferment in the school system. The Thanhist group wished to eliminate French influence, and to remove the language from primary schools; and among the Phnom Penh intellectuals there was a movement to introduce Annamite as the first foreign language. This was apparently not popular with the King, for measures emanating from the palace were calling for the Khmerization of the schools, though without Vietnamese; and while Thanh was advocating 'close relations with the Annamite Empire', Sihanouk spoke out against a Vietnamese government proclamation to unify all of the old Vietnamese Empire's territory, if it included Cochin-China. Perhaps in answer to this was the denial from Thanh's camp, in an article about his organization of a club for 'Khmero-Annamite rapprochement' in 1938, that the Khmer and the Vietnamese were preparing to fight one another. This was followed a week later, on 23 August 1945, by a long article on the similarities between the Khmer and the 'Annamites'. Thanh also recognized Ho Chi Minh's independent Vietnam, on 2 September 1945, and allowed a Vietnamese mission to be established in Phnom Penh.[3]

Two weeks later *Cambodge* was warning the populace of the imminent arrival of British and French troops to disarm the Japanese and by mid-October Thanh had been removed to Saigon, according to a communiqué signed by British Brigadier-General Murray, because of 'his activities contrary to the security of the allied troops and to the detriment of Cambodia'.[4]

The goals of the Thanh-*Nagaravatta* nationalists seem moderate today, but they shocked the traditionalists and may have contributed to the alacrity, even enthusiasm, with which the latter greeted British, then French, troops who began arriving in September 1945 to disarm the Japanese and restore French authority. The young rebels were imprisoned, Son Ngoc Thanh was packed off to exile in France, Sihanouk stayed on his protected throne, and among the seven members of the first ministerial cabinet after the French return there were three from Sihanouk's first independence cabinet from March to August and four who had been appointed by Son Ngoc Thanh. The Cambodian elite was very adaptable.[5]

Post-war Politics to Independence

The position of this elite was to be threatened more by certain democratic reforms which the French now introduced than by either the Japanese occupation of Indo-China or the re-establishment of the French protectorate. A modern constitution was promulgated, with regular elections, a cabinet responsible to the National Assembly, and tolerance for political parties. The first three elections, in 1946 for the Constitutional Convention, and in 1948 and 1951 for the National Assembly, were conveniently won by the Democrat Party which was both anti-French and anti-Sihanouk, with direct links to the Son Ngoc Thanh nationalists (and to more radical groups), who, as they returned from exile or were released from prison, joined it. Thus the democratic reforms which the French had hoped would secure Cambodian loyalty gave prominence and authority to a party eager for independence (Kiernan & Boua, 1982, pp. 89–113; Chandler, 1983a, pp. 178–80; Kiernan, 1984, p. 57). The goals of this largely urban party were even more threatening since in the rural areas armed resistance against the French was developing along with Vietnam's war for independence.

This armed resistance marks the first certain appearance of a Cambodian communist or Marxist organization which, at the time, in the 1940s, was only one among several armed groups fighting for independence with or without revolution. The earliest of these groups was not communist. In 1940 the first Khmer Issarak ('freedom') Committee had been set up by a Cambodian exile in Bangkok, Poc Khun. At the time this worried the *Nagaravatta* group who were afraid of Thai encroachment and who were, as we have seen, relatively pro-Vietnamese. After the dispersal of Thanh's government in 1945 Pach Chhoeun established another Khmer Issarak Committee along the Vietnamese border, but it was soon suppressed by the French (Kiernan, 1984, pp. 41–52).

During 1946–7 the Thai government under Pridi Panomyong and his collaborators sympathized with the Khmer independence movement and provided it with aid and facilities. There was also co-operation among the Thai-orientated and Vietnam-orientated Khmer groups, with the future leader of Cambodian communism, who soon took the name Son Ngoc Minh, joining the Indo-China Communist Party (ICP) in Thailand in 1946. Other future prominent communists, such as Tou Samouth, also joined the ICP at that time. The co-operation of different elements created what appear in retrospect to have been some very strange bedfellows. When Issarak forces seized the town of Siemreap in August 1946, Son Ngoc Minh was there under the command of future pro-American warlord Dap Chhuon, and they included rebel Prince Norodom Chantaraingsey, who ended his career as the Khmer Republic's most effective general during the 1970–5 war.[6]

Throughout 1945–7 groups were founded and then fell apart as leaders sorted out their ideological positions and political alliances. Stability, on the left, increased in 1948 when a Khmer People's Liberation Committee was formed in Battambang. Chantaraingsey refused to join on the grounds that it was pro-Viet Minh, but Dap Chhuon still commanded its troops. Its first manifesto called for 'an Indochinese Front for Independence', and Dap Chhuon exchanged congratulatory telegrams with Ho Chi Minh.[7]

A major reorganization of the revolutionary independence forces came on 17 April 1950, when two hundred delegates met in the south-west of Cambodia in a congress which established the Unified Issarak Front (UIF), under Son Ngoc Minh, and with five of fifteen identified leaders as members of the ICP. The congress also established a proto-government, the Provisional People's Liberation Committee, likewise headed by Son Ngoc Minh.[8]

The next step was the formation of a Cambodian revolutionary party, an event believed to have taken place most likely between February and June 1951, following a decision of the Second congress of the ICP to split into three national parties. The provisional Central Committee of the new organ was headed by Son Ngoc Minh with Tou Samouth as a member.[9]

By 1952 the Issarak and KPRP forces were winning in the countryside, controlling from half to three-fifths of the country, and the situation was becoming intolerable for the French and for the Cambodian right. In June Dap Chhuon, now a military pillar of the establishment, scattered leaflets in Phnom Penh calling for the King and the people to take action against the government. French tanks were patrolling in the capital, and the French Minister for Associated States declared that France would make no concession (toward independence) to a Democratic government.[10]

In these circumstances Sihanouk dismissed the government, then assumed personal leadership, while promising to achieve independence within three years. Sihanouk's declaration had a good deal of effect, for many outside the hard core of the Issarak and KPRP (Khmer People's Revolutionary Party) forces were fighting for independence and nothing more.

In January 1953 Sihanouk augmented his personal authority by abolishing both houses of parliament and proclaiming a special law which abridged all democratic rights. In February he launched his 'Royal Crusade for Independence', in the face of which many of the small Issarak groups broke up, with some of their leaders joining the royal army. The French, hard pressed in Vietnam, were persuaded to negotiate now that the Cambodian government seemed securely in conservative hands; so that by November 1953 the attributes of independence had been transferred to Sihanouk. His high-handed methods notwithstanding, Sihanouk had made good his pledge (Kiernan & Boua, 1982b, pp. 95–6; Kiernan, 1984, pp. 131–2; Chandler 1983a, pp. 186–8).

This first period of anti-colonial and revolutionary struggle, ending with independence in 1953, had been dominated in rural areas by men of peasant or small-town background, such as Son Ngoc Minh and Tou Samouth, who organized the peasantry and were close to the Vietnamese, and in Phnom Penh by the radical nationalists, also sympathetic to Vietnam at the time, who looked to Son Ngoc Thanh. In the meantime, another revolutionary current had been developing among Cambodian students in Paris who formed a 'Marxist Circle', which included such now familiar names as Saloth Sar (Pol Pot), Ieng Sary, their wives—the sisters Khieu Thirith and Khieu Ponnary—Hou Yuon, Thiounn Mum, and others active in DK. In Paris they studied Marxist classics, became acquainted with international movements of the left, and they seem to have had some affiliation with the French Communist Party. Saloth Sar in 1950 spent a month on a work brigade in Yugoslavia, unusual for someone of his supposed orientation. More orthodox was the journey he made with other members of the group to the International Youth Congress in East Berlin in August 1951, where they are said to have come into conflict with the Vietnamese delegates (Kiernan, 1984, pp. 120–1; Vickery, 1984, pp. 265, 275, ff.).

In spite of their ideological tendencies, they were out of touch with the domestic communists, whose experiences were entirely foreign to the elite students. In January 1953 several of the Paris group, including Saloth Sar, returned to Cambodia, and by August 1953 Sar reached the communist zone in Eastern Cambodia where he presented himself as a member of the French Communist Party. Sar and his fellow students were taken in hand by the Khmer Veterans and the Vietnamese and were instructed in combat and revolutionary politics, but they did not attain leadership positions, a circumstance which left a deep resentment in some of them.[11]

Independence and its confirmation by the Geneva Conference of July 1954 represented a defeat for all progressive currents of Cambodian politics from the KPRP through the Thanhist guerrillas to the urban Democrats. In contrast to Vietnam and Laos, the Cambodian revolutionary forces were allowed no regroupment zone, and were left with no choice but to lay down their arms and reintegrate with Cambodian society under Sihanouk and his conservative supporters. About one thousand of the leading KPRP cadre, including Son Ngoc Minh, withdrew to North Vietnam, while the rest who remained active changed from armed to political struggle in order to contest the coming elections as *krom pracheachon* (citizens' group)—in fact the new political face of the KPRP.

If Geneva disappointed the Cambodian left, it also added an unexpected difficulty to the plans of the right. The latter, under Sihanouk, had hoped to continue the dictatorial regime instituted with Sihanouk's January 1953 coup, but the Geneva accords required all three Indo-China countries to hold elections, in Cambodia before the end of 1955, under existing constitutions and with freedom for all factions, including the participation of former guerrillas. This made possible the open organization of the Pracheachon (Citizens) under Keo Meas, Non Suon and Pen Yuth, while the old Democrat Party was revitalized and pushed leftward by former students of the Paris Marxist Circle, such as Keng Vannsak and Thiounn Mum, possibly with organizational work by Saloth Sar. Because of the Democrats' previous successes, and the popularity which both groups had gained during the anti-French struggle, it was anticipated that in an honest election the parties of the left would win an easy victory.

The election did not proceed honestly and the right managed to unite in a way unexpected in view of their pre-independence electoral débâcles (Kiernan & Boua, 1982b, pp. 118, 157, 181). The result was total victory for the Sangkum, and from then until 1970, through subsequent elections in 1958, 1962 and 1966, no non-Sangkum politician sat in the National Assembly. This does not mean that the Sangkum was ideologically monolithic. The pragmatic Sihanouk was willing to co-opt talent from any source, even from among his leftist opponents, if they pledged loyalty and worked for the goals he defined. Thus, a number of former Democrats soon joined the Sangkum, as did Hou Yuon and eventually Khieu Samphan of the Paris student group, and Hu Nim, who had started out as a Thanhist, then joined the radicalized Democrat party in 1955, aftwards moving further leftward (Kiernan & Boua, 1982b, pp. 118, 157, 181).

For several years the leftists in the Sangkum probably believed that they could gradually achieve their original goals peacefully by pushing Sihanouk leftwards, and indeed the increasingly close relations which he cultivated with the socialist countries and his lip-service to 'socialism' easily encouraged such a delusion. Their efforts to educate Sihanouk in the complexities of international politics and economic matters, and the support they gave to his foreign policy, together with the access to publicity which their work within the Sangkum permitted, may have really contributed to some progressive drift within the country. Nevertheless, in any major domestic policy conflict Sihanouk inevitably came down firmly on the side of the far right. In the meantime the work of the left within the Sangkum served to distance these talented intellectuals from the KPRP/Pracheachon, which was being taken over by a different sort of leadership.

Polarization After Independence

The divisions among the different kinds of radicals began to assume importance after Geneva and the Sangkum victory of 1955. It was perhaps in 1956 that a new KPRP Central Committee was formed; it is said to have been divided into two nearly autonomous urban and rural sections with the former theoretically in control. It seems certain that from 1956 Tou Samouth headed the urban section which had overall responsibility although he was rarely present, while Sieu Heng, a veteran of the anti-French war, led the rural section; but statements about the identities of the remaining members are confused.[12]

Two distinct lines were also beginning to emerge, although one may not place much confidence in retrospective comments on who held which. One line, the dominant one, was that of the urban intellectuals who hoped to push Sihanouk leftward, and of the Vietnamese, who understood the utility of a neutralist Cambodia under a strong nationalist ruler for their own continuing struggle. They held that Sihanouk, owing to the successful conclusion of his independence campaign, was too popular to be overthrown, and that the policy of the left should be to encourage him in his anti-American stand. This was also the policy favoured by the Soviet Union, and was plainly supported by China, whose leadership maintained particularly close relations with Sihanouk.[13]

The other line was that Sihanouk and the 'feudal' class were the principal enemy, and their overthrow should be the first goal of the Cambodian revolution. This was the line eventually adopted by the party under Pol Pot's leadership, and it was probably his own conviction from the beginning, but there is now a tendency to deny that any other responsible party members held it in the 1950s and 1960s, and to affirm that it was a personal aberration encouraged by China. It is much more likely that this 'Pol Pot line' was the popular one among the rural cadre, except for those with a thorough internationalist (e.g. Vietnamese) indoctrination.[14] It was also popular with young nationalist radicals who, even if not affiliated with the KPRP, considered themselves (and were considered) of the left, who were heavily represented in the teaching profession, and who derived their ideology directly from Son Ngoc Thanh's movement of a few years earlier.

The reminiscences of one former activist indicate that even Tou Samouth, head of the Central Committee within Cambodia, was sympathetic to this more revolutionary line in 1957, for he called cadres to clandestine meetings to instruct them on the necessity to continue the struggle, saying 'we ourselves are the masters', an emphasis which was important in Pol Pot's programme years later.[15]

In 1960 government repression of the left, which had begun anew in 1959, continued, particularly against leftist intellectuals and newspapers in Phnom Penh, and in spite of the fact that one of the victims, Khieu Samphan and his *L'Observateur*, had published complimentary material about the neutralist tendencies of Sihanouk's regime. Four newspapers were banned, and their editors sent to gaol for a time. If they had sincerely been promoting support for Sihanouk because of his formal neutrality and anti-imperialism, they must have indeed been discouraged.

In September 1960 the Party held what became known as its Second Congress, attended by twenty-one members, in the Phnom Penh railway station. The old leadership was maintained, with Tou Samouth as Party Secretary and Nuon Chea his deputy, but Pol Pot moved into third position and the Politburo. Ieng Sary was also elected to the Central Committee, together with veterans Keo Meas, Son Ngoc Minh (absent in Vietnam), So Phim, Prasith, and Non Suon.[16]

Following this, the party undertook new journalistic ventures supporting Sihanouk's international position, and they began preparing for the 1962 National Assembly elections scheduled for June. In January, however, a group of alleged rural party members were arrested on espionage charges, and they implicated Non Suon. In May the latter was arrested, they were all sentenced to long prison terms, and the party newspapers were closed. No Pracheachon candidate stood for the election, and open, legal activity by the party came to an end. In July Tou Samouth disappeared—presumably murdered—although this was not known outside local communist circles until 1978;[17] and in between the January and May arrests there occurred another incident which, if true, complicates the analysis of the contradictory party positions.

In a speech on 15 February 1962, Sihanouk announced that a certain communist agent named Setha, 'alias "Samouth"', had recently come from Vietnam (and quickly returned there) with a message for the Pracheachon. The message, which in the circumstances would have been instructions from the KPRP leadership in Hanoi and was reproduced in a Cambodian government publication that year, purported to establish the party line on the coming elections.[18] The Sangkum was called treasonous, while the feudalists and national reactionaries were termed the enemy. Participation in the election was discouraged, since the results were fixed in advance; and the party should try to win over the intellectuals who had succeeded in gaining entrance to the Sangkum. As for the future, patience should be exercised until victory in Laos and Vietnam led to immediate victory in Cambodia.

If genuine, and presented as they were in a Sihanouk propaganda work there is no guarantee of that, these documents indicate a line midway between the two adduced above. Thus, the feudalists and the Sangkum, and implicitly Sihanouk, are the enemies, the leftist intellectuals who support him are misled and should be won over, but armed struggle in Cambodia would be premature and must await victories in Vietnam and Laos. Of course this looks very much like a Sihanouk manœuvre, and too much weight should not be given to it.

Following the June 1962 election, Sihanouk continued experimenting with leftist intellectuals, including Khieu Samphan, in ministerial responsibilities. Samphan immediately began calling attention to the country's economic weaknesses, proposing austerities, higher taxes on luxuries, limits on unproductive inflationary investments–in short, structural reform; but when the 1963 budget was prepared a large deficit was maintained, while increased luxury taxes favoured by Sampham came under severe attack from the right-wing and capitalist press.

While these controversial economic dicussions were going on, in February 1963, there were anti-regime student demonstrations in Siemreap, which then spread to other towns and were blamed on leftist subversion. Sihanouk published a list of thirty-four 'leftists' whom he accused of acting against his government. Interestingly, it included only one Pracheachon veteran, Chou Chet. All the others were intellectuals, including three in his own government, Chau Seng, Hou Yuon and Khieu Samphan. That is, the list, so far as Sihanouk knew, was not directed against real communists, but against the intellectual left who had tried to co-operate with him in his home-grown 'socialism' and neutralist foreign policy.

Although the Siemreap rioting had strictly local causes, it was used by Sihanouk and the entire Cambodian right to attack the left, who were blamed for turning the youth against the Sangkum. The witch-hunt gave Samphan's enemies a chance to damn his reform proposals, and he resigned on 1 July.[19]

At very nearly the same time there were new developments within the KPRP. Following the disappearance of Tou Samouth, Pol Pot had become Acting Secretary-General of the Party, and the change was consecrated at the Third Party Congress in February 1963, which saw the Party centre definitely taken over by former members of the Paris Marxist Circle and their domestic allies. The most active veterans within the country, Keo Meas and Non Suon were dropped entirely, and the retention of Son Ngoc Minh was to no effect since he remained in Vietnam.[20]

By mid-year the controversial leftist ministers had been forced to quit their posts; and in July, as repression of the left increased, it became known that Saloth Sar, Ieng Sary and Son Sen had disappeared from Phnom Penh. At the time they were presumed murdered, but the first two in fact fled to the eastern part of the country where they began preparing the rural revolution and Son Sen hid in Phnom Penh and fled a year later. From this point it seems certain that the Party centre was working for Sihanouk's overthrow as the revolution's principal goal.

In spite of their exclusion from ministerial posts, to which they were never thereafter allowed to return, leftists remaining in Phnom Penh, such as Hou Yuon, Hu Nim, Phouk Chhay, Chou Chet, and perhaps even Khieu Samphan, may have felt again after mid-1963 that they had reason to try to work together with Sihanouk toward a gradual socialist transformation. Sihanuouk was becoming increasingly hostile to the United States and its Asian allies, South Vietnam and Thailand. In August 1963 relations were broken with Ngo Dinh Diem's government, in November import-export trade and banks were nationalized in moves that recalled recommendations made earlier by Khieu Samphan, and during the last months of 1963 and early 1964 the termination of all American aid programmes was ordered. Finally, in May 1965, diplomatic relations with the United States were cut, a move that brought the approval of the entire left.

The urban intellectuals miscalculated, however, for at the same time the authorities were undertaking a new campaign of harrassment and suppression of former KPRP and Issarak cadres, driving many who had returned to civil life after 1954 back into a guerrilla struggle. All during 1964–5 active leftists and former Issaraks who had settled down after 1955 were harrassed and in some cases driven into dissidence again. This continued in 1966, with increased violence (Kiernan, 1984, pp. 211–12, 230–1).

Furthermore, the economic 'reforms' of 1963–4, albeit superficially leftist, did not lead to 'socialist' results, and the new institutions were not run by the left. Sihanouk's nationalization of foreign trade and banks in fact concentrated them, like the state industries constructed as Chinese aid projects, in the hands of his favourites, who treated them as personal fiefs from which to extract wealth.[21]

Thus, after 1963, economic conditions steadily deteriorated, and it is quite mistaken to claim that 'the reforms were clearly an economic success'.[22] The 'reforms' were in fact a cosmetic treatment to disguise further concentration of Cambodia's economy in the hands of Sihanouk's favourites, who were allowed to run them for their own profit.

It is not surprising that ultra-leftist statements emerged from some sectors of the Cambodian communist movement, which had apparently begun to call for a renewal of armed struggle, and such views would have begun to find favour with increasing numbers of the peasantry. Even their attachment to Sihanouk would not have made them immune to a call for revolution against wealthy 'capitalists and feudalists', for the peasants viewed Sihanouk as the 'good King' who could save them from his rapacious subordinates.[23]

September 1966 saw organizational changes of both the left and the right. The former convened a Party Central Committee meeting and adopted the name 'Communist Party of Cambodia', while the right consolidated its position in National Assembly elections.

For the first time Sihanouk allowed free multiple candidacies, instead of choosing a single candidate for each seat, and the outcome in most places clearly showed the application of wealth and power. Following this election, Lon Nol became Prime Minister (Vickery, 1982b, pp. 106–7; Kiernan, 1984, pp. 232–4).

The genuine strength of the left in some places, however, was demonstrated by the victories of Hou Yuon, Khieu Samphan and Hu Nim, in spite of a personal campaign by Sihanouk against them.

The new government immediately stepped up pressure on the left, and in many parts of the country both active leftists and former Issaraks and KPRP fighters were arrested, beaten, murdered. In addition, in early 1967, the state began forcible collection of the new rice harvest at below market prices, both to pre-empt illegal sales to Vietnam and to increase state revenue. In several places there was resistance to the rice collection, and anti-government tracts, presumably prepared by Party cadres, appeared. The most serious resistance began in Samlaut, in south-western Battambang province; some attacks on military units had occurred as early as January or February, but then in April widespread violence between villagers and military broke out and turned into a full-scale rebellion which was not finally put down until August.[24]

Even though unplanned, the Samlaut affair deserves to be called the beginning of the 'First Civil War', for conflict between left and right continued and increased, both in suppression of individual leftists by the authorities and in armed attacks by both sides in rural areas. Hou Yuon and Khieu Samphan disappeared from Phnom Penh in April and Hu Nim in October. Phouk Chhay, who had been active both in Cambodian-Chinese friendship activities and in new economic initiatives, including the organization of a state farm which was attacked by peasants early in the Samlaut uprising, was arrested at the same time. Most other intellectuals with a leftist reputation who escaped arrest fled during 1967–8 to the *maquis*.[25]

Fighting started again at the beginning of 1968, almost simultaneously in several parts of the country, including Samlaut, and all Party documents concur in claiming these events as a planned armed struggle, which seems likely since there was no longer a significant urban intellectual wing to urge co-operation with Sihanouk for the sake of wider international interests. The Vietnamese, and the Khmer cadres who had gone to Vietnam in 1954, still objected to the outbreak of open revolt, for a peaceful Cambodia, even under Sihanouk and Lon Nol, was essential to the Vietnamese war effort; and when Keo Meas went to Hanoi in 1968 to get the Khmers there to support the struggle, he was met by a refusal. Within Cambodia the Vietnamese seem to have had some success in impressing their views on the Eastern Zone, which delayed attacks on government forces for several months, thus showing early signs of the differences which would separate it from the Party centre until 1978 (Kiernan, 1984, pp. 270–1).

By 1969 even Sihanouk's neutralist foreign policy, which had endeared him to the local left and the international socialist bloc, was no longer certain. He was moving toward the United States, was increasingly critical of Vietnam, and in spite of formally good relations with that country, he permitted, perhaps even encouraged, anti-Vietnamese tirades in the Khmer-language press.

If many of the peasantry still stood in awe of him, as was shown by some of their reactions to the 1970 coup, the awe did not extend to Sihanouk's subordinates or to the urban business networks which held the countryside in subjection. Even if Cambodian society was not 'feudal', and the peasantry's enemy was urban business men rather than landlords, this did not make the revolutionary potential any less. It simply meant that if the Cambodian peasantry became revolutionary, they would direct their wrath against the towns (Vickery, 1984, Chap. 5, pp. 287–8, n. 117).

It now seems certain that the 18 March 1970 coup was an internal Cambodian affair, arising out of conflict among economic and political elite groups. Despite great interest in discovering major American responsibility, little evidence for this has appeared, and given Sihanouk's shifts during 1969, the American government would have seen little reason to remove him. If there was lower-level American encouragement in Saigon, it was perhaps a result of influence on those Americans by Kampuchea Krom militants, whose own interests required the removal of Sihanouk before he could establish a solid relationship with the American government.[26]

Still more surprising to all parties must have been Sihanouk's moves after his removal. Even if the Party had foreseen a coup against Sihanouk during the heyday of his cooperation with the Democratic Republic of Vietnam (DRV) and the NLF, they could not have expected that he would join with them in backing a *Cambodian* revolution; neither would this have occurred to those who planned, and finally carried out, Sihanouk's removal.

Indeed, Sihanouk in Peking claiming leadership of the revolution caused more disarray on the left than on the right. Had Sihanouk remained in Phnom Penh, again on good terms with the United States, with continuing economic decline and spillover from the Vietnam war, the Party might have eventually benefited from gradual peasant disaffection and an end to the problem of Sihanouk's hold on the people. More certainly, the intellectual left would have remained united, and most of them would have eventually rejected the Phnom Penh regime and gone over to the revolution. There would not have been the spectacle of old Pracheachon activists like Saloth Chhay and Pen Yuth, or former Marxist Circle members like Keng Vannsak, and other radical intellectuals like Hang Thun Hak, supporting Lon Nol's regime to the end.[27]

With Sihanouk on the revolutionary side, and his popularity maintained among peasants who suffered from attacks by American and Lon Nol forces, the revolutionary forces in the short term stood to gain, for any peasant hesitation in attacking the towns and government troops would be removed. This also increased the possibility, or danger, depending on one's theory of revolution, of a peasant revolution, with the mass of the revolutionary forces mainly concerned to destroy their enemy, the towns and then return to simple village life; while cadres who were known to hold a more moderate view of the process of revolutionary change invited the charge of sympathy with the enemy.

The coup against Sihânouk, and his response to it, split the intellectual left and allowed full reign to peasant, anti-urban tendencies within the Cambodian revolution. Sihanouk's switch also removed Vietnamese objections to

Cambodian armed struggle, but meant that Vietnam's Cambodian allies were latecomers on the revolutionary scene and operated under the disadvantage of having advocated apparent theoretical and tactical errors over the previous twenty years. As is now well known, the veterans who returned from Vietnam after 1970, and the domestic intellectuals who may have favoured a similar line, were pushed aside and, for the majority, physically eliminated during 1970–8, while anti-urban, peasant theories came to dominate the 'Pol Pot clique' among the Party leadership (Kiernan, 1984, Chap 8.; Vickery, 1984, Chap. 5).

Foreign Influence on the Cambodian Revolution

In the foregoing outline of the development of the revolutionary movement and its factions I have, in contrast to most treatments, neglected the international aspect, both the influence of other communist movements on the Cambodian groups and the effect of the international position of Sihanouk's government and its relations with communist powers. This was in part because I believe that the major determinants of the course of the Cambodian revolution were local ones (Vickery, 1984, Chaps. 1, 5), and that integrating their delineation with a discussion of foreign relations distracts from the more important aspects. It is also because I disagree with the inferences which most other writers have drawn about the international context of the Cambodian revolution.

The role of foreign governments and communist parties in the development of Cambodian communism and in the course taken by the Cambodian revolution is of interest both for factual history and for an analysis of revolutionary dynamics and Marxist theory. Did the peculiarities of DK arise out of native preconditions or did they depend on manipulation by outside forces? All participants, and most interested outsiders, have found it more comfortable to attribute the undeniable disasters of 1975–9 to foreign interference. For the PRK and their sympathizers, the evil foreign interference was Chinese, but for the DK leadership, Vietnam is the culprit. The former allege that Pol Pot was carrying out Chinese hegemonistic policies, while the latter contend that everything which went wrong in DK was the result of Vietnamese subversion via traitors within their midst who were following Vietnamese directives.

For once, there can be no question of Soviet directives, for the Soviet Union, after Sihanouk's overthrow, maintained relations with the Khmer Republic until the end, and thus perhaps disapproved of the tendencies in the

Cambodian *maquis*. As noted above, there may have been another urban Marxist faction on whom the Soviets were counting, and if so, their prognosis for Cambodian developments was as mistaken as that of all other outsiders.

At least one thing is of a priori certainty—the Cambodian revolution as it developed, at the latest from 1968, was not in accordance with Vietnamese wishes, and no more proof of this is necessary than that its policies were ultimately directed against Vietnam. By 1973 the Pol Pot group were even asserting that Vietnam was the principal enemy. Moreover, the Vietnamese agree with the Pol Pot group on the fact that in the 1960s they valued Sihanouk's neutrality for the Vietnamese struggle and felt that the Cambodian revolution should wait until after victory had been won in Vietnam. The Cambodian armed struggle, beginning in 1968, was thus objectively anti-Vietnamese, after 1973 explicitly so, and Vietnamese influence was certainly exercised to replace the Pol Pot line with a policy more friendly towards Vietnam.

Does this prove that the DK anti-Vietnamese policy resulted from some other outside influence? The PRK leaders, the Vietnamese and their friends see a Chinese hand behind Pol Pot, but the arguments depend too often on *ad hoc* allegations of intention which are undemonstrable, and often excessively tortuous.

In broad outline, Chinese and Soviet policy toward Cambodia throughout the 1950s and 1960s was identical to the Vietnamese—to maintain Cambodia's neutrality, even if it meant holding back the local revolutionary forces. In 1958 Sihanouk recognized China and signed a trade agreement with the DRV. Vietnam, as Pol Pot charges, was willing to maintain Sihanouk against the Cambodian communists, because neutral, non-communist Cambodia was valuable to the Vietnamese war effort. But China was also one of Sihanouk's main foreign supports, and provided economic aid which was important for the country's material progress and for strengthening Sihanouk's regime.[28]

The official line in the PRK, and also that of the SRV, is that the course of the Cambodian revolution under Pol Pot was determined by China's desire for hegemony over South-east Asia, and that the Pol Pot clique was carrying out Chinese policy. This line has been adopted uncritically by some foreign friends of the PRK, such as Wilfred Burchett (Burchett, 1981), and it is also reflected in the most thorough treatment to date of the history of the Cambodian revolution, Kiernan's *How Pol Pot Came to Power* (Kiernan, 1984), despite his recording of evidence to the contrary.

This tale of Chinese perfidy starts with the Geneva negotiations of 1954, and the failure to secure representation of the revolutionary side or a regroupement zone for the revolutionary forces as was done in Laos and

Vietnam. According to the Socialist Republic of Vietnam (SRV) and the PRK, they were betrayed by China, who sold out to the Western powers and then supported Sihanouk in Cambodia.[29] Pol Pot has blamed Vietnamese treachery for the same result, and Western writers have chosen one or the other line, more or less, depending on their relative Chinese or Vietnamese sympathies.[30]

In 1954 both the Vietnamese and the Cambodian revolutionaries were forced at the negotiating table to withdraw from gains they had made on the battlefield. Both the Chinese and the Russians urged this retreat, and the main reason was fear of military intervention by the United States, including the use of nuclear weapons.[31] This very real threat, which the Chinese and the Russians would have understood much better than the Cambodian Issarak and KPRP forces, sufficiently explains the Chinese and Russian positions; and there are no grounds to postulate at that date an intention to sabotage Vietnamese unification or to use Cambodia against Vietnam.

The Vietnamese, for their part, were persuaded that the retreat was temporary, and that their goal would be achieved in 1956 following the elections which the Geneva Accords had called for. Within Cambodia, not only had formal independence been granted to Sihanouk's government before Geneva, which thus entitled that government to a place at the conference, but a fundamental weakness of the Cambodian revolution had been revealed by that independence. Much of the revolutionary ardour in the countryside disappeared, for independence itself had been the issue, and there was insufficient popular support for further struggle in the interests of political or social revolution. Quite apart from the danger of American intervention, a clear assessment of the real balance of forces would have indicated to the Vietnamese, Chinese, and Russians, that insistence on support for the KRPR against Sihanouk was premature.

There has always been a dual thrust to the argument associating China with support for Pol Pot—the international aspect and the question of Cambodian domestic policies. On the first point, there is no doubt that as the Sino-Soviet rift widened, the Chinese were less interested in Asian communist parties of pro-Soviet tendency and they might eventually have regarded Pol Pot, because of his anti-Vietnamese position, as a more worthwhile ally. To that extent Cambodia was a casualty of the Sino-Soviet struggle.

This does not, however, implicate China directly in the domestic Cambodian political struggle, nor in fomenting Cambodian-Vietnamese disputes, at least not in ways that have been alleged.[32] Speculation that Pol Pot might have conferred with Deng Xiaoping and Liu Shaoqui in 1965, just before his anti-Vietnamese policy solidified, and hints that Deng may have been responsible for Pol Pot and his policies are misplaced. Further, the hypothesis that the defeat of the Cultural Revolution radicals by Deng directly contributed to the serious escalation of the Cambodian-Vietnam conflict is at odds with what is known of the ideologies and policies of the four parties concerned. Although the real rise of Polpotism began after the death of Mao, which undercuts PRK views of the matter, and continued after the defeat of the Cultural Revolution, the temporal coincidence is not evidence for causality (Kiernan, 1980, pp. 27, 52; Kiernan, 1984, pp. 222–3).

Equally unconvincing is the speculation that when Pol Pot was in Peking in 1965 he was '*likely to have been asked* by the Chinese, *as by the Vietnamese*, to refrain from . . . rebellion against Sihanouk, but *probably* did receive encouragement for his adoption of a hostile posture toward Sihanouk' (author's emphasis). The argument is based on 'Chinese policy interests [which] lay in alienating the Kampuchean Party from the Vietnamese'. Could this have occurred in 1965—when Vietnam was not an issue in the Sino-Soviet dispute, and when China was resolutely anti-American? If the Chinese were cultivating Pol Pot against Sihanouk at that time, it would more likely have been because they saw him as an anti-American ally in case Sihanouk wavered, as Marxists might have predicted, and as he did four years later, not because of Pol Pot's emnity toward Vietnam, which the Chinese might not yet have perceived. After all, there was at that time close Vietnamese-Chinese co-operation in training Cambodian cadres.[33]

The peculiarities of the Cambodian revolution are best explained through close attention to the details of Cambodia's socio-political situation, and the most that can be said about foreign influence is that no outside socialist power felt able, or would have been able, to intervene and put the revolution back on straight Marxist-Leninist rails until Democratic Kampuchea had thoroughly worn out its momentum and goodwill. The theory of clandestine Chinese support for Pol Pot since the 1960s could only be sustained if the Chinese leadership since then had clearly favoured DK-type policies. Nothing Deng Xiaoping has done in China indicates that he ever had sympathy for DK domestic policies, rather the contrary, and his interest in DK can only have been as a part of the international power game.

4 The Present Regime

The formation and history of the People's Republic of Kampuchea cannot be studied in isolation from its predecessor, Democratic Kampuchea; and although the PRK leaders quite correctly emphasize the dramatic break with DK, and the vast changes which have occurred since 1979, their regime nevertheless has its ultimate origins in the same revolutionary victory of 17 April 1975 as does the rival Pol Pot DK group. All of the members of the present leadership with any revolutionary background represent a continuity from the pre-DK days of which Pol Pot, Ieng Sary and Khieu Samphan were also a part, and nearly all of them either participated for a time in the DK administration, or in the case of some of those who had spent 1954–70 in Vietnam, would have participated had not the DK leadership shown that their participation was not wanted, even that their lives would have been in danger had they returned to, or remained in, Cambodia. Perhaps only two of the present top leaders are nearly free from suspicion of DK association, having returned from Vietnam but broken with Pol Pot before 1975, continuing to engage thereafter in the struggle inside the country. The two are Say Phouthang and Bou Thang, who are also ethnically non-Khmer, the former being Thai and the latter Tampuon, and they hold two of the more important positions—President of the Party's Central Organizing Committee and Minister of Defence.[1]

The continuity from DK is also explicit: 17 April has been accorded the status of a national holiday, although it has been given decreasing public attention since 1979 as the old revolutionary leadership realized that for most of the population whose support they wished to secure that date had exclusively negative connotations. By 1985 the celebration was restricted to a small group of leaders laying a wreath at a site from which the public were exluded; although the local press still published features on the war 'against Lon Nol and the Americans', including a map with indications of the routes followed by revolutionary forces as they entered Phnom Penh on 17 April 1975.[2]

Their argument is that the PRK represents the true revolutionary path from which the Pol Pot clique disastrously deviated. That true path winds from the war for independence from France, combined with class struggle against Sihanouk during 1946–54, through the 'anti-feudal' political struggle of the late 1950s and 1960s, and the second armed conflict, first against Sihanouk in 1968–9, and then against Lon Nol and the Americans to culminate in the victory of April 1975.[3]

It is unlikely that there is a consensus among the present leadership on the date of Pol Pot's break with the true revolutionary line. For Say Phouthang and Bou Thang it must be before 1975, when they became dissidents. The same is probably true for all of the post-1954 Vietnam regroupees, survivors of a much larger group whom Pol Pot began to have destroyed as they returned to join the fray in Cambodia after 1970. Some of the others, who worked in the DK administration after 1975, would no doubt have placed Pol Pot's deviation later, perhaps for some, as late as 1977 or 1978; and it must be assumed, although it would be impossible to get an honest answer on the subject today, that some at least of the present leadership approved the evacuation of the cities in 1975, the executions of the higher Lon Nol military leaders as traitors or irredeemably dangerous foes, and the communalization of most areas of economic life.

This does not mean that they are simply blood-smeared Pol Pot remnants, as a certain propaganda line would have it, who only broke with him for personal reasons (Becker, 1983; Shawcross 1984a, 1984b, pp. 36, 357–8). Having a theoretical conviction of the desirability of rapid social change, even immediate communalization, or a pragmatic view that in the dire straits of Cambodia's post-war situation strict organizational measures were required, does not mean that one approves of the continuing arbitrary murder or mass starvation of class enemies. Even Hou Yuon, considered one of the 'good guys' of the Cambodian revolution, if only because, having disappeared in 1975, he cannot be held responsible for any of the subsequent disasters, once wrote approvingly of the rapid establishment of high-level co-operatives of former urban dwellers on new land.[4]

Whatever they felt about the immediate tasks or the treatment of their enemies as they marched into Phnom Penh in April 1975, there is ample evidence that many among the old cadres soon after, and increasingly, came to believe that Pol Pot was indeed deviating from the line for which they had fought.

The announcement of the first group of high office-holders in 1975, and the subsequent reorganizations in 1978 revealed some of the attempts to balance power among the factions already discernible in pre-victory information or from pre-war events.

The regime which was announced publicly after the April 1975 victory was the Royal Government of National Union of Cambodia (RGNUC) headed by Prince Sihanouk as Chief of State, Penn Nouth as Prime Minister, and Khieu Samphan as Deputy Prime Minister, Minister of Defence, and Commander-in-Chief of the Armed Forces (Vickery, 1984, pp. 144–5).

The outside observer had to piece together the remaining membership of this first DK government from pre-victory sources and radio announcements, since no complete list was made public. Most of the ranking ministers in the RGNUC were pre-war Sihanouk loyalists who remained powerless in Peking, and who did not return to Cambodia until September, when they were promptly incarcerated. Real authority in their ministries was held by nominal subordinates inside Cambodia who gradually emerged into view in 1975–6. Two ministers who had always been in the interior, Hu Nim and Hou Yuon, intellectuals who had fled to the guerrillas in 1967, remained in 1975 respectively Minister for Information and Minister of the Interior, Co-operatives and Communal Reforms.

Associated with them, apparently, were Khieu Samphan, Poc Deuskoma, Vice-Minister of Foreign Affairs, and Tiv Ol—after 1975 a subordinate of Hu Nim in the Information Ministry. Another who could be assumed from his political background to belong to the same faction, was Norodom Phurissara, who fled to the *maquis* in 1972 and who appeared on a mission to Bangkok at the end of October 1975 as Minister of Justice.[5]

Another RGNUC faction inferable at the time included Saloth Sar, the Vice-President of the Supreme Military Command and Chief of the Army Military Directorate; Nuon Chea, Vice-President of the Supreme Military Command and Chief of the Army Political Directorate; Koy Thuon, Vice-Minister of Finance; Ieng Sary, Special Envoy from the Interior to Sihanouk and sections outside the country; Son Sen, Chief of General Staff; and the two sisters, Khieu Thirith (Mrs Ieng Sary) and Khieu Ponnary (Mrs Saloth Sar), who were respectively Vice-Minister of Education and Youth, and Vice-president of the Front Committee for the Capital (Vickery, 1984, pp. 144–7).

Almost totally omitted from the available information in 1975, Nuon Chea being an exception, were the veteran revolutionaries and communists who had started fighting the French in league with the Vietnamese in the 1940s, who formed the first Cambodian communist organization in 1951, and who in 1954 either went to Vietnam or stayed to form the legal Pracheachon ('Citizen') group which published newspapers and contested elections until 1962. Particularly remarkable was the absence of Non Suon, who had been the most publicly active communist around 1960, and whose name had figured in battle-front news of 1970–5. Their omission from public attention after victory could have been interpreted at the time as a desire to placate Sihanouk, who had always conidered them his deadly enemies, but it is now clear that there were sharp factional divisions in the revolutionary upper ranks.

Domestic Policies in Democratic Kampuchea

It was no doubt because of such factional divisions that many of the DK policies were carried out with exaggerated rigour, even though the policies themselves seem designed to punish entire classes of people whom the 1975 victors considered to be traitors.

Soon after the end of fighting on 17 April 1975 and the entry of the revolutionary forces into Phnom Penh, virtually the entire population was ordered to begin moving out of the city into the rural areas. Excepted from the general order were some factory workers and some skilled employees of technical services, such as the municipal water and electricity plants. The evacuees were given reasons such as the danger of American bombardment, and were told that the evacuation was only for three days, after which they would be able to return.

Subsequently, the DK leadership explained that the evacuation had been necessary both because there was insufficient food within the city, and because they had to clean out subversive networks established there by the United States and its Cambodian allies.[6] None of these reasons is totally without foundation. Although the United States has dismissed the first as propaganda, wartime activity in Indo-China had been such that the possibility of an American bombardment of Phnom Penh in the hands of the 'communists' was not something the new authorities could totally ignore. Food was indeed a problem. During the war years the population of Phnom Penh had expanded from 600,000 to about two million; by the end of the war it had to be supplied with rice by air from Thailand and many were on the verge of starvation. Also, intelligence networks had certainly been left in place by the defeated government and its foreign backers.[7]

Perhaps the greatest controversy among serious observers has been over the question of available food in Phnom Penh and in the countryside. The highest estimates of available food in the city, however, only show enough for a few weeks, and they lack credibility in view of the near starvation which was increasing daily even at the height of American aid.[8] Where would additional food have come from after the city's stocks had run out? Furthermore, over half the wartime population increase of Phnom Penh consisted of rural people fleeing the war, who were needed back in their villages to work in agriculture. It was also reasonable, given the degree of destruction of the country's productive central zone, to insist that all able-bodied people should engage in productive work, which in Cambodia meant essentially agriculture. There is even evidence that in some areas to which the city people were evacuated the food that was available and that which was distributed, was more abundant than that which the poor of Phnom Penh had been receiving during the last year of the war (Vickery, 1984, pp. 78–9). The evacuation of Phnom Penh can only be faulted in its modalities—excessive haste, neglect of available skilled personnel, and sudden removal of the disabled as well as the able-bodied.

There is some evidence of disagreement among the new leadership over the evacuation of Phnom Penh, or at least of its modalities. For temporary administration, the city had been divided on 17 April into five sectors under troops who had marched in from different areas and who, during the previous five years, had often operated quite autonomously. They directed the evacuees out of the city towards their own areas in the countryside. Witnesses report that in the eastern and southern sectors of the city they encountered troops, who appear to have been from the Eastern Zone, and who denied the fact of the evacuation, even telling people to return home. In some places the uncertainty continued for a whole day, before the evacuation policy was fully accepted by the Eastern forces (Vickery, 1984, pp. 78–9).

Whatever the validity of the pragmatic reasons given for urban evacuation, there was also an ideological reason, derived from the Cambodian communists' peculiar class analysis of their society, which also determined the position in which the evacuees found themselves once they reached the rural areas.

According to the Cambodian communist analysis, the population were to be divided into three categories, called 'Full Rights', 'Candidate', and 'Depositee'. Full Rights people comprised in theory poor peasants, the lower and middle strata of the middle peasants, and workers—altogether, those classes held to be revolutionary. Upper-middle peasants, wealthy peasants and petty bourgeoisie made up the Candidate group; while Depositees consisted of capitalists and foreign minorities (Vickery, 1984, pp. 81–2).

Such was the theoretical outline, but the position was modified by a person's behaviour or even by the actions or positions of other family members. A poor peasant could be demoted to Depositee if it were discovered, for example, that his father or brother had been a policeman; and if a Full Rights person was arrested for any reason his family would then become Depositees.

Moreover, all those evacuated from the towns after 17 April 1975 were considered as Depositees whatever their economic or social status, as were all peasants living in areas which had remained under Khmer Republic control until 17 April. This meant that virtually all workers or petty bourgeois were placed in that lowest and socially disadvantaged group and that the poorer peasants were *de jure* as well as *de facto* the privileged class. This result was quite un-Marxist in that there was no recognition of the proletariat as the revolutionary vanguard, or even as a progressive class.

Once the evacuees were settled in the rural areas the really operative class distinction which affected their lives was the dichotomy between 'new' people (the evacuees) and 'old' or 'base' people, the peasants who were officially either of Full Rights or Candidate status and who had lived in revolutionary areas before the end of the war.

After evacuation, the 'new' people were rapidly organized into agricultural production units, usually called co-operatives, which varied as to living conditions and discipline from zone to zone, depending both on objective factors such as the local economic potential, and on the attitudes and competence of the local authorities.

Cambodia under DK was divided into seven large zones, each comprising two to four pre-war provinces and subdivided into from three to seven regions.[9] The leaders of the zones had operated during the war with considerable autonomy, and sometimes represented different revolutionary backgrounds and tendencies.

The Eastern Zone, for example, was heavily staffed by old revolutionaries who had co-operated with Vietnam in the anti-French struggles of the 1940s–50s, and in the second Indo-China war of the 1960s–70s. The zone chiefs of the West and North-West were also of that group, but the latter did not dominate those zones as they did the East. The South-West Zone, on the other hand, was dominated by a man whose anti-Vietnamese views were well known, and its lower echelon cadres were more often composed of poor peasants during the struggle within Cambodia. In the North-West, intellectuals, particularly teachers, who had joined the revolution in the 1960s and after 1970, were prominent in the second-echelon leadership, the administrative committees of the zone's seven regions. All over the country, the chiefs of villages and co-operatives, and thus those who were in direct authority over the urban evacuees, were local peasants who had proved their loyalty to the revolution. They differed widely in terms of competence, humanity and political approach, and the fate of the 'new' people to a large extent depended on the personal qualities of their immediate supervisors (Vickery, 1984, Chap. 3).

In general, living conditions considered by zone during the DK period were best in the East, and in the adjacent Kratie Special Region, partly because of their agricultural potential, but also because of the orientation of their leadership. Another favourable place to live was Region 3, in the North-West, just west of Battambang city, where the agricultural potential was good and the leadership lenient. In the South-West working conditions and discipline were extremely strict, and executions more of a threat than in the East, but the tight organization ensured that food supplies were in most places adequate to prevent starvation, even though the zone had been relatively poor in normal times. Perhaps the very worst areas for death by starvation and overwork were those where urban evacuees had been assigned to carve new villages and fields out of forests, without adequate tools, food, or any experience in such work. Regions 5 and 6 of the North-West, in northern Battambang and western Pursat provinces respectively, were apparently the worst in this respect. A different type of situation, generally speaking, prevailed in the Central Zone, dominated by one of the most brutal of Pol Pot's military supporters. There, food shortages rarely reached starvation levels, but capricious brutality was an ever-present danger, and conditions varied considerably even among adjacent villages, depending on the character of the local leaders.

Economic activity was entirely managed by the state apparatus. There were no markets, no currency, no independent exchange; in most places no private garden production or independent food gathering, and by 1977 there was even a policy, ever more strictly enforced, of communal cooking and eating. Movement outside the basic unit, village or co-operative was forbidden without written authorization, which was rarely granted.

In principle, each locality was supposed to retain sufficient food from its production to feed its population and ensure seed, if required, for the following season. The remainder was collected by higher-level units for redistribution to deficit areas or to non-food producing workers, for the military and central administration, and for export. Likewise, in principle, essential commodities which could not be produced in the villages were distributed by the authorities. In addition to direct agricultural production, and work in those factories deemed essential, large numbers of people, in particular 'new' evacuees, were set to work building new water control and irrigation works, for the purpose of increasing agricultural production, particularly rice (Vickery, 1984, pp. 156–8; Stuart-Fox & Bunheang Ung, 1985).

With the entire population transformed into poor peasants, education beyond that which a poor peasantry would need was neglected, and even classes in basic literacy functioned only in a few of the more prosperous and well-run districts. Medicine was also at a very primitive level, both because over half the doctors had emigrated before April 1975 and medicines were not available, and because the DK authorities often refused to deploy medical personnel among the 'new' people (Vickery, 1984, pp. 75–8, 165–71).

Reports indicate that, by 1976, after one year of the new regime, agricultural production was well on the way to recovery from wartime damage. Then, however, instead of allowing some improvement in the quality of life, the authorities demanded larger deliveries of surplus produce, perhaps under the delusion that all the new applications of irrigation and fertilizer had realized the theoretical maximum of 3 tons of rice per hectare rather than the pre-war 1 ton. This led, from 1977, to further deterioration in living conditions, more executions as disciplinary measures, and increasing intra-leadership conflict over policy and methods. Thus, some of the top leaders, once the immediate post-war emergency was over, wished to relax discipline, to reintroduce some market activity and gradually restore urban life. Some lower-level cadres did not deliver the required quotas, in order to prevent starvation in their units, while others falsified statistics for the same reason.

All of these attempts either to oppose central policy, or to circumvent it, were treated as treasonous, and those responsible were usually arrested and executed. Thus, although there had been some removals and executions of members of the leadership group during 1976, throughout 1977 and 1978 periodic waves of arrests and executions swept through entire zones, most noticeably the North, the North-West, and last, the East, in May 1978. The South-West, which by then had become the favourite and most loyal of the zones to the party centre, provided the muscle for purges in the other zones, and southwestern cadres moved in to replace those purged. In general, 'new' people report 1977 as a year of increased hardship and brutal treatment from new cadres following the purges (Vickery, 1984, Chap. 3, *passim*, pp. 139–44).

Factions and Purges in Democratic Kampuchea

The scope of the purges, and the outline of the factional struggle from which they resulted, are reflected in the number of top leaders who dropped from public mention, beginning soon after the April 1975 victory. From the outside it seemed that Hou Yuon and Poc Deuskoma simply disappeared.[10] Then, in August 1975, Ieng Sary was appointed Deputy Premier in charge of Foreign Affairs and Son Sen, Deputy Premier in charge of Defence.

A major change occurred in April 1976 when, after elections on 20 March, Sihanouk resigned, the dissolution of the RGNUC was announced, and a new government structure was partially revealed. At the top was a State Presidium, with Khieu Samphan as Chairman, So Phim as First Vice-Chairman, and Nhim Ros as Second Vice-Chairman.

The Council of Ministers below the Presidium consisted of Pol Pot (Saloth Sar), Prime Minister; Ieng Sary, Deputy Prime Minister for Foreign Affairs; Vorn Vet, Deputy Prime Minister for Economy; Son Sen, Deputy Prime Minister for Defence; Hu Nim, Minister for Propaganda and Information; Thiounn Thioeun, Minister of Public Health; Ieng Thirith, Minister for Social Action; Toch Phoeun, Minister for Public Works; and Yun Yat (Mrs Son Sen), Minister for Culture, Education and Learning.

In addition, the Ministry of Economy had six committees whose chairmen held ministerial rank. Five of these were Non Suon for Agriculture, Cheng An for Industry, Koy Thuon for Commerce, Mey Prang for Communications, and Phuong for Rubber Plantations. The head of the sixth committee, for Energy, was probably Thiounn Mum.[11]

Several of the names announced in the reorganization had not been made public before; and among them, finally, were some of the veteran communists from the 1950s. Such were the two Vice-Chairmen of the State Presidium, So Phim and Nhim Ros, who were also Secretaries respectively of the East and North-West Zones, Non Suon of the Agriculture Committee, Phuong of the Rubber Committee, and Nuon Chea, Mat Ly and Chou Chet of the National Assembly Standing Committee which was announced at the same time. Chou Chet, in addition, was Secretary of the Western Zone.

Another reorganization occurred on 27 September 1976, when Pol Pot was replaced by Nuon Chea as acting Prime Minister, a change which remained in effect until at least 19 October. Then, on 25 October, the name Pol Pot reappeared as Prime Minister on a message sent to Hua Guofeng (Vickery, 1984, p. 148).

Later, in 1978, Ieng Sary claimed that the reorganization of April 1976 had been an attempted coup by pro-Vietnamese traitors, which appears absurd given that Khieu Samphan became Chief of State and Pol Pot Prime Minister, Sary, however, was obviously referring to the prominence given to men from the old communist group in the State Presidium, the Standing Committee of the Assembly, and the committees of the Economy Ministry (Vickery, 1984, p. 148).

If not a real coup, there was probably an attempt to change the regime's leadership and modify its direction, an attempt which nearly succeeded with Pol Pot's deposition in September; but he returned the following month and began to eliminate his enemies. Over the next two years Non Suon (November 1976), Koy Thuon (January 1977), Toch Phoeun (January 1977), Hu Nim (April 1977), Tiv Ol (June 1977), So Phim (May 1978), Nhim Ros (June 1978), Vorn Vet, Cheng An and Mey Prang (November 1978) were arrested and executed.

As the zonal and regional opponents of Pol Pot were eliminated, they were most frequently replaced by cadres from the South-West Zone, under Ta Mok, and it is apparent that the main area of conflict was between a Pol Pot group of intellectuals and the military in the South-Western zonal forces and another group of intellectuals plus the old revolutionary cadres from the pre-independence struggle period, both those who had remained in Cambodia after 1954 and those who had gone to Vietnam. In 1975 the latter held important central government posts as well as leading positions in the West, North-West, North, and in particular the East, where they maintained much of their authority until 1978. The two main points of disagreement were policy regarding Vietnam and domestic socio-economic organization. Pol Pot considered Vietnam to be the country's main enemy, whereas his opponents wished to maintain the policy of alliance and co-operation which had prevailed between Vietnamese and Cambodian communists before 1975. Inside the country his opponents objected, in varying degrees, to the extreme communalization and poor peasantism of the Pol Pot policies (Vickery, 1984, pp. 137–8, 144–50, 196–202; Kiernan, 1984; Chap. 3 above).

The East Zone cadres in Phnom Penh who had expressed scepticism about the evacuation order, the various zone and region leaders under whom post-1979 refugees report reasonable treatment, and who later disappeared into Tuol Sleng prison, and their dossiers from there which show their mystification about the strange events after 1975, all testify to the opposition, passive or active, to the Pol Pot line among significant numbers of the DK higher leadership (Vickery, 1984, pp. 74, 106, 111; Kiernan, 1980, pp. 7–74).

Because of the geographical distribution of DK factions, life in much of the Eastern Zone differed considerably from the convential DK horror picture, and in many places was as tolerable as could be expected in the conditions left by the destruction of the war of 1970–5. The Pol Pot terror did not pervade the East until the latter suffered a concerted central government assault in May 1978, as a result of which the survivors retreated to the eastern border region, or into Vietnam, and requested help from the latter to overthrow Pol Pot. Among those survivors were several of the PRK leadership's nucleus—Heng Samrin, Hun Sen, Chea Sim and Ouk Bun Chhoeun are examples. Pol Pot had deviated from the old revolutionary line in two ways—in his enmity towards Vietnam, and in ignoring the purpose of the revolution, which was to improve the standard of living, not just to turn the rich into poor peasants—a criticism of Pol Pot imputed to So Phim (Vickery, 1984, p. 137).

By late 1978, after destroying the main stronghold of their opponents in the Eastern Zone in May and June, the Pol Pot faction had won the internecine conflict, through the simple expedient of executing all opponents, real or imagined, *en masse*. Had there been no foreign support for the surviving opponents, Pol Pot's DK would very likely have continued its bleak existence with a population cowed under fanatical poor-peasant cadres, and might have stabilized in a peasant autarky at a very low economic level. For change to occur at that time, foreign intervention was essential, and the displacement of the Pol Pot faction by their opponents was due to the Vietnamese invasion, which in turn was a reaction to DK attacks across the Cambodian-Vietnamese border, attacks which were in part for the explicitly aggressive purpose of reconquering provinces inhabited by Khmers but under Vietnamese administration for the past two centuries (Vickery, 1984, pp. 190, 192–3, 195; Stuart-Fox and Bunheang Ung, 1985, p. 128; Kiernan, 1984, pp. 414–16).

The DK-Vietnam Conflict

There was a time when communists believed that wars could not happen between socialist states, because the contradictions which led to wars would disappear with the advent of socialism. The overthrow of capitalism and the victory of the proletariat would remove the impulsion towards imperialism; and socialist states would work co-operatively for mutual benefit and the interests of the international proletariat. This was more implicit than otherwise, however, 'because Marx and Engels never devoted much attention to the problem of the foreign policy of a socialist state' (Ulam, 1971, p. 141).

The official view expressed in a Soviet textbook was that 'socialist foreign policy and the methods of implementing it were evolved by Vladimir Lenin'. He showed that 'in the long run the policy of any state is determined by its economic and social system'. Capitalist society is founded on private ownership of the means of production and on the exploitation of man by man, and the driving force behind its foreign policy is the desire to consolidate the exploititive system and expand the sphere of exploitation. 'By virtue of its social nature, capitalist foreign policy is one of expansion and aggression' (Ponomaryov *et al*., 1969, pp. 9–10).

Socialism is different. Public ownership of the means of production eliminates exploitation, and planned economic development rules out anarchy of production, crises and struggle for markets. The 'inner laws of socialist society make the socialist state an irreconcilable adversary of aggression and conquest'. Socialist foreign policy 'combines patriotism and dedication to the interests of the country with internationalism' (Ponomaryov *et al.*, 1969, p. 11).

Emphasizing the Marxist importance of the socio-economic basis of society, the text continues, 'close co-operation among socialist countries is founded on objective prerequisites, namely identical economic and social systems and the common objective of building socialism and communism', which 'gives rise to a community of foreign policy interests and tasks'. It is not at all easy, however, 'to shape new international relations founded on socialist internationalism', for 'capitalism has left to socialism a legacy of many features that are alien to its nature', such as 'nationalistic and chauvinistic prejudices inculcated by the bourgeois system' (Ponomaryov *et al.*, 1969, p. 11).

Thus, socialism by its very nature avoids the type of war known to capitalist states, but for true socialist peace, 'identical economic and social systems' are required; and even then (in a book written in 1969 after the Sino-Soviet dispute had begun), there may be difficulties, owing to remnants of bourgeois nationalism (Ponomaryov, 1969, p. 17).

By 1975 such difficulties were all too clear. Armed conflict not only could, but had, occurred among the states of 'actually existing socialism'. The Soviet interventions in Hungary and Czechoslovakia, and the Sino-Soviet conflict were sufficient evidence for that. It was clear that the removal of capitalism did not of itself settle border conflicts ('nationalistic and chauvinistic prejudices') or ensure that all 'socialist' regimes would have identical views on relationships with the non-socialist world, and that even socialist states would resort to armed force to protect their perceived interests in these areas. It should be noted, however, that those conflicts had been qualitatively different from wars among capitalist states—they had not been in aid of controlling markets, for the conquest of territory, or for the acquisition of cheap labour. The Sino-Soviet split, interestingly, began in disagreement over how best to deal with their major capitalist enemy, the United States, and its military dimension, which remained very limited, a minor border conflict, was indeed a chauvinistic remnant and would no doubt never have occurred if the ideological and strategic disagreement had not been present (Zagoria, 1962, pp. 153, 385; Clubb, 1971, pp. 511–12).

With respect to Marxist theory, it might also be well to consider whether the economic and social systems of China and the Soviet Union, even within socialism, did not differ sufficiently to render conflict likely even in those terms. One non-socialist student of the Sino-Soviet relationship, moreover, implicitly recognized the importance of identical, or similar, socialist systems in conflict avoidance. In a prognosis in 1963 that the split would never be total he wrote, 'both parties are very much aware of the weaker position they would assume relative to the non-Communist West . . . both parties are aware that a split would drastically, perhaps mortally, weaken the international communist movement' (Zagoria, 1962, pp. 384–5).

In spite of this evidence it was expected that the new revolutionary governments in the three countries of Indo-China could remain at peace because of the similarity of their regional interests, their common struggles against France and the United States, the absence of any real bones of contention, and the common background of their revolutionary leaderships. On the contrary, the most violent warfare yet witnessed between socialist states has been that between Democratic Kampuchea and Vietnam.

With respect to the question in general, it must be emphasized, and from the theoretical point of view it is sufficient, that no 'socialist' state yet in existence conforms to Marxist prognoses for the overthrow of capitalism by communism, that is, by a proletarian revolution in a highly industrialized society in which capitalism has reached its greatest potential development, and in which agriculture is no longer a peasant sector, but under capitalist management. In contrast, nearly all states of 'actually existing socialism' were relatively poor and underdeveloped, with weak industry, a small proletariat, and peasant agriculture as the dominant economic sector where the majority of the population lived. This in itself means that no prediction about socialism based on Marx's view of the nature of the capitalism–socialism transition is a valid touchstone against which to assess the quality of socialism in Indo-China. Marx's socialism and actual socialism are quite different phenomena, and 'nationalist and chauvinist prejudices' in particular would be especially prominent in the latter.

All these considerations were particularly significant in Indo-China where all three countries were poorer, less developed industrially, and more peasant-based than any of the European socialist states. They also differed significantly among themselves in their pre-war social and economic systems, and pre-1975 students of the area neglected to give sufficient attention to the possibility that these differences might persist even after common revolutionary victory.[12] Indeed, the Cambodian communist leadership forced their country into a social and economic system totally unlike that of Vietnam or of anything seen previously in any other socialist country.

There was also an unusually severe legacy of left-over chauvinist prejudices as well as deep differences between the Vietnamese and Cambodian party leaderships which were not obvious to outside observers until after 1975. The first Cambodian communist leadership had grown out of the Indo-China Communist Party as comrades of the Vietnamese; but from 1960 the Cambodian party was gradually taken over by a group of younger leaders who had not fought with Vietnam against the French, who had a traditional anti-Vietnamese chauvinist outlook, and whose idea of revolution was much more peasant-populist than Marxist.[13]

Serious contradictions had arisen even before 1970. Vietnam, for the purposes of its own war effort, desired a peaceful Cambodia, and therefore supported Prince Sihanouk's regime. They advised the Cambodian party against revolution, telling them to wait until after victory in Vietnam. Cambodian revolutionary activities before 1970 were thus opposed, not supported, by Vietnam—something which caused resentment among the Cambodians and convinced them that the Cambodian revolution must be entirely independent, not in the least internationalist.[14]

The Cambodian leadership established a peasantist, egalitarian society, not even a worker-peasant alliance, let alone a regime relying on a vanguard proletariat. And instead of 'socialist internationalism, applying the ... Marxist principle of proletarian internationalism to ... relations with socialist countries', they adopted nationalistic prejudices as major articles of policy (Ponomaryov *et al*., 1969, p. 14).

As noted above, failure to successfully implement policies laid down by central authorities were almost invariably treated as wilful sabotage and treason; and the alleged treason was usually held to have been in favour of Vietnam.

To the extent that DK emnity towards Vietnam resulted from the personal propensities of the DK leadership, it is not open to analysis, or even absolutely to certain demonstration. They were a new group of petty-bourgeois intellectuals who grew up at a time when the Cambodian government-inspired media and the school system were permeated with chauvinism, largely directed against Vietnam, and this no doubt affected their outlook, however seriously they may have taken Marxist theory. Later, when they reached an age of active political involvement, with ambitions for leadership, the bourgeois chauvinist remnants may well have been re-sensitized in their ideology by the fact that their rivals in the independence and revolutionary struggles, both the non-Communist rebels led by Son Ngoc Thanh, and the older Cambodian communists associated with the Indo-China Communist Party, had held pro-Vietnamese positions.[15]

The nationalist sensibilities of the men who gradually attained party leadership after 1960 were exacerbated by Vietnam's reluctance to support armed revolutionary struggle in the late 1960s, when the Cambodian leaders considered the time to be ripe. The Cambodians refused to place the general Indo-China struggle, which in fact meant the war in Vietnam, ahead of purely Cambodian interests, and they interpreted Vietnamese policy as an effort to secure Vietnamese domination over Cambodia.[16]

After the Lon Nol coup of March 1970 and the outbreak of full-scale war inside Cambodia, the Cambodian party leaders were very circumspect about the modalities of Vietnamese aid, refusing joint commands, and trying wherever possible to get along without Vietnamese troops. Although the conduct of one's battles with one's own forces is approved in Marxist, and Maoist, revolutionary theory, the Pol Pot group went much further. The old Khmer communists who started to return from Vietnam to participate in the war were gradually eliminated, Vietnamese troops were sometimes attacked, and Khmer civilians who aided Vietnamese forces in the interests of the revolutionary war against the Khmer Republic and the Americans were massacred (Kiernan, 1984, pp. 372–3, 386–9).

Finally, by 1973, senior party officials were putting forward the line that Vietnam was an enemy, at least enemy number two, if not the principal enemy. This extreme view, identifying the foreign power which since 1970 had given the most aid to the Cambodian revolution as a national enemy, is indeed left-over bourgois chauvinism, and it indicates a total rejection of proletarian or socialist internationalism (Kiernan, 1984, pp. 362, 389). It meant that the Cambodian communist leaders, or the small 'Party Centre', even before the nature of their socio-economic plans had been revealed, had adopted a line which was quite un-Marxist, and unlike anything followed by previous socialist states.

The anti-Vietnamese position adopted within the inner circles of the Cambodian party meant that once the war against mutual enemies was over in 1975, the inevitable disagreements between any neighbouring states in times of political tension would be more than usually difficult to solve. The most obvious problem left over from colonial and post-colonial times was the border between the two countries which, although defined in administrative documents and marked on maps, had never been accurately delimited on the ground (Delahaye, 1928).

Thus, immediately after the end of the war, in April 1975, there were skirmishes in border areas, and in particular disagreement over the occupation of some of the offshore islands; but these conflicts were defused by early 1976, even if the causes of conflict had not been resolved, and 1976 was a year of peace between the two countries.

Then, in early 1977, the Cambodians increased pressure on certain disputed zones left over from Sihanouk's deal with the Vietnamese in 1967 and 'the escalatory rounds of armed clashes . . . probably began when the Kampucheans attempted to drive the Vietnamese forces out of disputed zones they felt had been illegally occupied by the Vietnamese between 1965 and 1975'. By April–May Cambodia began to initiate raids and artillery fire, not only in the disputed areas, but in what they acknowledged as Vietnamese territory; and Vietnam answered the challenge by sending several thousand troops into the border zones. There followed proposals for peaceful negotiated settlement which foundered; and from July to September 1977 the Vietnamese apparently really did violate Cambodian territory. In September the Cambodians retaliated, and in December 1977 there was a major Vietnamese invasion, following which conflict continued until the outbreak of full-scale war at the end of 1978 and the Vietnamese call for the overthrow of the Cambodian government (Heder, 1978, 1980a; Vickery, 1984, pp. 193–5).

Among serious analysts there is no disagreement over who started hostilities. In 1978 'most intelligence analysts in Bangkok agree[d] that Cambodian raids and land grabs escalated the ill will . . . until peace was irretrievable'; and those sympathetic to the Democratic Kampuchean position at that time have at most argued that 'although the Kampucheans may have fired the first shots, they considered their actions a response to *de facto* Vietnamese aggression by long-term occupation of Kampuchean land'.[17] The last statement refers to Vietnamese occupation of areas which some Cambodians still claimed after Sihanouk's agreements with the DRV and NLF in 1967 and the unilateral Vietnamese recognition of Cambodia's borders as they stood in that year.

The DK authorities were apparently claiming a unilateral right to resolve in their favour any ambiguities remaining in the delineation of the border in 1967. There is no doubt that ambiguities existed, but a unilateral claim to an exclusive privilege to readjust a border agreed to with another country can have no validity in international law, and military actions undertaken to enforce such claims are hostilities pure and simple. The Cambodian attacks in disputed zones, and in particular in undisputed Vietnamese areas, were violations of international law, and they justified, in traditional international practice, a military response.

It has become fashionable in the last five years in certain milieux to suggest that because the Vietnamese intervened in Cambodia for pragmatic reasons (to defend themselves against DK attacks), rather than for purely altruistic, humanitarian interests, their intervention is thereby less justifiable, perhaps even quite illegitimate (Shawcross, 1984b pp.70–1). The important point for anyone now concerned about the human rights issue is that the change wrought by Vietnam immediately, and enormously, improved the level of human rights, even if their generals had in fact been more concerned with the security of their own country.

Furthermore, defence of one's country against attack has always, in international law, been considered a much more legitimate justification for military action against another power than mere concern with that power's neglect of human rights within its own boundaries. Thus, had the Vietnamese invaded Cambodia merely in order to help improve the situation of the Cambodian people, in the absence of any direct provocation by DK, they would have been more clearly in violation of international law than they are now alleged to be.

It must also be emphasized, with respect to Vietnamese timing, that until May 1978 there were anti-Pol Pot, and relatively pro-Vietnamese Cambodians in rather high places, a circumstance which had always held out the hope that the internal opposition would be able to change DK policies and avoid conflict with Vietnam. Pol Pot accused the Vietnamese of mounting one plot after another, via sympathetic Cambodian cadres, to overthrow his regime, and while Pol Pot's historical remarks may not be accepted *ipso facto*, his anti-Vietnamese charges for the post-1975 period argue for a Vietnamese concern with Cambodian domestic policy. Their delay in acting until late 1978 demonstrates that they were in fact observing the principles which they are accused of violating.

The Vietnamese case, aside from self-defence, rests on the argument that their aid was requested by a Cambodian opposition which had broken with Pol Pot, and which has now become the new government. Formally, this is true, although the relative balance of forces is worthy of attention, and in any such argument one must be certain that the indigenous group asking for foreign support are not mere creations of the interested foreign power.

If the indigenous element of the new coalition had not been substantial, and its position enjoying considerable popular support, one would have expected them to suffer massive rejection, particularly when the foreign power with whom they were allied, Vietnam, has for generations been considered by Cambodian chauvinists as the 'hereditary enemy'. Instead, the Salvation Front-Vietnamese campaign from late 1978 through early 1979 met with almost complete popular approval, to such an extent that the Vietnamese troops moved forward faster than expected and outran their logistics.[18]

While it has been said that Vietnam imposed its solution on an unwilling Cambodia, with the aid of a few puppets, one serious commentator has noted Cambodian opinion that the Vietnamese have exaggerated their contribution to the anti-DK campaign of 1979, when in fact they marched along the major roads while the Khmer population disarmed and overthrew the DK forces out in the villages (Chanda, 1980, p. 25). Had those villagers not been enthusiastic about changing their regime, they would have fought against the Vietnamese, whom they would have seen as the 'invaders', and the latter would very likely have bogged down somewhere in eastern Cambodia, just as the DK coalition, now in opposition, is bogged down in north-western Cambodia in spite of foreign backers much more powerful than Vietnam.

The Vietnamese invasion of Cambodia was thus a legitimate act of self-defence, and it was also undertaken in support of one faction of the previous Cambodian regime, just as the latter, when they were in revolutionary opposition, had accepted Vietnamese and Chinese aid in their war against Lon Nol's Khmer Republic, and in the same way that Lon Nol had required American, Thai and (Republican) Vietnamese aid to maintain himself after overthrowing the legally constituted government of Prince Sihanouk. With respect to the reliance on foreign support for survival and the acquisition of state power by force, the status of the PRK is no more invidious than that of its two most recent predecessors. Since Lon Nol's Khmer Republic was rapidly granted international recognition, and since DK was also recognized by most of the world and given Cambodia's seat in the United Nations, there would seem to be few valid reasons for withholding similar recognition from the PRK.

The Formation of the PRK

The PRK government which undertook the country's restoration had its origins in the Congress of 200 of those people who had taken up arms against Pol Pot in the Eastern Zone, and who met on 12 December 1978 in their 'liberated zone', proably near Snuol, to form the National Union Front for the Salvation of Kampuchea. A fourteen-person Central Committee was formed, with Heng Samrin as President and Chea Sim as Vice-President. Other members still active in the PRK leadership were Mat Ly, Hun Sen, Mean Saman, Meas Samnang, Neou Samom, Chan Ven, Hem Samin, and Prach Sun.

It is significant that those whose party affiliations were evoked in Front literature—Heng Samrin and Chea Sim—were described as *former* members of the Communist Party of Kampuchea, and that Pen Sovann, Say Phouthang and Bou Thang, soon to appear prominently in government and party positions, were absent from the Front at its formation.[19]

Then, on 1 January 1979, a Congress of Representatives of all revolutionary organs met to decide on the 'principles of action' of the Cambodian state revolutionary power, and a week later, 8 January, following the victory in Phnom Penh, the Kampuchean People's Revolutionary Council, with Heng Samrin as President, was proclaimed. This was to remain the government of Cambodia until the first parliamentary election of May 1981 (PRK, 1980, pp. 124–5).

The membership of the KPRC, in addition to President Heng Samrin, comprised: Pen Sovann, Vice-President, and in charge of National Defence; Hun Sen, in charge of Foreign Affairs; Chea Sim, in charge of the Interior; Keo Chenda, in charge of Information, Press and Cultural Affairs; Chan Ven, in charge of Education; Dr Nou Beng, in charge of Health and Social Affairs; Mok Sokun, in charge of the Economy and living conditions.[20]

The new KPRC seemed to meld the Front leadership under former communists Heng Samrin, Chea Sim and Hun Sen who had also been members of the DK East Zone administration, with non-Front Pen Sovann, Keo Chenda and Nou Beng who were in Vietnam between 1954 and 1970, and who then returned to Cambodia during the war, but broke with Pol Pot before 1975; Mok Sokun was one of the Vietnam group too, but Chan Ven was a 'new person' evacuee during 1975–9. The dichotomy is not that clear, though, for the Front also included Vietnam veterans Ros Samay, as its Secretary-General, and Meas Samnang, while Pen Sovann was to claim membership in the same 'Communist Party'.[21]

Heng Samrin immediately addressed a telegram to the President of the UN Security Council to apprise him of the new situation, stating that the KPRC 'now controls the entire territory of Cambodia' (PRK, 1979, p. 13); and on 12 January 1979 the new official designation of Cambodia, the People's Republic of Kampuchea, was proclaimed.

The major concerns of the KPRC during its first year in power were to recreate normal social and economic life from a void. Personnel had to be found for newly established posts at a time when hardly anyone in the country had performed other than agricultural tasks since 1975 and when nearly all former urban dwellers were moving around the country in search of their homes and families. There were no facilities for training or education. Food had to be gathered and distributed just when most people, freed from DK discipline, were throwing down their tools and eating whatever was available, including seed and work animals. Basic health care was non-existent, medicines had disappeared, and there were only fifty or sixty doctors left in the country.

Not only were there too few qualified people to staff the services which the PRK wished to re-establish, but many of those who were available refused to work in their specialities, preferring the more lucrative market work, or emigration across the Thai border. During 1979 only about one-third of the rice requirement was produced; and it was foreign aid, first from Vietnam and the Soviet Union, later from Western sources as well, that prevented starvation in the newly recreated towns, and provided medical care. Until April 1980, when a new currency was established, trade was by barter and state salaries paid in kind, mostly out of foreign aid supplies. Without that aid, urban life and a normal administration could not have been re-established, and, simply in order to avoid starvation, a DK-like rejection of urban life would have been required (Vickery, 1984, pp. 78–9, 152–4, Chap. 5; Chap. 9 of this book).

An increasing, and perhaps unexpected, concern was national defence, as it became clear that the DK remnants and other opposition groups would be rebuilt and supported by ASEAN, Chinese and United States aid on the Thai border.

By 1980, large-scale population movement had ended, most people had settled down, an administration functioned, and the most implacable opponents of the new regime had crossed into Thailand. The countryside had fed itself with the crop left in the fields when the DK administration fled in January 1979, with a small winter crop at the end of 1979, and by virtue of a policy of complete *laissez-faire* which permitted food-growers to consume their crops and anything else they could forage. At the same time, the towns, normally dependent on local agriculture, had been supplied by foreign aid, which permitted the new administration to function. The next rice crop was expected to be good, and there was even talk of self-sufficiency by 1981 (Vickery, 1984, p. 224).

Throughout 1979–80 the government gradually fleshed itself out in terms of organizational structure and personnel. During this time the KPRC was the sole overt organ of state power, and it assumed both executive and legislative functions. In the latter area, Decree-Laws (*kret-chbap*) were issued, and it was thus a government of revolutionary dictatorship.

At the central level new ministries were created, and new personnel appointed to them, although it is not possible to assume that the date when a new office or official was first publicly mentioned is the date of the inauguration of that department. One of the original ministerial group, Mok Sakun, died in April 1979 (Vickery, 1984, p. 209; *Summary of World Broadcasts*, 16 May 1979). In October several new ministries were created: Trade, under Taing Sarim; Industry, under Meas Samnang, a Front Central Committee Member who retained his post as President of the Trade Union Organization; Agriculture, under Men Chhan; Finance, under Chan Phin, also Director of the State Bank. The Social Affairs portfolio was split off from Health and given to Neou Samom; and Ros Samay, Secretary-General of the Front, was named Minister for Special Affairs, Economy (where he replaced Mok Sakun), Co-operation with Foreign Countries, Tribunals, and for 'drafting the constitution'. Some of these people must in fact have held their positions before they were formalized in KPRC Order No. 6, for Khun Chhy, named there as 'Vice-Minister' of Posts and Telecommunications, had already been mentioned as 'Minister' of that portfolio in June.[22]

During 1980 other new names appeared in ministerial and other high central government positions. By June of that year, Ouk Bun Chhoeun was Minister of Justice, and by November Chea Soth, who had been PRK ambassador to Vietnam, appeared as Minister of Planning (*Kampuchea*, **41**, June 1980, p. 56, September 1980, **62**, November 1980).

In terms of past activities and affiliations, the leadership was still divided between two groups—former DK personnel and old revolutionaries who had been in Vietnam between 1954 and 1970 or later. The former were Heng Samrin, Chea Sim, Hun Sen, Men Chhan and Ouk Bun Chhoeun, but they seemed to be outweighed by Vietnam veterans Pen Sovann, Chan Si, Chea Soth, Meas Samnang, Khun Chhy, Taing Sarim, Ros Samay, Chan Phin, Nou Beng, and Keo Chenda. Foreign media speculation was convinced of this imbalance and held that Pen Sovann was regime strongman, with his double ministerial responsibility, including the control of the army, and his apparent control of the Party. Some even spoke of the 'Pen Sovann Regime', and heralded the end of Cambodian independence at his hands.

The next phase in state organization came in 1981 with elections, the adoption of a constitution, the restructuring of state organs, and the emergence of the party into full view after its Fourth Congress. National Assembly elections took place on 1 May, the Party Congress convened at the end of May, the new Assembly opened its first session on 24 June and adopted the new constitution. The other new state organs were a State Council and the Council of Ministers. KPRC President Heng Samrin became President of the State Council and KPRC Vice-President Pen Sovann was named President of the Council of Ministers, i.e. Prime Minister. Say Phouthang, President of the Party's Organizing Committee, took up his first government post as Vice-President of the State Council. Most of the ministers in the new structure continued in the same posts from the KPRC, although some of the original ministers of the KPRC were moved up to, perhaps more symbolic, posts in the State Council or in the Standing Committee of the National Assembly. Such were Chea Sim and Nou Beng in the Assembly's Standing Committee, and Chan Ven and Men Chhan in the Council of State.[23]

During the last half of 1981 there was a major shake-up, but the causes are still unknown. The first move was the July promotion of Chan Si, until then

Director of the Military Political Commissariat, to replace Pen Sovann as Defence Minister. Then, in December, Pen Sovann was removed from all his posts, replaced as Party Secretary by Heng Samrin, and after some hesitation by Chan Si as Prime Minister, continuing as Minister of Defence. Finally, after still further hesitation, Bou Thang moved from Chairman of the Party's Propaganda and Education Committee to the post of Defence Minister. As it appeared in the contemporary local press, Heng Samrin replaced Pen Sovann as Party Secretary at the Second Central Committee Plenum on 4 December. Then, for a month, no Prime Minister was mentioned in the local press, where prominence was given to Heng Samrin and Chea Sim. When mentioned, Bou Thang is still only referred to as President of the Party Propaganda Committee. In January, *Kampuchea* ran an article on the anniversary of the 7 January overthrow of DK, and Chan Si was named as both Prime Minister and, still, Minister of Defence. This dual role continued at least until the second week of February, when *Kampuchea* announced that the National Assembly had chosen Chan Si as Prime Minister and Bou Thang as Deputy Prime Minister and Minister of Defence.[24]

Pen Sovann's removal took all foreign analysts by surprise. Until then he had been seen as Hanoi's proconsul in Phnom Penh, and in those terms it was unthinkable that a Hanoi man could be overthrown, least of all by perhaps more nationalist Khmers. Thus it was decided that Pen Sovann must have really been Moscow's man in Phnom Penh, and he had been overthrown because he seemed to be playing a Soviet card against Vietnam.[25] The Heng Samrin group, then, rather than being nationalists, as they had been regarded previously, were the real agents of Vietnam. Most of the commentary was based on the assumption that all shots in Phnom Penh had to be called by Hanoi; but one observer felt he saw clear signs of Sovann's anti-Vietnam swing in the structure of his Political Report to the Fourth Party Congress. I have analysed this below, and find that the argument does not hold up.[26] Neither does Sovann's visit to the Soviet Union shortly before appear significant. Visits by Khmer leaders to Moscow and to other East European countries have continued, as have Soviet visits to Cambodia; in fact, the tempo may have increased after Sovann's fall. Moreover, Soviet influence has steadily increased, and the Russians are now the most important providers of aid. The explanation for Sovann's sudden removal must be sought, I believe, in domestic politics, not in foreign power rivalries.[27]

Outside the government proper, the Party and the military may be the real centres of power in the PRK; and the most important person in the former may be Say Phouthang, rather than the Party Secretary. Phouthang, since at least April 1980, has been head of the Central Organization Committee of the Party which decides on all appointments of Party personnel; and because of the multiple hats worn by the PRK leadership this means appointments to many posts in the administration. The Party also seems to dominate the military, whose importance grows as the country continues to be threatened by enemy forces on its western border. Ever since 1979 the military have been under Party leaders with a Vietnam background: Pen Sovann, Chan Si, and now Bou Thang, whose only overt post before assuming the Defence Ministry was as head of the Party's Propaganda Committee.[28]

Say Phouthang and Bou Thang may be pivotal figures in the PRK leadership. Both went to Vietnam in 1954, and both returned in 1970; but they then broke with Pol Pot before 1975 and are thus untainted by association with DK at its worst. Moreover, they are of non-Khmer ethnic minorities—Thai and Tampuon respectively, and are thus perhaps viewed as less likely to manifest the Khmer chauvinism which brought disaster to the DK. Potentially interesting aspects of their ethnic positions might become prominent in the future. Bou Thang belongs to the minority area which straddles the Khmer-Vietnamese border and whose people have for years caused problems for Khmer and Vietnamese governments of all political stripes; and Say Phouthang, from the Thai branch of Khmer communism which showed considerable independence before being obliterated by Pol Pot, might have an interesting role to play if relations with Thailand shift.

Between early 1982 and early 1985 the government was very stable, with only minor changes in leading personnel. Then the surprise death of Prime Minister Chan Si in December 1984 led to his replacement by Hun Sen, the youngest of the leadership group, who retained his Foreign Affairs post, and who soon afterwards announced several further imminent changes in the ministries.[29]

Table 1 shows leading state personnel in the KPRC period (1979–81), in the new structure adopted in 1981, after changes in late 1981 and early 1982, and following further change in 1985. For the State Council and National Assembly Standing Committee I have only listed names of those who were prominent in the KPRC government.[30]

With respect to factional divisions, and in contrast to the Party leadership, Vietnam veterans still outnumber former DK cadres, but the balance has shifted towards the latter with the disappearance of Pen Sovann and Chan Si, and the elevation of Hun Sen to Prime Minister. Bou Thang's emergence as new strongman in the military, however, may maintain the old balance. The Vietnam veterans' group was also depleted by the late 1985 removal of Keo Chenda, who had moved from the Council of Ministers to dual responsibility—PRC President and Party Secretary—in the

Table 1 Leading state personnel, 1979–1981

Post	1979–80 KPRC	1981–2	1982–4	1985 (changes)
		State Council	*State Council*	
President	Heng Samrin	Heng Samrin	Heng Samrin	
Vice-Pres.	Pen Sovann	Say Phouthang	Say Phouthang	
		Chan Ven	Chan Ven	
		Men Chhan	Men Chhan	
		Nat. Assembly		
		Chea Sim	Chea Sim	
		Math Ly	Math Ly	
		Nou Beng	Nou Beng	
		Ministry	*Ministry*	
Pres. (PM)		Pen Sovann	Chan Si	Hun Sen
Vice-Pres.		Hun Sen	Bou Thang	
		Chea Soth	Hun Sen	Say Phouthang
		Chan Si	Chea Soth	
Defence	Pen Sovann	Chan Si	Bou Thang	
	Chan Si			
Foreign	Hun Sen	Hun Sen	Hun Sen	Hun Sen
Plan.	Chea Soth	Chea Soth	Chea Soth	
Interior	Chea Sim	Khang Sarin	Khang Sarin	
Agriculture	Men Chhan	Kong Samol	Kong Samol	
Industry	Meas Samnang	Keo Chenda	Meas Samnang	
Comm. Post	Khun Chhy	Khun Chhy	Khun Chhy	Tea Banh
Home & For. Trade	Taing Sarim	Taing Sarim	Taing Sarim	Chan Phin
Economy	Mok Sokun			
	Ros Samay			
Econ. Co-op. w. Soc. bloc				Taing Sarim
Finance	Chan Phin	Chan Phin	Chan Phin	
Nat. Bank	Chan Phin	Cha Rieng	Cha Rieng	
State Affairs		Sim Ka	Sim Ka	
Education	Chan Ven	Pen Navuth	Pen Navuth	
Health	Nou Beng	Yith Kim Seng	Yith Kim Seng	
Soc. Affairs	Neou Samom			
Disabled & Soc. Affairs				(name?)
Information	Keo Chenda	Chheng Phon	Chheng Phon	
Justice	Ouk Bun Chhoeun	Ouk Bun Chhoeun	Ouk Bun Chhoeun	
Pres. Office		Ung Phan	Ung Phan	Khun Chhy

Phnom Penh city government, from all his posts. The reasons for this are unclear, however, and it may have been as much a question of personality as political factionalism. More serious is the reported removal of Khang Sarin, which had not yet [January 1986] been confirmed in the PRK press.

The increasing elevation to prominence of men with no revolutionary background is interesting, up from one, Chan Ven, in 1979, to four in 1984, Kong Samol, Pen Navuth, Yit Kim Seng and Chheng Phon, and to seven at the end of 1985. They do not constitute a power faction, certainly not in the posts they hold, but Chheng Phon has also been elected to Party Central Committee alternate.[31]

Below this highest ministerial level, the administration is full of people without revolutionary background, many of whom were employed under Sihanouk and Lon Nol; and with time more of them will probably appear in positions of prominence.

Among the PRK's major concerns, increasingly, has been defence, for which an army is slowly being rebuilt, which absorbs material resources and personnel badly needed elsewhere. This has been inevitable. Although DK forces were almost totally destroyed after the 1979 campaign, a foreign-backed rehabilitation campaign for them began soon afterwards, with food and medicine channelled through the refugee camp system and arms, mainly from China, via Thai military channels. This operation was backed by ASEAN and the United States, who have also provided various types of direct aid, financial and military. In July 1982, a Coalition Government of Democratic Kampuchea was put together in order to cover the more effective DK troops with the greater respectability of Prince Sihanouk and Son Sann, whose own forces are much weaker. A war situation, particularly in western and northern Cambodia has thus continued, and while it does not threaten the existence of the PRK state, the continuing acts of sabotage and terrorism sap morale within the country, and the support given to the coalition by the world's largest and its most powerful country cause Cambodians to worry that DK may be brought back with international support.

The economy, in which both agriculture and industry are below their pre-war levels and are still admittedly inadequate, gives cause for concern. The country is not yet self-sufficient in rice, salaries are extremely low, and state employees are disadvantaged with respect to the agricultural and market sectors which have little reason to desire integration with the state apparatus. Because of these hardships, much attention is devoted to the formation of a citizenry loyal and hard-working in spite of prolonged difficulties; and long hours are devoted to political education at all levels and in all organizations. The political courses are particularly important for state employees, most of whom were brought up in the Sihanouk–Lon Nol era when a *fonctionnaire* post was ticket to status and relative wealth, instead of a duty to serve the country at a lower income than a skilled mechanic or market-stall operator. Certainly connected with this was the boost given to the major mass organizations through the holding of National Congresses in 1983 (see pp. 117–18).

On the positive side, the new state has established itself and has lasted longer than its two most recent predecessors—Lon Nol's Khmer Republic, and DK—and with a much better record than either. Also important is that the PRK has become certainly and increasingly Khmer, the number of Vietnamese advisers and experts, in every office in 1979, has regularly decreased, and in this respect too, the PRK looks better than any of its opponents. Vietnamese troops are still there, and are still needed for defence, but with each year they are less visible in the towns, their garrisons are not prominent, and they are in less contact with the Khmer civilian population. When Cambodians have to deal with authorities and the administration, they deal with fellow Khmers.

If living standards are minimal, they are liveable, there has been considerable freedom of movement and choice of work, all children again go to school, and restrictions on personal, intellectual and political freedom are hardly more rigid than under Sihanouk in the late 1960s, nor more than would be expected in a small country subject to attack from abroad and, like the two Germanies, to subversion by enemies who are difficult to recognize.[32]

There is reason for concern in that the undoubted progress seemed to be slowing down in 1983–4, undoubtedly because of the resources put into defence and the virtual blockade of Cambodia maintained by China, major western powers, and their allies among Cambodia's neighbours. An important new development in this respect was the destruction of all enemy bases along the Thai border in the first two months of 1985. The PRK thus seemed militarily stronger, or at least its opponents weaker; and the new Prime Minister, Hun Sen, has announced that by 1987 the question of the PRK's political existence will have been resolved, and that by 1990 the Vietnamese forces will be able to return home.[33]

5 Social Structure

Historical Survey

Traditional Cambodian society comprised three main classes–royalty, officials and peasants. Very few Khmers became merchants, and to the extent that an urban population outside the court and officials existed, it was mainly composed of non-Khmers–generally Chinese. This division of society probably goes back to the Angkor period when national wealth was produced from the land, and collected by the officials who channelled it to the court and the religious apparatus, where it was largely used for building temples and supporting the specialized populations attached to them. Part of the revenue collected by officials remained in their hands in lieu of salary, but this was accepted as the way the system naturally functioned. Each performed a function believed essential for the welfare of society, in which the king's role was quasi-religious and ritual.

Even after the Angkor state disappeared, the old divisions of society persisted. For the mass of the population, social positions were fixed, and it would have been almost inconceivable to rise above the class into which one had been born. Occasionally, perhaps in time of war, or for exceptional services to a powerful patron, someone from a peasant background might move into the official class and thereby change the status of his immediate family; and clever children might be educated in an official family or else at court, to become officials; but this occurred too rarely for any expectation of social mobility to be part of public consciousness.

The possibilities of accumulating wealth were also limited. Land was not owned privately, but in theory belonged to the king. An energetic peasant could not accumulate land or wealth through hard work and abstemiousness in order to move up the scale to rich farmer, entrepreneur or merchant. The only possibility for change lay in an official career. Even there, life was hazardous. Officials were of course more or less wealthy, and the status of a family as such might continue for generations; but their position was not legally assured, and could be ended precipitously at royal displeasure–for instance, if an official showed signs of accumulating too much wealth or power. There was no guarantee of the inheritance of accumulated wealth; indeed, it was more likely to revert to the state, and there was thus no incentive, or possibility, to use wealth for long-term constructive purposes or entrepreneurial investment.

Village and family organization, especially in comparison with China, Vietnam or India, was weak. Khmer villages were not cohesive units, as in Vietnam, dealing collectively with officials; and beyond nuclear households, families easily disintegrated. Family names did not exist, records of previous generations were not kept, ancestors were not the object of reverence. Corporate discipline over the individual by extended families or by village organizations was weak, and once a person had fulfilled obligations to the state—through payment of tax or corvée—there was little constraint on his activities. Paradoxically, it was thus likely that great anarchic personal freedom prevailed in a society in which there was no formal freedom at all.

Since the fifteenth century at least, and particularly during the eighteenth and nineteenth centuries, Cambodian society was subject to almost continuous disruption and instability. Frequent warfare displaced large sections of the population, the capital was often moved, villages disappeared, and all organizations beyond the immediate family declined in importance.

The colonial period, beginning for Cambodia in 1863, stabilized traditional society, for the French tried to rule indirectly, through the old Cambodian administration. Taxation, however, increased, thus forcing peasants to seek more cash income than before, and the colonial authorities legalized private property in land to transform it into a commodity and to provide an inducement to higher productivity.

Despite these changes, the result was neither concentration of land holdings nor capitalist development of agriculture. Potential capitalists in Cambodia were first of all foreigners, mainly Chinese, who were prohibited from owning land, or if Cambodians, they preferred the traditional elite occupation of office-holder. In either case, they extracted wealth from the agricultural sector through usury, taxation, or payment for favours, not by direct intervention to increase production. Cambodian agriculture was persistently smallholding, but with peasants caught in networks of debt and traditional obligations.

Well into the twentieth century, then, the Cambodian social structure remained much as it had always been: at the very top, a royal family; in the middle, a small class of bureaucrat-aristocracy who depended on royal favour and tradition for their status and wealth. At the bottom were the ordinary people, engaged in agriculture or service occupations, and constituting, before the 1950s, about 90 per cent of the population. The small commercial sector was mainly foreign, especially Chinese.

In the 1950s and 1960s significant changes occurred in the old structure. With independence, the bureaucracy increased severalfold, providing opportunities for many to move out of agriculture into urban life. The school system was expanded to meet the demand, and an entire new *petit-bourgeois* sector appeared. As some industries were created, a small proletariat formed, consisting first of former peasants, but by the late 1960s increasingly of urban school-leavers who could no longer find places in the administration. After 1970, in particular, the military, which until the 1960s had been very small and not seen as an attractive career, became the most important section of the official class, acquiring the wealth and prestige which had accompanied official positions in traditional Cambodia. Officers were first drawn from among the corps of civilian officials, then from among the new *petit-bourgeoisie*; that is, they were almost entirely an urban group.[1]

The Democratic Kampuchea Transformation

The revolutionary victory of 1975 brought an abrupt end to the traditional social structures. The official ideology of the dominant Pol Pot faction was that the only progressive classes were the poor and the lower-middle peasants. All other sections–in particular the urban population, including even the urban working class, the proletariat–were class enemies. The new DK authorities moved swiftly to put their class analysis into effect. All urban dwellers were evacuated to the countryside where they were forced to adopt the life of poor peasants or other menial labourers. Some workers were kept on in those factories deemed to be essential, but they were not considered a privileged revolutionary proletariat. They were regarded instead as unreliable townsfolk to be replaced by new workers brought from the peasantry as soon as feasible.[2]

The abolition of money, markets and any other means of accumulating wealth, together with enforced communal dining and widespread prohibition of foraging for additional food, ensured that virtually no one was able to work his way out of the near egalitarian poverty to which the society was constrained. Even at the top there were serious efforts to ensure that the new political rulers should not become an economically privileged class. As a French-woman who spent 1975–9 in the DK Foreign Ministry has described, even there, in addition to their office duties, they grew their own food, cooked and ate in common, and were severely punished if they even ate a piece of fruit in private (Picq, 1984, pp. 96, 113–14, 118–19).

Also in accord with DK ideology was the slight economic superiority which the poorest peasants, those who had been in revolutionary 'liberated' zones before April 1975, enjoyed over the urban evacuees who were sent out to their villages. They usually continued to have *de facto* possession of houses and sometimes gardens and fowl; and even when communal dining was enforced, breaches of the regulations by poor peasants were often tolerated. They could therefore gather extra food and consume it in private with greater safety than the urban evacuees. The poor peasants were also more trusted, and their class supriority was both an economic and a political one (Vickery, 1984, pp. 92, 115, 117, 134, 141).

The People's Republic of Kampuchea, Since 1979

Although the goal of the Vietnamese and their Cambodian allies in 1979 was to overthrow DK, this was not for the purpose of effecting a counter-revolution and restoring pre-war society. Both the Vietnamese and the new PRK leaders believed in socialism, though without the excesses of DK and there was the intention that wide class differences should not redevelop.

Certainly, poor peasantism was no longer in vogue, and the proletariat was to be given its due Marxist prestige, although it was recognized that Cambodia would long remain an agricultural country, and that industry should develop to complement, and to meet the needs of the agricultural sector. The state would continue to own the major means of production, land, equipment and real estate, so that no new exploitative bourgeoisie could reappear.

There would be no attempt, however, to maintain the DK suppression of urban-rural differences. The initial Salvation Front Programme promised that the former urban population would be allowed to return to their homes; thus, Phnom Penh and other towns would be resettled, and schools, medical facilities and religious practices, as these were all traditionally conceived, would be revived. This meant that an urban infrastructure, with a civil service and tertiary sector, would reappear, but differences in economic advantage were to be limited.

The DK experience left the PRK successors in one way in an unusually favourable position to undertake such reconstruction. The dirty work had already been done by their opponents whom they overthrew. The old parasitic groups had been severely weakened, if not completely destroyed, excessive urban growth had been reversed, and the entire population had been inured to hard work. Moreover, the reaction of the PRK's Western neighbours and their Great Power supporters to the PRK victory meant that those survivors of the old privileged classes who would accept nothing less than a complete counter-revolution could easily, and probably with tacit

PRK assent, flee abroad rather than remain within Cambodia to subvert the new authorities.

The PRK, then, intended to rebuild a society with normally functioning and interrelated urban and rural sectors after nearly four years in which such distinctions had been effaced and the urban sector abolished. Moreover, it was soon admitted that, except for food, the urban commodity supply would operate through a free-market system, and that the countryside, at least for a time, would not be coerced either directly or indirectly into supplying non-producers with food. There would thus be, as in all societies with urban centres, part of the population whose basic livelihood would have to be assured by the labour of others; and there would be a market trading sector with the potential for evolving into a new bourgeoisie. There was thus the inherent possibility of a re-emergence of the type of society which DK wished to destroy and which the PRK leadership still wished to avoid.[3]

Checks operating against a complete revival of the old structure were state ownership of all land and major means of production such as factories and transportation, as well as state monopoly of financial institutions and foreign trade. Peasant land would thus not be subject to sale or transfer for repayment of debt. Traditional usury was effectively blocked, and the authorities declared that for a time there would be no state coercion of the rural sector to supply the towns.

To be sure, market traders would make profits, but these could not be used to acquire agricultural land, industrial property, or real estate for rental income. Such profits could only be reinvested in continued market trading or in personal consumption.

A risk for the new PRK leaders in their partial return to pre-DK structures was the dependance on former bourgeois and official personnel from the Sihanouk and Lon Nol regimes, since the PRK socialist leadership did not even have the numbers or competence to fully staff the upper levels of their own administration. Would not the mass re-employment of pre-revolutionary personnel overwhelm the revolution; and could the former bourgeoisie and *fonctionnaires* be relied on to perform the tasks with which they were to be entrusted? Would not PRK socialism become bourgeoisified through such large-scale co-optation of former members of the bourgeoisie and *petit-bourgeoisie*?

A peculiarity, perhaps unique in world revolutionary history, was that a situation which would have seemed to the former Cambodian bourgeoisie and officials unacceptably and oppressively revolutionary and authoritarian before 1975 could be offered as a return to social freedom and personal liberty in 1979. Again it must be emphasized that the PRK's task was facilitated by the circumstance that Pol Pot had already accomplished the requisite revolutionary spade work, and a socialist system which the urban and private sectors would have violently resisted if it had been imposed by the same revolutionary leadership in 1973, conceivable if the war had ended then, appeared as a relief from unmitigated misery. The royalist and republican officer corps had been destroyed after 1975, as had the financial and commercial bourgeoisie; and the survivors of those groups preferred to flee abroad in 1979 rather than stay to fight the new system. As for the peasantry, before Pol Pot they might have strenuously objected to total land nationalization, but in 1979, without other restraints, it was part of a package which represented a return to freedom of cultivation and consumption under conditions of normal family and village life.

The PRK authorities were therefore able to invite the educated elite, the technically and administratively trained, to return to tasks for which they were qualified, and this without having to promise them any kind of class or economic privileges, since the change from peasant status to teacher or administrator, even for exiguous remuneration, was sufficient inducement. Most of these who would not accept the change on those conditions, i.e. who insisted on previous levels of status of salary differentiation, sooner or later fled abroad. Some others, though few, remained for a time, or even still remain in Cambodia while refusing to take up state positions for which they are qualified. Thus, there are fluent French- and English-speakers who prefer to sell fruit from a street stall and make more money than for example, as an interpreter, and other highly qualified people who became market traders rather than administrators.

PRK society as a result comprises a very thin stratum of proven revolutionary socialists in most of the top administrative offices and positions of authority, and below them, throughout the administration and service occupations, people from the same groups who occupied such positions before 1975. All of these are remunerated according to a very narrow scale of very low salaries, such that significant economic or social stratification on the basis of income is impossible. Department chiefs in ministries earn no more than factory workers, who, if skilled, and with special allowances, may take home more than their factory boss.

Most market activity is in the hands of people who engaged in such work before 1975, and the initial finance for the resumption of trading in 1979 came from wealthy individuals who were fortunate enough to have preserved hoarded wealth throughout the DK period. Here then, former wealth has permitted the perpetuation of a relatively affluent status under the new regime, but unlike pre-war times, this wealth cannot be parlayed into other economic areas or political status. Other relatively privileged economic groups are the independent artisans, who earn several times an official salary. They are, economically, at a much higher relative level than pre-war, but their wealth buys no privileges beyond immediate consumption.

Class divisions have only re-emerged to a very limited degree, although there are levels of status and authority. Economically, the working class is relatively (that is, with respect to other groups), much better off than before 1975, as are the peasantry, freed from the danger of usury and the threat of land loss.[4] In terms of perceived status within the whole society, the Foreign Ministry guide-interpreter, or the school teacher, whose salaries are lower than that of a skilled worker, nevertheless rate higher, certainly at least in their own estimations, and probably in the worker's as well. Part of this status consciousness is deliberately fostered. Cadres, in particular Party members, are supposed to be a vanguard, setting examples for society, and in return receive respect. This is not meant to be translated into economic privilege, however.

One area in which important changes have occurred since the 1950s is the family, in particular the relative positions of men and women. As education, the civil service, and the urban sector rapidly expanded after independence, women participated in the first two in a much smaller proportion than men. This was the effect of tradition rather than official policy. Most peasants saw no reason for girls to have more schooling than was required for basic literacy, and in the 1960s secondary-school classes were still 80–90 per cent male. Women who moved into the urban sector at that time, if they were not simply following parents or husbands, worked in service areas, and later—the first places where they achieved some economic independence—in some of the new industries, particularly textiles and pharmaceuticals. Teaching also absorbed many of the women who completed secondary school in the 1950s–60s, and contributed to a new economic independence for them. During the 1970–5 war, the general social collapse and increased recruitment of women into the military and civil service served to break down traditional sex divisions still further.

Under DK a strict sexual equality was instituted, but at a rigorous level which did not benefit women in any absolute sense. Official sexual equality has been maintained under PRK, and more women are obviously being taken into responsible official employment, which may of course be no more than the inevitable result of the imbalance between the sexes after DK, when many more men than women lost their lives.

Statistics on the excess of women over men are unreliable, but there are now certainly far more women, both in towns and in agricultural villages, who are forced to live independent lives, either alone or with children. Because of this, traditional divisions and limits on female activities will probably not re-emerge. Even before the war, Cambodian women were becoming impatient with their inferior status, and were quick to take any new opportunities for freedom and equality which arose. Given official PRK policy, and the economic egalitarianism which will be inevitable for many more years, women are unlikely to revert to social, intellectual and economic dependence.

Different levels of authority do, however, occasion various privileges, or the lack thereof. This is most apparent in housing. Ministers have taken over the dwellings of pre-war millionaire businesmen, and those further down the official hierarchy have smaller quarters. Similarly, those in the highest positions have official cars, just as they would in wealthier countries of either the socialist or capitalist camp. I was struck, however, on my one visit to a minister's private quarters, which was incidentally the largest private dwelling I have ever entered in Cambodia during any regime, that the only great advantage he possessed was space. His furniture was as simple and as sparse as that in many poorer houses, we drank the cheapest local liquor, such as any worker might have offered guests, and the minister's wife was cooking over charcoal pots like those used in the homes of ordinary workers or low-level officials.

Although most of the pre-war intellectuals and administrators whose ambivalence toward serving the PRK could not be overcome have left, and those remaining are reconciled to working loyally within the new system, there is inevitably tension resulting from the different backgrounds and expectations, and probably disappointment that so few of the luxuries to which the pre-war urban population was accustomed, are again available.

The basic sectors of pre-war society—agricultural, urban manufacture and tertiary—have re-formed, and in general, except for the revolutionary cadres in top political positions, are occupied by the same people as before. Unlike pre-war society, there is no hereditary upper class, nor an economic elite living on unearned income. Although the existing socio-economic sectors are determined by the country's objective circumstances, and cannot be to any great extent modified without DK-type violence, a question for the future is whether these sectors will continue to be occupied by the same people and their descendants, forming, if not classes, in a sense castes.

For the present and the next generation such a perpetuation of social divisions seems to be occurring. The first groups of former students able to continue higher education, and thus to take over places in the administrative, technical and political sectors were from the relatively privileged pre-war groups, because only they had the requisite preparation. Most of the two thousand or more students now in higher education abroad, and who are expected to return over the next four or five years, are of this type, and it will be interesting to see whether future generations in higher status positions come from among the children of the present corps via better schools, or whether egalitarian access to education and therefore to the more desirable positions will prevail.

One area in which pre-war survivors have not been recruited is the military. The old officer corps really was a group subject to extermination under DK, and nearly all survivors have fled abroad. The new military leaders are men of poor rural background who participated in the revolution, but then split with Pol Pot. Some of them, moreover, are from the non-Khmer minorities who were totally outside mainstream, particularly urban, life before 1975.[5] At the very least, this suggests that the military, and its officer corps, will not recreate the same socio-political niche as that occupied by their pre-1975 predecessors.

Part II
Political Systems

6 The Party

The ruling party of the PRK, the People's Revolutionary Party of Kampuchea [PRPK], implicitly and explicitly derives from earlier Cambodian communist parties. The party dates its foundation from 1951, when the Khmer People's Revolutionary Party (KPRP) was formed; and they claim to have held the Third Party Congress in January 1979, following the tradition which places the Second Congress in 1960, and which ignores the subsequent developments of party organization under Pol Pot.[1]

The founding date of the first Cambodian 'Communist' Party has long excited controversy both within the ranks of Cambodian revolutionaries and among foreign students of the revolution; and the true date is probably unknown. Apart from Pol Pot's aberrant historical treatment, all sources agree on the year 1951, and there seems little reason to doubt that much. Strangely, perhaps because of the party's clandestine nature, no pre-war documents on its origin have surfaced, and the first party history to fall into outside hands was one prepared by East Zone authorities in 1973, captured by the government side, and made available to scholars in English translation.[2]

This Party History placed the founding on 30 September 1951, with the formation of a provisional Central Committee termed 'party formation and propaganda committee', pending the First Congress, which thus, according to that view, would have been held sometime later.[3] At the Fourth Party Congress in 1981, however, it was claimed that the First Party Congress had been held on 19 February 1951, implicitly right after the Second Congress of the Indo-China Communist Party had decided on a three-way split,[4] but then in 1982 the PRK authorities decided that their founding date was June 1951.[5]

Examination of the sources and their treatment suggests that there is something arbitrary about all these dates. Ben Kiernan, relying largely on the memories of participants in the 1950s events, French intelligence reports and Vietnamese documents and publications, has compiled the largest amount of material yet published about the origins of Cambodian communism.[6] Here we find that, on 17 April 1950, a Congress of two hundred delegates established the United Issarak Front and a proto-government, the Provisional People's Liberation Central Committee (PLCC); and two months later,

19 June, Son Ngoc Minh, the president of the new organizations, speaking in the name of the PLCC, declared Cambodia independent. Kiernan also cites a Vietnamese popular treatment of the period for details on numbers of Cambodian ICP members and party branches to fill out his story.[7]

Then Kiernan writes that on 8 February 1951 'the nine cadre committees' of the ICP in Kampuchea met in a 'plenary session' called by Le Duc Tho for the purpose of forming a national communist party in line with the decision of the ICP Second Congress of early February, and that in September 1951 the KPRP provisional Central Committee was established, with this last detail from the 1973 Party History integrated with the earlier information (Kiernan, 1984, pp. 82–3).

None of these sources is absolutely clear on the founding of the party. The Vietnamese publication, *Dât Nu'o'c*, merely says the ICP Second Congress decided that each country should have its own party in conformity with its own conditions, and it says the Cambodian party was founded in June 1951. Another publication in which one of the authors of *Dât Nu'o'c* participated also states that the party was founded in June, but relates it to a March 1951 joint congress of the Vietnamese, Khmer and Lao Fronts, an event also mentioned by Kiernan. There is no mention here of the Khmer party resulting from the dissolution of the ICP or of the cadres committees' meeting under Le Duc Tho. Yet a third Vietnamese work on Cambodia, published in 1979 and the apparent source of the material in the two others just cited, also omits mention of the ICP Second Congress Decision, and says that the Lao and Cambodian parties were established together with the Vietnamese Lao Dong Party because of the maturity of the revolutionary forces in 1951. Then it mentions the joint Front congress of March and in June the founding of the Cambodian party by the decision of a group of communists in that country.[8]

The Vietnamese work is also interesting in that it places Son Ngoc Minh's declaration of independence at 19 April 1950, rather than 19 June; but even more curious is that the PRK has chosen to place that event a whole year later, at 18 June 1951.[9]

In retrospect, it seems strange that one current of scholarship adopted with so little question the September date for the party's founding, particularly since information which tends to cast doubt on it, and not just in Pol Pot propaganda, was available. As noted above, *Dât Nu'o'c*, which Kiernan cited for other details, gave a June date; and in Kiernan (1984) the author cites a Vietnamese document of August 1951 containing the Khmer party's statutes, which had been approved by the 'Cadre Committee of Cambodia', presumably one of those called to a meeting in February by Le Duc Tho; and a

French intelligence report noted by Kiernan, in reference to those statutes, stated that 'until August 1951, the Cambodians admitted to the Party were few in number', indicating that the party had been formed before August, rather than in September. Kiernan also cites another Vietnamese document which said that 'by late 1951' the 'newly-formed' Khmer Party had a thousand members, and one wonders if that document might not have contained some more precise notation of date (Kiernan, 1984, pp. 83–4 and n. 118).

The September date is not reflected in any other Khmer or Vietnamese source; and no other important organizational event, which might have been confused with a founding congress, occurred in September 1951 either. The Vietnamese, since at least 1979, have preferred June 1951 as the date; and if confusion existed, it would have been over the validity of some earlier date in 1951 rather than a later one.

It is now clear that such controversy within Khmer and Vietnamese ranks really did exist, for during the Fourth Congress of the Cambodian party in May 1981, Chea Sim in the opening address, Pen Sovann in the Political Report, and the Congress Resolutions all proposed the date of 19 February 1951 for the First Congress of the Khmer People's Revolutionary Party, ancestor of the People's Revolutionary Party of Kampuchea which issued from the Fourth Congress. According to this view, that first congress was an application of the decision of the Second Congress of the ICP to establish separate parties in each of the Indo-China countries.[10]

Evidence of uneasiness within the Cambodian leadership over their choice of date appeared scarcely a month after the Fourth Congress in an article on the founding of the Issarak armed forces on '19 June 1951'. It stated that early in 1951 unified command over the revolutionary forces was required, and in June the 'Issarak Army' was formed under the direct leadership of the Khmer People's Revolutionary Party, without any allusion to the party's founding date (*Kampuchea*, **92**, 18 June 1951, p. 3).

In just over a year, however, the official Cambodian view changed, and on 26 June 1982 a party circular informed the public that exactly thirty years earlier, on 28 June 1951, after the ICP decided to split into three national parties 'the ICP members in Kampuchea held a Congress under Son Ngoc Minh to create the Khmer People's Revolutionary Party'. This announcement coincided with the celebration of the thirty-first anniversary of the establishment of the revolutionary armed forces, a date announced a year earlier (*Kampuchea*, **145**, 24 June 1982).

Although the surviving party members clearly considered that the party continued to exist, and there were some public references to it during 1979, its organization and leadership were not clear, and throughout 1980 and early 1981 until the Fourth Congress in May of the latter year, I have found no mention at all of the party in the two principal press organs (*Kampuchea* and *Kong tap padiwat*). This low-key treatment was no doubt in response to the unpopularity of any version of 'socialism' after the DK experience; and indeed in 1979, Ros Samay, then Secretary-General of the Front, admitted to a foreign journalist that they had to move slowly because socialism and the party had been discredited by Pol Pot.[11]

Ros Samay in fact, on two occasions, suggested that the new leadership rejected the old party and intended to form a new one. In response to an AFP interviewer who asked precisely whether a new party would be formed or the old one preserved after purging it of those who served DK, Samay said that the old party had been transformed into an instrument of repression of the Pol Pot clique, whereas the party leading the Cambodian revolution must be genuine; and a month later Samay told Hungarian journalists that 'we consider one of our most urgent tasks the establishment of a new Communist Party . . . [which] we already set to organizing' following the January 1979 victory.[12]

Similarly, in a January 1979 Front publication, Heng Samrin, Chea Sim and Bun My of the Front's Central Committee were described as *former* members of the Cambodian Communist Party, Samrin as East Zone committee member, and the other two as members of the committees of regions 20 (East) and 3 (North-West) respectively.[13]

This view was evidently not shared by the entire leadership, for in March 1979 Pen Sovann in his capacity as Vice-President of the government told a political education course that 'we have a correct party which adheres to Marxism-Leninism' (*SWB*, 13 March 1979); and a week later a telegram sending greetings to the Lao party was signed by Pen Sovann as First Secretary of the Central Committee of the Communist Party of Kampuchea, demonstrating that the name of Pol Pot's party was still being used (*SWB*, 21 April 1979). The following month, Bou Thang was mentioned as President of the party's Education and Propaganda Committee (*SWB*, 24 May 1979), and in June a report broadcast about a political reorientation course referred to the Party Secretary in charge of Phnom Penh, although not by name, and to the Central Committee of the Revolutionary Party of Kampuchea (*SWB*, 18 June 1974).

Quite possibly, the party leadership was revealed in the announcement of the group which met a visiting Japanese Communist Party delegation in July. They were Pen Sovann, Chea Sim, Ros Samay, Keo Prasath, Say Phouthang, Bou Thang, and Chan Si(?); and the Japanese only later met for talks with Heng Samrin together with the seven just mentioned and Chea Soth.[14]

The next significant reference to the party was in Pen Sovann's address to delegates of the Second Front Congress in which he spoke in the name of the Central Committee of the Communist Party of Kampuchea, again using the post-1960 name of the Pol Pot faction (*SWB*, 8 October 1979). The same name was mentioned publicly again in the publication of the first Draft Constitution of 28 July 1980, which referred to a meeting of the Central Committee of the Communist Party on 18 April of the same year;[15] and three Central Committee decisions of the first half of 1980 relating to the organization of the Women's Association, the Salvation Front, the Trade Unions, and the Youth Organization, were all issued from the Central Committee of the *Communist* Party of Kampuchea and signed by Say Phouthang, 'for the Central Standing committee'.[16]

There were also references in 1980 to persons holding positions which would certainly be understood as party functions, even when there was no mention of the party itself. Thus, in a report on the 1980 Cambodian New Year celebration, some of the leading cadres listed as present were Pen Sovann, Chea Sim, Say Phouthang, 'president of the Central Organization Committee' and Bou Thang, 'president of the Central Committee on Propaganda and Education'.[17]

The Fourth Party Congress, May 1981

The Party did not completely emerge from its closet until the Fourth Congress held in Phnom Penh on 26–29 May 1981, which was attended by 162 delegates with full voting rights, including eight women, forty-two members of minority groups, and thirty-four military personnel (*Kampuchea*, **90**, 4 June 1981, p. 5).

The Congress approved a political report from the Central Committee, an economic programme for several years in the future, a report on construction of the party and its statutes, and a set of resolutions. Delegations came to the Congress from the 'fraternal proletarian parties' of Vietnam, Laos, the Soviet Union, Afghanistan, GDR, Cuba, Bulgaria, Czechoslovakia, Hungary, Poland and Mongolia, listed in that order (*Kampuchea*, **89**, 28 May 1981).

The opening address to the Congress was given by Chea Sim in his capacity as Vice-President of the Front, and indeed, until the Congress was over, no one was identified in the press by party role.

In his address, Chea Sim referred to the thirty years of the party's existence, and to the thirtieth anniversary of the founding of the revolutionary armed forces which was to be celebrated a couple of weeks later (*Kong tap padiwat*, 28 June 1981). He divided the thirty-year history of the party into three phases:

the struggle against French colonialism, the struggle against aggressive American imperialism, and the overthrow of DK, which he described as 'the genocidal regime of Pol Pot, Ieng Sary and Khieu Samphan, the associates of expansionist Peking'.

Chea Sim went on to say that the party had held three previous congresses. The first was on 19 February 1951, in order 'to apply the resolution of the Indochina Communist Party concerning the establishment of Marxist–Leninist parties' in the three Indo-China countries. That congress established the Khmer People's Revolutionary Party, and chose a central committee with Achar Mean, 'Son Ngoc Minh', as Secretary-General. Under that party's leadership the revolutionary struggle in 1954 ended nearly a hundred years of French Protectorate; and it is interesting that in this connection Chea Sim did not mention 'independence'.[18]

The Second Congress was held on 30 September 1960, and it was called because 'the revolution inside and outside the country was in confusion which required a change in political line'. The Second Congress chose a new Central Committee with Tou Samouth as Secretary-General. The new line was 'peace, neutrality, and opposition to American imperialism and its allies'.[19]

Chea Sim then jumped to 1970 without any allusion to the very serious internal party conflicts of the 1960s, the mysterious disappearance of Tou Samouth, his replacement by Saloth Sar/Pol Pot, and the confusion within the party over the line to adopt towards Sihanouk. The problem in 1970 was American aggression—there was still no mention of Sihanouk or Lon Nol—and under 'the Party's correct leadership', and with the aid again of Vietnam and Laos, a 'historic victory' was achieved on 17 April 1975, only to be perverted by the policies of Pol Pot.

As Pol Pot was being ousted, the Third Party Congress was held on 5 January 1979, i.e. two days before the entrance of the PRK forces into Phnom Penh.[20] The congress chose a 'Party-building commission' which turned into a Central Committee, very similar to the 1973 formulation of the organizing procedure in 1951, and Pen Sovann was chosen as that Party Central Committee's First Secretary. It should be noted that in this part of Chea Sim's remarks the party is given no name, although a few sentences later he referred to 'our Kampuchean People's Party', in either case in disaccord with First Secretary Pen Sovann's remarks of 1979.

Towards the end of his speech Chea Sim said,

> this is a congress of a new era, and an era of independence and socialism . . . from this 4th congress, for the first time and forever more our party will come out openly in all

tasks of leading the state power and the whole people for the purpose of defending and building a new country.

Finally, he defined the three immediate tasks of the Party Congress as (1) define the political line ... (2) develop party leadership in all areas ... (3) choose a new Central Committee.[21]

Following Chea Sim's opening address, Pen Sovann read the political report. This 'Political Report of the Central Committee' takes up eighty-four pages in French translation, and it was only very briefly summarized in the local press at the time, although copies both in Khmer and in French translation were apparently available then for interested observers.[22] In addition to the intrinsic interest which the first political report of a communist party in such circumstances would in any case have, curiosity about Pen Sovann's report has been enhanced by his sudden political eclipse half a year later, and by the deductions about his political position made by certain journalists largely on the basis of this report (Chanda, 1981a, pp. 24–6).

The report comprises five parts: (1) history of the independence struggle; (2) the struggle of the past two years for reconstruction and defence; (3) on the defence of national independence as the basis for building the nation according to true socialism; (4) the immediate tasks and objectives of the Cambodian revolution; (5) building the party.

In part 1, after brief reference to Angkorean glory and subsequent decline, the report lists the various movements of resistance to French colonialism, including both the real and the mythic, an example of the latter being the statement that Prince Yukanthor was 'arrested, then incarcerated in the prison of Koh Tralach [Pulou Condore] in 1900 [and then] disappeared mysteriously'.[23]

As Sovann's historical treatment reaches the 1930s we begin to find remarks which led Nayan Chanda to infer that Sovann wished to play down the Vietnamese role in Cambodia and link revolutionary Cambodia rather with the Soviet Union, an attitude which is said to have led to Sovann's downfall in December 1981(Chanda, 1981a, pp. 24–6).

Indeed, Sovann said,

> Thanks to the beneficial influence of the October Revolution in Russia on the three Indochina countries, and in the light of international communism, a message from which toward the beginning of 1930 ... [said], 'the primary and necessary task of all the Indochinese communists is to create a revolutionary party of the proletariat ... this party must be unique, and in Indochina, only this party represents the communist organization' [p. 4].

This is an accurate paraphrase of comintern policy of the time; but Sovann deviates from accuracy, as Chanda noted, a few sentences later in saying that the Indo-China Communist Party 'inspired resistance movements ... in order to conquer independence and freedom for each nation [of Indo-China]'. What Chanda missed, however, is that this passage upholds the modern Vietnamese line on the role of the Indo-China Communist Party.[24]

When Sovann reached the 1950s and the founding of the first Cambodian 'Communist' party, the true date of which is still not at all clear, he opted for 19 February 1951 as the date of the First Congress and founding of the Khmer People's Revolutionary Party, which would thus have been founded immediately after the Second Congress of the Indo-China Communist Party took a decision to split into three national parties. Chanda points to a Vietnamese party history which says that the Cambodians set up a preparatory committee for the foundation of their party only in June 1951, indicating a time lag after the Indo-China Communist Party decision. Whatever the truth here, and given the extreme historical confusion on this point, I fail to see that a split between Sovann and the Vietnamese may be inferred. Moreover, Sovann also mentions—to be sure in a contextually confusing manner, treating it before mention of the February date—the 'provisional Central Committee of National Liberation', founded on 19 June 1951, and headed by Son Ngoc Minh, also Secretary of the party, whatever its founding date. With respect to Sovann and Vietnam, his remark that the new party 'was in a way an *avant-garde* group of the Khmer people and nation' is again the Vietnamese line.[25]

Several pages of the report are then devoted to the Pol Pot disaster, in which there is no lack of hyperbole; and Maoism is blamed as the ideological basis for Pol Potism. In an effort to make the very strongest accusations, Sovann at one point accused the Pol Pot group not only of exaggerated nationalism and Maoism, but also of 'trying to make Cambodia a society of slaves suitable for the feudal regime, to orient the latter towards Trotskyite utopian socialism [and] ... in the manner of Qin Shi Huangdi', etc. (p. 9).

Nayan Chanda felt that in his recounting of the overthrow of DK Sovann gave surprisingly little attention to the Vietnamese role in Cambodia's rescue, that, for example, 'he barely touched on the assistance currently provided by some 200,000 Vietnamese troops', 'he made no reference to a 'special relationship' with Vietnam or to solidarity within an Indochinese bloc'. With these remarks Chanda seems really to be chiding Sovann for not treating the Indo-China situation in the terms conventionally adopted by the Western press; and on the last point Chanda is simply wrong.

Sovann, in several different contexts, said that Cambodia 'reinforced the ties of militant solidarity and unshakeable ties with Vietnam, Laos . . .' (p. 13); 'the alliance among the 3 Indochina countries is more solid than ever' (p. 23); 'international proletarian solidarity, and first of all the solidarity of the three Indochina countries' (p. 28); we must 'reinforce the solidarity among the three countries of Indochina, affirm without delay the meaning of the militant solidarity among Cambodia, Vietnam and Laos' (p. 29); 'develop unceasingly the militant indefectible solidarity with the two intimate fraternal countries, that is Vietnam and Laos' (p. 30); and finally, 'our three countries, Cambodia, Vietnam and Laos constitute a single family within the large family of the socialist countries in the world' (p. 74). As for the 'special relationship', it is rarely mentioned by Cambodian personalities at all, which may reflect a distaste for it, but Sovann on that point cannot be contrasted with his colleagues.

Thus, the contrasts which Chanda believed he discerned in Le Duan's answering speech are illusory. Duan did speak, as Chanda remarked, of the brotherhood of the parties, although Chanda got the terms reversed. Le Duan's phrasing was, 'the Kampuchea People's Revolutionary Party, of which the Communist Party of Vietnam is a brother born in the same way from the victorious Indochina Communist Party'.[26]

The 'passing remark' to solidarity with the Soviet Union which Chanda wished to contrast with the tenor of Sovann's speech was in fact a statement that the strength of the three revolutions in Indo-China was 'first of all the strength of the community of socialist countries in which the Soviet Union is the pillar and firm prop', which seems not very different from Chanda's 'contrasting' *Pravda* quote, 'Moscow as the principal defender of Kampuchea . . . and the main prop in the country's development of socialism'. Moreover, this remark of Duan's came at the end of a paragraph invoking Cambodia's revolutionary victory as a feat of the country's firm will to 'become the master of its fate', and continuing with 'it is a victory of the correct political line of a Marxist-Leninist party, constantly raising high the banner of national independence . . . and of proletarian internationalism which have victoriously joined together'. These are hardly remarks designed to chide Pen Sovann for independence or to downgrade the importance of the Soviet Union for Indo-Chinese socialism.

Near the end of his speech, and in a *similar* manner to Sovann, Le Duan spoke again of the Soviet Union:

> the people of Vietnam together with the peoples of Kampuchea and Laos intimately and unceasingly tighten the bonds of solidarity with all the revolutionary forces of

our time, first of all in order to consolidate friendship in struggle and all manner of cooperation with the Soviet Union and the other countries of the socialist community in the untiring struggle.

The steps in Pen Sovann's removal have been described above, and I would agree that he was on the way out by the time the Fourth Congress was held, but it is impossible, from the content of his remarks at that time, to infer that the reason was an effort at rapprochement with the Soviet Union to which Vietnam objected.

The second part of Sovann's political report, on the period 1979–81, reviewed the progress made in the economy, education and health care, with numerous statistics; then he described the development of the armed forces, the development of the country's political organization, and the country's foreign relations—all matters which are discussed in other sections of this book.

In the third part, on the defence of national independence, he reiterated several times a theme I noted above in Le Duan's speech, 'patriotism *and* international proletarian solidarity', usually linked, even 'in the first place', with 'the solidarity of the three Indochina countries' (p. 28). Otherwise this section gives most of its attention to the dangers of Chinese enmity and subversion and the attacks by Chinese-, American- and ASEAN-supported forces on the Thai border.

The final section of part three discusses the economy, culture, education and health in the 'transitional stage' on the way to socialism; and here we find remarks which may contrast with Vietnamese views as well as provide interesting insights to the political tendencies of Pen Sovann.

Thus he starts, 'Kampuchea [before the revolution] was a feudal country', a conception which was part of the 1960s Pol Pot group analysis, contrasting with the Vietnamese view of the time which held that Sihanouk was a progressive patriot.

Then Sovann went on to warn against trying to move too fast in the present period of transition:

> It is not as easy as we think to accede to socialism . . . we must not be dogmatic and lack imagination in literally transposing specific principles which are only suitable for fraternal countries . . . It is necessary to know how to interpret general laws according to the character and concrete realities of our country . . . We must study the experiences which fraternal countries have had in the edification of socialism and know how to procede to judicious choices . . . there is no socialism which is available to us in its initial form; it must be founded on the thought, the intelligence and the creative labor of each people in function of its possibilities in each country

... We must traverse, step by step, the transition period to be able to accede to socialism.

All of these remarks are eminently reasonable, and do not contrast with what Vietnam seems to have had in mind for Cambodia since 1979; and their immediate target would seem to have been any among the PRK leadership who still admired DK policies. On the other hand, having emphatically denied that DK was socialist at all, Sovann might well have been obliquely criticizing the overly ambitious Vietnamese policies of rapid progress towards socialism during 1975–9, much of which he must have observed at first hand; and he was insisting that there must be no attempt in Cambodia to move towards socialism too fast.

In the fourth part of his report, on the immediate tasks, Sovann devoted most attention to economic development, and the policies outlined are very much those which have remained in effect. Particularly interesting is his insistence that the state should not be 'too austere with the free markets ... it should encourage consumption and provide necessary intiatives for the stimulation of production, and for life in circumstances where state commerce has very limited possibilities for development'. So far, the country is still following that advice, but in early 1981 those remarks could have been understood as a warning against policies like those of Vietnam in the 1970s.

Then, discussing political organization, Sovann referred to difficulties encountered in the *khum* elections which had been held between January and March 1981, just a few months before the party congress. In some places there had been delays in holding the elections and in others 'bad elements had been elected', in which case 'the elections must be reorganized' (p. 64). Moreover, some *khum* had still not conducted their elections at the time when Sovann was giving his report, and he urged the creation of 'favourable conditions for the elections'.[27]

Next, Sovann spoke of the necessity to define the attributes of party, state, and mass organizations. The party, he said, determines the political line, controls its application, and forms cadres; the state power directs current affairs, in particular the economy and government functions; and the mass organizations inspire the masses to follow the political principles of the party and the state. Sovann may have intended some criticism of the excessive meshing of state, party and Front in the PRK, but in fact he was accumulating more functions than anyone else.

The final paragraphs of part 4 were devoted to miscellaneous matters. He advocated support for religious traditions and for monks, who are members of the Front, which aids them in understanding current events. Intellectuals were also praised: without them, 'socialism cannot be built' (p. 66).

One more subject which may indicate a Pen Sovann line different from that of his collaborators is the section on ethnic minorities (p. 67). It is extremely brief, and plainly refers exclusively to the hill ethnic groups, without regard for Vietnamese, Chinese or Cham. Moreover, it speaks only in vague terms of 'development', without addressing at all the important, and sticky, questions of use of minority languages in education, and whether rapid assimilation into Khmer life is seen as the desirable goal.[28]

Following this, Sovann noted the need for state aid to families of war dead and soldiers on active duty; he welcomed the return of Cambodians living abroad who 'really desire to return and participate in building the country'; and he also welcomed 'wayward people' (that is, DK adherents) who 'have abandoned their earlier ways and who wish to join the Front in order to serve the country' (p. 67).

He regretted that too little had been done to develop mass organizations for women, workers and youth. With respect to women, he emphasized health protection as the major task of a mass organization, youth organizations would be concerned with education, the inculcation of patriotic sentiments, and the formation of future party cadres, while workers' organizations should help workers understand the new revolutionary political line and their role in the edification of society, and should also solve the problems related to their living conditions.

The last of the immediate tasks concerned the 'international situation and the Party's foreign policy' (p. 71). Following remarks on the increasing tension since the Second World War between the socialist bloc led by the Soviet Union and the imperialist and reactionary forces led by the Americans, Sovann expressed appreciation for the Soviet peace initiatives, which Cambodia supported. Together with the 'treason of the clique in Peking' and their collusion with the United States, he also blamed Thailand in particular for the current troubles in Indo-China, but he insisted that 'we desire peaceful negotiations concerning the border problem of the two countries, Thailand and Cambodia' (pp. 73–4). Following this were references to Indo-Chinese solidarity, Soviet aid and an expression of gratitude to India for its recognition of the PRK

In the fifth part of his report, on 'the organization of the Party according to authentic Marxism–Leninism', Sovann first summarized the main events of party history since 1951. After the French left Cambodia in 1954, power remained in the hands of the 'feudal' class and Sihanouk; and the party adopted a policy of political struggle under Tou Samouth, which prevented the Americans from 'satellizing' the feudal class and forced the latter to 'obey the aspirations of the people'. Then Pol Pot, after returning from France in 1953, succeeded in rising to party leadership, and on 27 May 1962, his agents assassinated Tou Samouth and other party leaders, which is the first definite statement on the death of Tou Samouth.

Curiously, these remarks by Pen Sovann repeated the 'Pol Pot' analysis of Cambodian society of the 1960s, and attributed it to Tou Samouth, in a manner which I suggested above may well reflect the true situation. This indicates the tactics which Pol Pot may have adopted—take over and develop, even exaggerate, the native rural, and thus popular, elements in the Cambodian revolutionary *élan*.[29]

Thus, Sovann continued, Pol Pot destroyed the real Marxist-Leninist party and turned it into an instrument serving the Peking expansionists. During this period 90 per cent of true Cambodian communists were killed. Because Pol Pot damaged the prestige of the *communist* party, the name would be changed to People's Revolutionary Party of Kampuchea, which proves a determination to reorganize it on the basis of Marxist-Leninism and to distinguish it clearly from the party of Pol Pot.

After Pen Sovann's political report, the remainder of the first day of the Congress was taken up with speeches by leaders of foreign delegations, of which Le Duan's has been noted above.

The second day opened with Heng Samrin's Economic Report, which was summarized in the local press as concentrating on three points: economic and cultural reconstruction since liberation, the direction and duties in the future, and the programme for 1981. He also spoke about the organs of economic management. He emphasized in particular that economic development would be based first of all on agriculture and the concurrent development of culture and health (*Kampuchea*, **90**, 4 June 1981, p. 5). Say Phouthang then read a report on party building, but no details were made public.

On the final day of the Congress, 29 May, Hun Sen, perhaps foreshadowing his rapid rise in the hierarchy, was chosen to announce the composition of the Party's new Central Committee, Politburo and Secretariat; Chea Sim read the Resolutions; and Pen Sovann, the newly-announced Secretary-General, made a brief closing speech.

Among the important resolutions of the Congress was one on the need to hold fast to both patriotism and international solidarity; and in the latter instance solidarity with, in this order, Vietnam, the Indo-China countries, the Soviet Union, all fraternal socialist countries, and with all revolutionary and progressive forces in the whole world.

The resolutions also included a résumé of party history from the founding of the Indo-China Communist Party in 1930, through the founding of the first Cambodian party, the Khmer People's Revolutionary Party in 1951, to the close association of the Cambodian people with the peoples of Vietnam and Laos in the victories over, first, French colonialism, and second, over American imperialist aggression leading to the 'historical victory on 17 April 1975'.[30]

The published text contains no specific allusion to Cambodian independence, the Geneva Accords, or party reorganization during the 1950s and 1960s, except to remark that after mid-1960 the Pol Pot clique utilized the 'revolutionary banner' to undertake obscure manœuvres to take control of the party and transform it into an organ for betraying the revolution. Likewise, the DK perversion of party ideals after 1975 led to chauvinism, war with Vietnam, and incidents on the Lao border, as well as to a genocidal policy within Cambodia itself.

Other resolutions concerned defence of the country as one of the most immediate tasks; the rebuilding of the economy, emphasizing agriculture as the primary sector; the restoration of cultural activities, education and health care; solidarity of the people, via the Front and other mass organizations; and the last two sections were on foreign policy and the edification of Marxist-Leninism.

Party Leadership

The composition of party organs, made public on the last day of the Fourth Congress, was as shown in Table 2.[31]

The twenty-one party leaders may be divided into groups in several possibly significant ways.[32] First is the divison between those who apparently, in many cases certainly, spent all or most of the period 1954–70 in Vietnam ('sent by the party to fulfill duties abroad', as the assembly biographies have it), and those who remained in Cambodia, part of the time as DK cadres.

By far the largest number were in Vietnam after 1954. Only Heng Samrin, Chea Sim, Hun Sen, Math Ly, Heng Sam Kay (Heng Samrin's elder brother), Sim Ka, Rong Chream Kaysan, and Chan Seng are not listed as having been sent abroad; and the positions of the first six as DK East Zone cadres until 1977 (Hun Sen) or 1978 (Heng Samrin, Chea Sim, Math Ly), or perhaps even later (Heng Sam Kay) are well attested. Rong Chream Kaysan probably served in his native Koh Kong on the south-western border with Thailand, and he is said to have broken with Pol Pot in 1974, remaining thereafter in armed

Table 2 Composition of party organs, Fourth Party Congress

Central Committee	Politburo	Secretariat
Pen Sovann**	Pen Sovann	Pen Sovann
Say Phouthang**	Heng Samrin	Say Phouthang
Heng Samrin*	Say Phouthang	Bou Thang
Chea Sim*	Chea Sim	Hun Sen
Bou Thang**	Bou Thang	Chea Soth
Hun Sen*	Hun Sen	Chan Si
Chea Soth**	Chea Soth	Chan Phin
Chan Si**	Chan Si	
Chan Phin**		
Lim Nay**		
Chey Saphon**		
Math Ly*		
Soey Keo**		
Khang Sarin**		
Heng Sam Kay*		
Rong Chream Kaysan		
Lay Samon**		
Sim Ka*		
Chan Seng*		
Alternate members		
Men Sam An (f.)		
Kim Yin**		

* former DK cadre
** Vietnam veteran

opposition. The early whereabouts of Chan Seng are mysterious, although he undoubtedly served under DK. His biography jumps from 1948 when he joined the revolutionary struggle to 1970 when he again took up arms, leading some to suppose that he may have spent the intervening years in Sihanouk's prisons.

Of course, all of the twelve who went to Vietnam in 1954 had been fighting for independence before that date, as had Chea Sim, Math Ly, Rong Chream Kaysan and Chan Seng among those who did not go to Vietnam. Interestingly enough, Heng Samrin and his brother were not in the pre-1954 struggle, joining the revolution only in 1959 and 1955. Most of the Vietnam group returned to Cambodia when war broke out in 1970, but all are said to have broken with Pol Pot by 1975 (as early as 1971 in the case of Lay Samon), generally in 1973–4, and the latest was Soeuy Keo in 1975. Thus, only the six former East Zone cadres are acknowledged to have worked for DK. Two of the group, Chan Phin and Kim Yin, did not even return to Cambodia from Vietnam until 1979; and Men Sam An, the only woman, who only joined the revolution in 1970, is said to have then gone abroad and subsequently returned to 'remain in the army working against Pol Pot'—rather vague language which may indicate that she too spent some time as a DK cadre before, like Kaysan, joining the early anti-Pol Pot dissidence.

Five of the group belong to ethnic minorities: Say Phouthang and Rong Chream Kaysan are Thais from Koh Kong; Bou Thang, a Tampuon and Soeuy Keo, a Kachoh, are from north-eastern hill minorities; and Math Ly is a Cham.

In age they are rather young. Only Say Phouthang (b. 1925), Chea Soth (1928), Math Ly (1925), and Kim Yin (1928), were born before 1930; Hun Sen and Men Sam An were born in 1951 and 1953; and the rest in the 1930s.

Thus, in 1981, the party leadership was dominated by veterans of the independence struggle of 1946–54 who had then gone to Vietnam until 1970. This was only to be expected since they represented the oldest Cambodian communist tradition, their group as a whole had been massacred by Pol Pot, and they were proven friends of Vietnam. The only really anomalous members of the group are Heng Samrin and his brother, who neither fought actively for independence nor served in Vietnam, and who remained with DK until quite late; and in fact Heng Samrin's rapid rise to prominence has never been explained.

In the intervening four years, this leadership group has remained remarkably stable. The only serious upset was the unexpected removal of Pen Sovann from all his posts in December 1981 and his replacement in all three party positions by Heng Samrin. Lay Samon was also dropped from the Central Committee at some date which I have not discovered, for his name no longer appears in the 1984 list. The ranking order in the Central Committee changed somewhat, with Chea Sim moving up to number two under Heng Samrin, and Say Phouthang dropping to number four below Chan Si, who moved from eighth to third place.

By August 1984, Men Sam An had become a full member of the Central Committee, and in November of that year, during a national meeting of party cadres, eight new alternate members, unnamed at the time, were elected. A *Far Eastern Economic Review* article mistakenly called them full members, but the five names provided there—Chheng Phon, Mean Saman, Tea Banh, Sar Kheng and Nay Pena—were correct. They were mentioned in subsequent radio broadcasts or the PRK press as 'alternate members of the Central Committee'; and they are maintained in their new positions after the

Fifth Party Congress in September 1985. Another alternate member named in the press, Say Chhum, was probably also one of the eight elected in November.[33]

Chheng Phon is the first person without any revolutionary or definite communist background to be appointed to a party leadership position. Before 1975 he worked in the theatre, both as performer and teacher; and under DK he was evacuated to the countryside as one of the disfavoured 'new people'. He is not, however, entirely without leftist credentials, and he may represent a tendency which is finding new favour. As his National Assembly biography relates, he was expelled from a theatre school in 1957 'due to a political contradiction . . . subsequently, he founded a group to research and preserve traditional dances, and after that he became a professor of art at the University of Fine Arts in Phnom Penh'. The period elided between the 1950s and 'subsequently' included study in China in 1961–4, together with other Cambodian leftist intellectuals who found Sihanouk's regime uncomfortable, the most notable being Hang Thun Hak. They returned in the 1960s when Sihanouk had entered his pro-Chinese period and became prominent in the fine arts departments of the new universities then being established. The group to 'research and preserve traditional dances' was very much influenced by Chinese folk and ethnic dance styles of the time, and this influence visibly continues in the performances of the state dance groups which are under Chheng Phon in his capacity of Minister of Information and Culture.[34]

In spite of the Chinese influence in their studies, the 'Hang Thun Hak group', who became particularly prominent under the Khmer Republic (1970–5), were considered to be the nucleus of a pro-Soviet Cambodian communist group, and as such were energetically hunted down by the DK authorities.[35]

Mean Saman became the second woman among the party leaders, and, born in 1956, is the youngest. She fought in the 1970–5 war, and then is said to have gone abroad (Vietnam?) for a time before returning to oppose the Pol Pot clique. Since 1979 she has been President of the Women's Association.

Tea Banh, according to the National Assembly biography, was born in 1945, and is thus of an age group not otherwise represented among the party leadership. He joined the revolution in 1962, and fought in the 1970–5 war, but then broke with Pol Pot in 1974. In 1979 he became military affairs chief in his native Koh Kong, and was later taken into the Ministry of National Defence where he was Vice-Minister and Deputy Chief of Staff of the Army from 1981, until named Minister of Communications, Transport and the Postal Service in April 1985. He is no doubt a man to watch, for joining the revolution in 1962 when party fortunes were at their lowest, when Sihanouk was at the high point of his leftist internationalism, and when living conditions for the Cambodian population were at their best, required unusual commitment. The pre-1975 break with party leadership by one who had no old revolutionary or Vietnam experience indicates an independent character; and his high military positions combined with relative youth give him great potential for top leadership in the coming years.

One of the new alternate Central Committee members, Nay Pena, was rapidly promoted to full membership in the Central Committee in March 1985 and the reasons are not apparent. No biography has been published, and he refused an interview with Ben Kiernan during the latter's visit to Phnom Penh in December 1985. Besides his central party position he was also, until the Fifth Party Congress in October 1985, party secretary of Preah Vihear Province in the country's far north.[36]

The party leadership in early 1985, after the changes revealed in the 1984 'Liste des dirigeants' and further changes reported in the press, would seem to have been as shown in Table 3, although the lists may be incomplete. In particular I have been unable to discover the two other alternate members appointed together with Nay Pena, Mean Saman, Chheng Phon, Tea Banh, Sar Kheng and Say Chhum.

In comparison with the 1981 line-up, the balance shifted away from the Vietnam veterans, who decreased from twelve out of twenty-one seats in the Central Committee to nine out of twenty-six. Even though the backgrounds of some of the new members are unclear, it is unlikely that any of them were of the old Vietnam veteran group.[37]

Below the central level there are provincial and municipal (Phnom Penh, Kompong Som) party organizations, and district organizations wherever there are enough members. Some of the Central Committee members were also secretaries of Provincial Party Committees, for example Rong Thomea Kaysan in Koh Kong, Heng Sam Kay in Svay Rieng, Chan Seng in Siemreap, Kim Yin in Kompong Thom, and Nay Pena in Preah Vihear. In 1984–5 these lower-level organizations were of at least two types, 'Provincial Party Committee', and 'Directorate [*khana aphibal*] of Party Affairs', examples of the latter being the organizations in Kandal Province under Hem Samin and the Phnom Penh municipality under Keo Chenda—both Hanoi veterans. As I shall discuss further below, the second type was probably appointed directly by the central party organs when there was insufficient membership to form a fully-fledged committee.

Table 3 Composition of party organs, 1984

Central Committee	Politburo	Secretariat
Heng Samrin*	Heng Samrin	Heng Samrin
Chea Sim*	Chea Sim	Say Phouthang
Say Phouthang**	Say Phouthang	Bou Thang
Bou Thang**	Bou Thang	Chan Phin
Hun Sen*	Hun Sen	Khang Sarin
Chea Soth**	Chea Soth	
Chan Phin**		
Khang Sarin**		
Math Ly*		
Chey Saphon**		
Soeuy Keo**		
Lim Nay**		
Sim Ka*		
Rong Thomea Kaysan		
Heng Sam Kay*		
Men Sam An (f.)		
Kim Yin**		
Nay Pena		
Alternate members		
Mean Saman (f.)		
Chheng Phon		
Tea Banh		
Sar Kheng		
Say Chhum		

* former DK cadre
** Vietnam veteran

Party Membership and Growth

The total party membership has not been officially revealed, and before the Fifth Party Congress in October 1985 the reticence was no doubt due to the membership being very small. In his report to the Fourth Party Congress in May 1981, Pen Sovann said that 90 per cent of the real communists had been killed by Pol Pot, which, if taken literally as referring to party members and compared with pre-1975 estimates, would leave hardly one hundred remaining in 1979. Sovann continued, 'since then' [1979?] the number had increased tenfold, and was thus, inferentially, again at around one thousand. Two months later, Keo Chenda, in answer to questions, would only say that the number of members was 'much less' than five thousand; and another analyst in early 1984 still believed party membership to be under a thousand.[38]

The low figures, and apparent slow growth, indicate that the Cambodian party is looking for commited, ideologically-prepared members who will function as a real vanguard and leadership group, and do not intend to open up party ranks to all comers who might wish to join for opportunistic reasons. They may have drawn lessons from the Vietnamese experience in the south after 1975 and wish to avoid the same problem.[39] This impression of selectivity was reinforced by the remarks of a few middle-level officials in Phnom Penh in 1984 who commented on the long process involved in becoming a party member.

Below the party is the organization of 'core groups', in which people are prepared for party membership. In his 1981 Party Congress Political Report, Pen Sovann said there were about four thousand core group members.

Other figures mentioned by national leaders, although difficult to relate among themselves, are Keo Chenda's remark early in 1984 that 'we now have almost 100 new members', possibly referring to the Phnom Penh municipality—seven party branches, and 1060 core members divided into ninety-two groups. In August 1985 a report on preparations for the coming Fifth Party Congress referred to eighty-nine representatives of party branches attached to central ministries and offices.[40]

The Fifth Congress of the PRPK

The Fifth Congress, convened during 13–16 October 1985, was the major political event in the PRK since 1979. Advance media attention was given to the activities of provincial party congresses in electing delegates, discussing a draft political report, and suggesting new articles for the party 'constitution' (statutes?). It was also announced in advance that new members would be elected to the Central Committee.[41] The Congress was attended by 250 full-rights delegates from twenty-two party divisions. Twenty-five were women, forty were of ethnic minorities, and eight were from the central party organs (*Pracheachon*, **2**, 14 October 1985, p. 1).

A large measure of reorganization has resulted from the Fifth Congress. First, the Central Committee was expanded to thirty-one full and fourteen alternate members, and its composition noticeably altered. The shifts in personnel may be indications of the direction in which the PRK intends to move and of how the factional tendencies in the PRK leadership are to be balanced.

The new Central party leadership is as follows, listed in the order in which they were named in the party newspaper, *Pracheachon*, immediately following the congress.[42] Politburo: Secretary-General Heng Samrin, Chea Sim, Hun Sen, Say Phouthang, Bou Thang, Chea Soth, Men Sam An, Math Ly, Nay Pena; alternates—Chan Seng, Nguon Nhel; Secretariat: Heng Samrin, Hun Sen, Bou Thang, Men Sam An, Nay Pena; Party Inspectorate, or Control Commission ['Central Committee for the Inspection of the Party]: Say Phouthang, Chan Seng, Sim Ka, Men Sam An, Say Chhum, Mean Saman, El Vansarat.

The Party Inspectorate seems to be a new creation of uncertain significance. Its position in the leadership announcement, and Say Phouthang as President, suggested that it replaced the Committee for Organization, which was not mentioned at the same time. Later press articles devoted to leading cadre activities, however, show that the Organization Committee still exists and is now headed by Men Sam An, although at the end of 1985 Say Phouthang still took precedence over her.[43]

Table 4 Central party leadership, 1985

Central Committee	Other principal positions held
Heng Samrin*	President, State Council
Sim Ka*	Minister for the Inspection of State Affairs
Heng Sam Kay*	Party Secretary, Svay Rieng Province
Sar Kheng§	Director of Central Party Office
Kong Korm†	First Deputy Foreign Minister
Say Chhum§	Party Secretary, Kompong Speu Province
Nguon Nhel†	Party Secretary, Phnom Penh City
Sam Sundoeun†	Youth Organization President
Nay Pena†	Minister of the Interior
Ho Non (f)†	Deputy Minister in the Office of the Council of Ministers
Bou Thong§	Minister of Defence
Say Phouthang**	President, Party Inspectorate
Koy Buntha§	Deputy Minister of Defence
Chan Phin**	Minister of Finance
Kai Kim Yan†	Party Secretary and President, PRC, Battambang Province
Chay Sang Yun†	Deputy Chief, General Staff, Armed Forces
Kim Yin**	Director-General, National Radio; Vice-President, Committee for 'Misled People'
El Vansarat†	Deputy Chief, Central Political Department, Armed Forces
Math Ly*	President, Federation of Trade Unions

Hul Savoan†	Military Commander, Region 4, Siemreap/ Oddar Meanchey
Yos Son†	Ministry of Foreign Affairs
Rong Phlam Kaysan§	Party Secretary Koh Kong Province
Chea Soth**	Minister for Planning
Chea Sim*	President, National Assembly and Front Central Committee
Som Kim Suor (f)†	Editor, *Pracheachon*, party newspaper
Chan Seng*	Politburo
Hun Sen*	Prime Minister, Minister for Foreign Affairs
Khoy Khhun Huor†	Party Secretary, Preah Vihear Province
Men Sam An (f)§	President, Central Committee for Propaganda and Education; President, Central Committee for Organization
Mean Saman (f)§	President, National Women's Organization
Lak On (f)§	Party Secretary, Ratanakiri Province
Alternate members	
Thong Khon†	President, PRC, Phnom Penh City
Ros Chhun	Deputy Minister for Planning
Hun Neng*	Party Secretary, Kompong Cham Province
Chea Chanto†	Deputy Minister in the National Bank
Chhay Than†	Deputy Minister for Finance
Lim Thi*	Party Secretary, Kandal Province
Tea Banh§	Minister for Communications, Transport and the Postal Service
Say Siphon†	Vice-President, Trade Union Organization
Som Sopha†	Unknown
Chheng Phon†	Minister for Information and Culture
Sam Sarit	unknown
Pen Navuth†	Minister for Education
Neou Sam†	Party Secretary, Siemreap Province
Kham Len§	Member, State Council

* DK cadre
** Vietnam veteran;
† 'New' people neither DK nor Vietnam veteran.
§ Revolutionaries who broke with Pol Pot by 1975.

Four of the pre-Congress full members, Khang Sarin, Chey Saphon, Soeuy Keo and Lim Nay, all Vietnam veterans, were dropped. This leaves only four certain members of that group: Say Phouthang, Chea Soth, Chan Phin, and Kim Yin. Only Say Phouthang seems to retain a position of real power, as head of the Party Inspectorate, although the authority of that new body is not clear. It is possible that Say Phouthang has been pushed upstairs to a ceremonial position, while greater power still resides in the Committee for Organization under Men Sam An.

Former DK cadres number at least eight full members and two alternates. Two, Heng Sam Kay and Hun Neng, are brothers of more powerful figures, Heng Samrin and Hun Sen.

Four more men from the military have joined Defence Minister Bou Thang as full members of the Central Committee, reflecting the importance of the Defence establishment in Cambodia's current international position. Koy Buntha, like Bou Thang, was a revolutionary who broke with Pol Pot very early, while the other three, Chay Sang Yun, El Vansarat, and Hul Savoan are young newcomers. Nine others are either Provincial Party Secretaries or Presidents of Provincial PRCs, or both.[44]

Of the sixteen new full members, twelve were 'new people' outside the DK apparatus during 1975–9. They include Deputy Foreign Minister Kong Korm, who fought on the revolutionary side in 1973–5 and was then demoted to evacuee status; and Yos Son, also of the Foreign Ministry; Nguon Nhel, Party Chief of Phnom Penh; Sam Sundoeun, head of the Youth Association; and Som Kimsuor, editor of the new party newspaper, *Pracheachon*. Of similar background is Education Minister Pen Navuth, who joined Chheng Phon among the alternates, and these fourteen, with possibly six or seven more, may be counted as a new 'faction' among the leadership.[45]

No doubt of equal significance is the fact that at least three more of the new members, Koy Buntha, Lak On and Kham Len, although revolutionaries, are said to have broken with Pol Pot by 1975, reinforcing that tendency—neither DK nor strictly Vietnam veterans—already rep resented by several powerful figures in the party and army leadership. Sar Kheng and Say Chhum are probably also associated with this background, and in published photos some of the other new members seem too young to have been either of the Vietnam group or DK officials, and if they were not anti-Pol Pot revolutionaries they were probably 'new people' under DK.[46]

The rise of these two groups among the leadership bodes well both for Cambodian independence and for smooth integration of pre-revolutionary intellectuals and administrators into the new system. One of them, Nguon Nhel, is already an alternate member of the Politburo, although that body is still led by the old nucleus of former DK cadres and Vietnam veterans.

The predicted change in the post of Secretary-General did not occur, although Heng Samrin's background makes him an unexpected occupant of that post. A feature of the PRK from the removal of Pen Sovann until the Fifth Congress, however, seemed to be that the driving force in the Party was not the Secretary-General, but the President of the former Organization

Committee, now of the Party Inspectorate, Say Phouthang. This view, though, may now have to be altered, depending on the role of the new Party Inspectorate.[47]

In general, then, the results of the Fifth Congress show an erosion of the position of Vietnam veterans in the Cambodian Party, and thus relatively a gain in the power of former DK cadres, but also a rapid rise to positions of responsibility by younger people who do not represent a pro-Vietnamese tendency, and who may never have been active in the revolutionary struggles at all. The Cambodian Party is certainly not a Vietnamese puppet organization, and although this should be seen as a positive development, the problem of a resurgence of Khmer chauvinism must be kept in mind.

Since the Fifth Party Congress, much new information on party organization and development, in particular with respect to province and lower-level branches and total membership has become available. As noted above, two types of provincial organization existed, and since the Fifth Congress a third, 'Provisional Party Committee', has appeared in Phnom Penh and several provinces, a designation which in some cases would seem to represent a demotion.

An article in *Pracheachon* two months after the Fifth Congress stated that under normal conditions Party Committees are chosen by the party members of each locality in a congress.

> It is only in special circumstances such as in our country at present, when the Party has to be rebuilt, and when in many base areas there is not yet a Party organization to organize a congress, that the higher level organization designates a Provisional Party Committee [*Pracheachon*, **21**, 27 December 1985, p. 3.]

As new information on party membership indicates, this explanation for the sudden proliferation of 'Provisional Provincial Party Committees' is disingenuous, but in fact the article, entitled 'Democracy Within the Party', may have been protesting against this development, for it continued, 'and when conditions are right, it is absolutely necessary to organize regional Party congresses in order to elect full-rights committees'.

For, together with the transformation of several Provincial Committees into Provisional ones, has come an apparent explosion of party membership. According to estimates by Ben Kiernan on the basis of unofficial interviews with well-informed people, party membership since the Fifth Congress is 9-10,000.[48]

The Provincial and Municipal Party Secretaries, the nature of their committees, and pre-Fifth Congress incumbents, are set forth in Table 5.

Table 5 Provincial and Provisional Party Secretaries, 1985

Battambang	Kai Kim Yan*	provisional	Lay Samon
Kampot	Som Chen*	full-rights	no change
Kandal	Lim Thi	full-rights	Hem Samin
Koh Kong	Rong . . . Kaysan(?)	?	
Kompong Cham	Hun Neng	provisional	
Kompong Chhnang	Dok Narin	provisional*	no change
Kompong Speu	Say Chhum	provisional	no change
Kompong Thom	So Han*	provisional	Nguon Nhel
Kratie	Nhem Heng	provisional	
Mondulkiri	?		
Preah Vihear	Khoy Khhun Huor	provisional	Nay Pena
Prey Veng	Yuth Buntha	?	Thong Boret
Pursat	Ros Sreng	provisional*	no change
Ratanakiri	Lak On	provisional	Kham Len
Siemreap	Neou Sam	provisional*	Chan Seng
Stung Treng	Veng Khhuon	provisional*	Thang Bai
Svay Rieng	Heng Sam Kay	provisional*	no change
Takeo	Pol Saroeun		
Phnom Penh	Nguon Nhel	provisional*	Keo Chenda
Kompong Som	Lim Nay	provisional	no change

* with names means person is also President, Provincial PRC;
* with category means change from non-provisional;
(name) means pre-Fifth Congress incumbent, no recent information.

The Political Report to the Fifth Congress

The political report read to the Fifth Congress by Party Secretary Heng Samrin differed considerably from Pen Sovann's report to the Fourth Congress. It consisted of three main parts: (1) 'Seven Years of Unity and Struggle to Defend the Revolutionary Gains and to Revive the Nation'; (2) the longest part, 'The General Strategic Tasks and the Home and Foreign Policies of the Cambodian Revolution'; and (3) 'The PRPK is the Sole Leader of the Cambodian Revolution'.[49]

There is very little historical comment. The 1979 victory is said to mark the revolution's complete break with the regime of the Pol Pot clique, 'disciples of Maoism', although the 'Chinese ruling circles, in collusion with the US imperialists and the Thai ultra-Rightist reactionary forces, have continued to help the Pol Pot remnants'.

Nevertheless, the PRK, in co-operation with 'Vietnamese volunteers', have generally been successful. 'The past seven years of victorious struggle have proved that the Kampuchean revolution's own forces, combined with the Kampuchea-Vietnam revolutionary alliance, constitute the direct factor of victory and the vitality of the cause of safeguarding the revolutionary gains'.

The discussion continues to 'Rehabilitating the economy and building the new culture'. Here reference is made to the 'assistance of fraternal socialist countries—primarily Vietnam and the Soviet Union', in rebuilding the economy. Important successes in agricultural production are claimed, which 'allowed us, during the first days of our regime, to avert famine'. In spite of successes, there is consciousness of current difficulties. Thus, 'the economy, already backward, is unbalanced in many fields', 'material and technical bases [have] not been restored to the pre-war level', and here special mention is made of communication lines and waterworks. In industry there are difficulties caused by lack of energy, spare parts and raw materials. Finances 'cannot span the gap between expenses and income', which obviously means that *state* income is insufficient for state expenditure.

There is a cryptic acknowledgement of manpower drain to the defence effort in 'labor . . . is dispersed at present in order to face the needs of the struggle and those of production and construction'. And moreover, there is a lack of qualified specialist personnel.

Gradualism is emphasized in all remarks about the building of socialism. The birth of the PRK meant mastery of the country 'by the labouring masses [note *not* 'the proletariat'] to build the country through a gradual passage towards socialism'; and the economy, culture and education have been restored and 'oriented towards socialism'.

This theme continues in more detail in Part 2. The Cambodian socialist revolution should obey general laws, 'but should have particular features'. The potential for building a good society which should have been in place after the 'national democratic revolution' of 1975 was destroyed by the Pol Pot clique, and thus 'moving from a national democratic revolution to a socialist revolution . . . should take dozens of years of national rebirth, economic restoration and elimination of the severe consequences of the genocidal regime in order to create conditions permitting the transition towards socialism'. This is a clear acknowledgement that socialism in Cambodia is not for tomorrow, and that no further 'great leaps' are envisioned.

The subsection on 'Domestic Policy' calls for 'making every effort to complete economic restoration, reorganize production and build socialist education and culture'. The state must gradually build a national economy with socialist norms, progressively build material and technical bases of socialism. By 1990, every effort must be made to create great socio-economic changes to advance the revolution. Part of this effort is the first five-year plan of 'socio-economic restoration and development' between 1986 and 1990, the economic provisions of which are discussed below.[50]

The ideological guidelines for the next five years are to 'rely mainly on one's own strength' in economic restoration, but also strengthen economic and technical co-operation and economic planning co-ordination with Vietnam, 'which is an indispensable factor for bringing into full play the great potential of Cambodia's agriculture and forestry', a remark which would seem to indicate plans for the symbiosis of Cambodia's agricultural potential and Vietnamese industrial production. At the same time, 'cooperation with the Soviet Union and the other fraternal socialist countries' will be stressed, 'in order to build the material and technical foundations of socialism'.

Gradualism is again emphasized. The 'task of transforming the non-socialist component of our economy is now only at the initial stage', there are still 'several economic components operating simultaneously', and the party and state must 'build a national economy in conformity with the conditions of the country, and reorganize production *in the direction of socialism*' (author's emphasis). Then there is a prescription, in contrast to statements in 1981, identifying four components of the economy which are to be developed, in order to 'mitigate the weaknesses' of the state sector: the four are state, collective, family-run and private. In 1981 the three recognized sectors were state, co-operative and family. Since 'family' economy was private, the addition of an explicit private sector refers to private artisanal and entrepreneurial activities, which have become too important to ignore, and which cannot be converted to collectives.

Discussion of the Front and other mass organizations includes an interesting provision on building up the trade unions as 'the training school of the working class for economic and administrative management . . . [they] must take part in state management and in the management and defence of production bases'. This sounds very much like an intention to gradually evolve something like the Yugoslav workers' management system (Lydall, 1984).

Remarks on other mass organizations include reference to the Youth Union as 'a [political] reserve army . . . the school of communism for young people . . . [which] has the responsibility of presenting its elite members to become Party members'. Mobilization of women is 'to achieve equality between men and women'; and mass organization policy for ethnic minorities evokes the same goal of 'total equality in all fields'. Buddhism and Islam are mentioned in a short paragraph on 'achieving freedom of belief', and on 'mobilizing all of the people', including the followers of those faiths, 'to defend and rebuild the country'. Finally, in this section, 'Cambodian compatriots living abroad' are to be persuaded 'to turn their sincere feelings toward the fatherland' in order to help 'carry out national restoration and reconstruction'.

The statement on Foreign Policy emphasized continuation of the policy followed to date and set out first in the Front declaration of December 1978; and there is no significant change here.[51] Different paragraphs contain different nuances of emphasis, however. First is the call to 'strengthen and consolidate the bloc... among the three countries—Cambodia, Vietnam, and Laos—making it more powerful ... on the basis of Marxism-Leninism and socialist internationalism'; and then the declaration that 'co-operation and mutual help between the PRK and the Soviet Union and other fraternal socialist countries on the basis of Marxism-Leninism and socialist internationalism ... is the foundation of the internationalist line and foreign policy of our Party'. Thus still, and in contrast to some foreign press interpretations in 1981, the PRK intends to rely on *both* Vietnam and the Soviet Union.

Part 3, on the PRPK as the 'sole leader of the Cambodian Revolution,' boldly asserts its origin in the Indo-China Communist Party 'founded by President Ho Chi Minh'; there is no allusion to the Cambodian party's separate founding in 1951, and the text continues with reference to struggles against the French and Americans. Then, 'pseudocommunist' Pol Pot usurped party leadership, introduced the 'reactionary ideology' of Maoism [and] abandoned is working-class position'. The true line was restored after 7 January 1979.

Some weaknesses in the party are mentioned: 'popularization and implementation of options and policies ... are still slow and lack depth ... [and] responsibility'. Ideological work 'is lagging behind the requirements of the revolution'; and 'the organizational system ... is still too thin and weak', is 'incomplete at district and especially at grass-roots levels', and 'has not taken deep root among the workers and peasants in state enterprises and farms'. Expansion 'should be insisted on among workers, women, members of the armed forces and in [villages] with special attention to be paid to regions with ethnic minorities'. A major problem is immediately recognized, for in recruitment 'greater consideration should be given to quality than ... [to] number', but 'narrow-mindedness' should not result in demands for 'too high qualifications for being Party members'.

As a whole, the report reflects a realistic view of Cambodia's situation, in particular its economic and political weaknesses. Although socialism is emphatically the goal, gradualism in its implementation is to prevail, if only because of the serious weakness of the party and the obstacles in the way of increasing either its membership or effectiveness. There is also clear implicit recognition that the party weaknesses derive from general apathy to socialist goals mong the mass of the population, and there is also an apparent reluctance to force the issue.

7 The Constitution

Background

The present PRK constitution is the fourth in Cambodia's history, following those of Sihanouk's monarchy, Lon Nol's Khmer Republic, and Pol Pot's Democratic Kampuchea.

Modern constitutionalism in Cambodia began with decisions taken by France during the Second World War, presumably with the hope of gaining popular support for the resumption of the French Protectorate following the end of hostilities.[1]

The first constitution, which went into effect in May 1947, provided for a government dominated by a strong National Assembly very much like that of the Fourth French Republic. The power given to the Assembly led to crises with King Sihanouk in 1949, and particularly in 1953, when Sihanouk dissolved the Assembly and ruled personally until after the Geneva Accords of 1954 reimposed democratic practices. Such constitutional conflicts only ended after Sihanouk's party swept all seats in the 1955 elections.[2]

Following the destitution of Sihanouk on 18 March 1970, Cambodia at first remained under the same constitution and National Assembly elected in 1966, with Lon Nol continuing as Prime Minister. After various modifications of the system, a new constitution was promulgated in April 1972.

The Khmer Republic Constitution was designed to institute a strong presidential government, inspired no doubt both by the United States example and by that of de Gaulle's Fifth Republic. The Executive consisted of the President and Vice-President, elected directly for five-year terms. The Prime Minister was chosen by the President, and the other ministers were proposed for the President's approval by the Prime Minister. The Council of Ministers was responsible to the President, not to the Assembly, and there was no requirement that any of them be chosen from among the elected representatives.[3]

The Democratic Kampuchea constitution was announced on 5 January 1976 after an alleged 'Special National Congress' of 25–27 April 1975.[4] The state apparatus consisted of an Assembly, an executive body elected by the Assembly and to which it was responsible, and a Presidium chosen by the Assembly. The Assembly had 250 members, representing peasants (150 members), other workers (fifty), and the army (fifty); and it thus resembled Sihanouk's Council of the Kingdom and Lon Nol's Senate in representing corporate bodies rather than administratively-defined population groups.

The Constitution of the People's Republic of Kampuchea

In the first point of the Salvation Front's eleven-point declaration of 28 December 1978, they promised a new constitution guaranteeing equality, liberty and true democracy; and by April 1979 Heng Samrin referred to drafting of the new constitution as though it had already begun (Service d'Information du FUNSK, 1979; *SWB*, 10 April 1979). Then, in the political report of the Front's Second Congress in September 1979, the second of three points in section 3 on 'participat[ion] in the building of a solid revolutionary state power' said, 'participate energetically in the proceedings of general elections to choose a general assembly to engage in drafting a new constitution'.[5] This was restated somewhat in the third of the five points in the programme of activity set forth in the final communiqué: 'Participate energetically in the building of a solid state power; prepare . . . for general elections to choose a National Assembly and establish a constitution in appropriate circumstances'.[6] This would be similar to the situation still existing in Laos where the Assembly chosen in 1975 has not yet fulfilled its tasks of providing a new constitution (Chou Norindr, 1982, p. 54).

Both these statements placed the election of an assembly before the writing of a constitution, as though the latter would be the first task of the former. Next, in a reorganization of ministries under the KPRC, Ros Samay, among other duties, was named minister in charge of drafting the constitution.[7]

If the intention in 1979 had in fact been to elect an assembly and then draft a constitution, matters proceeded rather differently in 1980. According to a statement published in early 1981, a *council* had been formed by decision of the KPRC of 11 January 1980 to prepare a constitutional draft. It was chaired by Heng Samrin and its Secretary-General was Minister of Justice Ouk Bun Chhoeun (*Kampuchea*, **78** and **79**, of 12 and 19 March 1981). Then, according to *Kampuchea*, in August 1980, a *committee* to draft a constitution had been appointed at an unspecified date. It was chaired by Heng Samrin, with Pen Sovann as Deputy Chairman and Ros Samay as Secretary-General.[8] Just over a month later, *Revolutionary Army* announced still another *committee* charged with drafting the constitution. This one was chaired by Say Phouthang and there were to be fourteen members, unnamed.[9]

With seeming appropriateness, three draft constitutions eventually appeared, but it is not entirely possible to attribute responsibility among the three drafting bodies. What was presumably the first draft was dated 28 July 1980 and among the administrative acts out of which it developed the last was a meeting on 21 July 1980 at which representatives of both the council for preparation of the constitution and a drafting committee were present.[10]

It would appear from this that a Drafting Committee was subordinate to the Council, but there remains the question of two committees and uncertainty as to whether the second superseded the first or whether they were in some sense in competition. The second possibility is suggested by their announcement in different news organs and the different leadership, particularly in retrospect, indicates different party factions.[11]

Another draft constitution also dates from 1980, presumably somewhat later because the organization of the text has been tightened, resulting in fewer articles, down from 107 to 105.[12] Presumably, it was this second 1980 draft which was discussed in detail at a three-day national Cadres Congress ending on 16 February 1981, although the press gave no details of the discussions or of any modifications introduced into the draft text.[13]

It was no doubt as a result of this congress that a third draft was prepared, with significant differences from the preceding texts, and published in March 1981 after a public meeting of ten thousand people at the Olympic Stadium in Phnom Penh to greet its completion.[14] At about the same time as the third, and nearly final, draft of the constitution was being discussed and accepted, the KPRC issued a decree on elections to the National Assembly; and this decree refers for authority to the declarations of the First and Second Front Congresses and to Decision No. 32 of the KPRC itself. The elections were held on 1 May, and during the first sitting of the National Assembly—24–27 June 1981—the third draft, with some minor changes, was adopted as the PRK constitution.[15]

Thus, although the first Assembly was not elected, as originally conceived, to write the constitution, it was elected in advance to adopt it. The seemingly contradictory relationship between a constitution which authorizes an assembly, and an assembly which must ratify the constitution, is of course a problem in any state starting out anew; and as will be noted below, some of the constitutional provisions apply to the future, but not to the institutions actually in existence.

All versions of the PRK constitution start with historical preambles, which will be discussed comparatively below. Then come chapters on the Political System, the Economic System, Culture and Social Action, Rights and Duties of Citizens, the National Assembly, the Council of State, the Council of Ministers, Local Government, Courts, National Symbols, Effects and Amendments. In the 1981 drafts the second and third have been combined as 'The Economic System and Policy on Culture and Social Affairs', reducing the number of chapters from eleven to ten.

The Main Features of the Final Constitution

The nature of the political system is defined by the country's official name, stated in article 1, 'People's Republic of Kampuchea', and it is said to be 'moving step by step toward socialism'. Article 2 says all power belongs to the people, who exercise it through the National Assembly and the various organs of state power which the people establish and which are responsible to the people. 'The people have the right to remove any representative in whom they lose confidence'.

The description of the political system continues with Article 3, which says the Front for Construction of the Motherland, and other revolutionary organizations of the populace, are the firm supports of the state; and article 4 establishes the People's Revolutionary Party as the leading force in all revolutionary tasks.

Article 5, on national solidarity, emphasizes the equality of all ethnic groups, and in particular states that 'the languages and writing, together with the good traditions of the minority peoples are to be respected'. The state also has the obligation to aid in the development of minority groups, especially those in undeveloped areas far from the centre.

The right to practise religion is guaranteed by article 6, unless religious activity is used to endanger security, public order, or the general welfare. Article 7 establishes equality of sexes, and declares the state's special interest in the welfare of women and children; article 8 continues with the duties of parents to educate and care for their children in order that they become good citizens, and it also establishes that children are obliged to care for their parents.

Article 9 deals with the obligation of all to defend the country, although the modalities of joining in the country's defence are not specified. It also states that the armed forces must retain the respect of the population and not act against the people's interests.

The chapter on the political system ends with article 10 on foreign policy, which is 'independence, peace, and neutrality'. In addition, Cambodia 'tightens the bonds of solidarity and cooperation with Vietnam, Laos, and the Soviet Union, and other fraternal socialist countries'.

Chapter 2 on the Economic System and Cultural and Social Policy starts off with a declaration that 'the national economy is under state leadership' (article 11). There are three economic sectors—state, communal and family (article 12). Articles 13 and 14 further define the state sector. The state is involved in the development of agriculture, industry which serves agriculture, commodity production, commerce, communications and transport;

and state property consists of land, forests, seas, lakes, ponds, natural resources, economic and cultural centres, defence bases, and other state constructions.

Articles 15–18 discuss individual economic rights. An individual may use and pass on rights of inheritance to the plot of land, to be further defined by law, which the state gives to each family as a house and garden plot. In addition to that 'private' plot and the land allotted by the solidarity group to each family for production, a farmer may borrow additional land from the state to cultivate according to his abilities; and he has the right to receive the fruits of that labour. It is forbidden to buy, sell or pawn land; and no one may use agricultural land or forests for their own purposes without official permission. Finally, authorized private property and profits from work are protected by law and may not be confiscated.

In the realm of commerce the state has a monopoly of foreign trade; and state trading within the country is to be developed. Nevertheless, the populace may sell family agricultural and handicraft produce, so long as such trade is in accordance with state policy (article 19). Taxation and sale to the state may be established by law (article 20).

The remaining articles of Chapter 2 deal with education and social welfare. Culture, education, and the development of language and literature in accordance with the needs of a new society are among the state's interests, while all influence and remnants of reactionary, corrupt culture are to be eliminated (article 21). Education, pedagogy and schools are to be closely linked to society. Educational facilities at all levels, from pre-school centres to tertiary institutions, will be developed by the state according to national requirements; and adult literacy programmes will also be instituted (articles 22–23). Article 23 adds that educational co-operation will be established with the fraternal socialist countries, and relations will be established with other countries as well. Article 24 states that the state will protect ancient temples and art works, and develop internal tourism and cultural exchanges with other countries.

Health care is the subject of articles 25–29. Sport is encouraged, health care is free, particular attention is given to mother and child care centres, with women entitled to ninety days' pre-natal paid holiday. Special care is afforded those suffering from the effects of revolutionary combat, as well as for state employees disabled by age or illness, and for the support of the aged, crippled, widowed and orphaned in general.

Chapter 3, on rights and duties of citizens, guarantees the usual human rights: equality before the law, without regard for sex, religion or race. The exercise of these rights, however, may not be separated from the fulfilment of citizens' obligations (article 30). Freedom of speech, press and assembly are declared, but such freedoms may not be used to offend the honour of others, to offend good social customs, or disrupt public order or national security (article 37).

Electoral rights are spelled out in article 31. All citizens aged 18 may vote, and at age 21 may stand for election. This includes members of the armed services and monks who under pre-revolutionary regimes were deprived of political rights. Deprivation of voting rights may be determined by electoral laws.

Arbitrary arrest and detention without due process of law are forbidden (article 35), and the state guarantees the inviolability of residence and secrecy of the mail, that is, search of domicile may only be undertaken as authorized by law. Freedom of movement and freedom of residence will also be regulated by law (article 36).

Citizens' obligations are also spelled out in detail. Citizens must respect the principles governing social life, act according to state policy and protect state property (article 39). They must conform strictly to the constitution and laws, and they are obliged to serve in state activities, i.e. national defence is an obligation and citizens must defend the motherland and serve in the armed forces (articles 40–41).

The three final articles of this chapter, 42–44, are unexpected and seem fashioned for concerns peculiar to the PRK in its present conjuncture. Loyal citizens of the PRK living abroad are protected by the PRK authorities; the PRK offers asylum to foreigners who have been prosecuted for struggling for peace, democracy, national independence and socialism, and for freedom of scientific and cultural activity in the interests of social progress. Finally, foreigners living in Cambodia must respect the laws of the PRK and will enjoy the protection of the PRK.

The constitution next takes up the organs of government. In Chapter 4 on the National Assembly that organ is established as the 'supreme organ of state power', the highest organ representing the people, and the only organ entitled to make laws.

The National Assembly is chosen by general, direct, secret vote and serves for five years. The number of representatives and modalities of election are to be determined by law.

The State Council is described in Chapter 5 as the organ representing the PRK and as the permanent organ of the National Assembly. As such, it assumes some of the Assembly's duties when the latter is not in session. The State Council reports to the National Assembly, it is chosen from among members of the National Assembly, its officers and members are chosen by the National Assembly, and it serves for the same period of time.

The duties of these two organs are set out in ten points for the former and nine for the latter. The State Council organizes elections for the National Assembly and calls the latter into session, a provision for the future which was obviously not operative for the election of 1981.[16] The Assembly passes and amends the constitution and the laws and watches over their application. The State Council promulgates and interprets the laws. The Assembly establishes domestic and foreign policy and decides on economic and cultural programmes and the national budget. The Assembly also elects and removes its own officers, those of the State Council, and those of the Council of Ministers. Ministries themselves may be established or dissolved by the Assembly. When the Assembly is not in session such changes in ministries are decided by the State Council at the request of the Council of Ministers. The Assembly votes taxation, determines amnesties, and ratifies or abrogates international agreements presented to it by the State Council.

The latter reviews judicial proceedings, and decides on commutation, reduction of sentences and reprieve. The Council also receives letters of credence of foreign diplomats, and ratifies or abrogates international agreements except when decision by the Assembly is required.

The third major state organ, the Council of Ministers, is treated in Chapter 6, articles 64–70. This body is 'the governnent of the PRK; it is the organ governing society directly and which directly takes charge of economic development'. The Council of Ministers is responsible to the National Assembly, or to the State Council during the interim between Assembly sessions. Among the eleven enumerated functions of the Council of Ministers are: drafting laws and other bills for submission to the Assembly and State Council, application of the constitution, laws, and domestic and foreign policies; the formulation and application of economic and cultural programmes and the national budget; the elimination of defects remaining from the old society, the improvement of living standards; and attention to public health.

The Council of Ministers is responsible for state organs from the central government down to local level, it directs cadres, workers and state employees, it is reponsible for the proper functioning of People's Revolutionary Committees at all levels, and it modifies or abrogates improper decisions taken by all such state organs. The establishment of the boundaries of all administrative units is the responsibility of the Council of Ministers.

The development of national defence forces is a ministerial responsibility, as is the application of international agreements. Following this, Chapter 7, articles 71–78, defines lower-level organs of government—the People's Revolutionary Committees. Administratively, the PRK is divided into provinces and municipalities directly under central government authority. Provinces are further divided into districts (*srok*) and the latter into subdistricts (*khum*). The municipalities under central control are divided into wards (*sangkat*). Each of these divisions has a People's Revolutionary Committee. The committees of the two lowest levels, *khum* and *sangkat*, are chosen by the respective populations in general, at direct elections by secret ballot. Then at each higher level the committees are chosen by representatives of the subordinate level committee, Front, and mass organizations affiliated with the Front. The province and muncipality committees are elected for five years, equal to the National Assembly, while the lower-level committees have a life of three years.

These committees are responsible both to their populations and to the higher-level state organs. They execute and apply directives of higher-level organs and supervise the activities of lower levels, in the interest of carrying out state policies, developing the country and maintaining order. In the case of dereliction of duty by a committee, or committee member, dissolution or dismissal may be carried out, in a manner to be established by law.

The judiciary is the subject of Chapter 8, articles 79-86. In the PRK there are civilian and military courts. Special courts may be created by the State Council for special purposes when required. A court consists of a judge and 'people's councillors', as established by law, and cases are decided by majority vote of that council. Court proceedings are public, except when otherwise established by law, and national minorities may use their own languages. Defendants have the right of defence, either by themselves or by a lawyer. Further details of organization and procedure are to be established by law.

Chapter 9 describes the PRK's coat of arms (article 87)—the flag with a five-tower silhouette of Angkor Wat, in contrast to the DK three-tower emblem—[17] the national anthem (to be decided by the National Assembly), National Day, 7 January (article 89), and the capital, Phnom Penh (article 90).

The tenth and final chapter establishes the constitution as the basic law of the PRK with authority over all other laws, which must be in conformity with the constitution (article 91). Article 92 adds that all decrees and decisions of the KPRC before the promulgation of the constitution remain in force until replaced by laws; and the final article, No. 93, vests authority to amend the constitution in the National Assembly, by a two-thirds vote.

Changes from Earlier Drafts

The least significant changes were the decreasing number of articles as language was tightened and articles merged. The July 1980 draft contained

107 articles in eleven chapters, the later 1980 version had eleven chapters with 105 articles, while the March 1980 draft was down to the ten chapters and 93 articles of the final constitution.

Other changes, however, reflected clear divergence of opinion about the organization of the new Cambodian state. They also reflect different ways of adapting features of the 1979 constitution of the Socialist Republic of Vietnam (SRV), which plainly served as a model. Even the preambles underwent far-reaching changes. The first paragraph of the 1980 drafts vaguely evoked the thousands of years during which the Cambodian people struggled to preserve and construct their country. Only in the 1981 drafts is there specific reference to 'the culture of Angkor'. The preambles of 1980 referred to the great influence of the October Revolution of the 'Russian people' on the people of Cambodia—a statement missing from the 1981 preambles. Likewise missing from the latter, and more surprising, is the 1980 reference to 'the victory of 1954', which 'gave independence and sovereignty to our country', and which was lauded in the 1979 Vietnamese constitution.[18]

The second paragraph of the 1980 preamble evokes the violation and exploitation of Cambodia by the French colonialists, while the 1981 drafts speak of the French colonial conquest of Vietnam and Laos, unmentioned in 1980, along with Cambodia.

All the texts then speak of American aggression following the French, the joint Indo-China struggle against them, and the victory of 17 April 1975. They all similarly state that the fruits of that victory were denied by the genocidal policies of the Pol Pot/Ieng Sary/Khieu Samphan clique acting under the direction of the Chinese hegemonists and expansionists. The 1981 texts add remarks on the DK aggression against Vietnam, the March draft stating that they violated 'the borders of Vietnam', while the final text says 'violated the territory of Vietnam'.

Salvation, all texts agree, came in 1979, 'thanks to the ... Communist Party of Kampuchea, the Front ... and the active support of fraternal socialist countries ...' (1980); 'because of ... the party ... the Front ... and the help of the army and people of Vietnam, the people of Laos, and the support of the fraternal socialist countries' (March 1981); 'because of the Party ... the Front ... together with help from the people and army of Vietnam and the support of the fraternal socialist countries' (July 1981).

Following the 1979 victory, the 1980 texts emphasize the roles of the Communist Party and the Front in the country's reconstruction, while the 1981 versions emphasize the Kampuchean People's Revolutionary Council, ignored in the 1980 drafts. Similarly, the 1981 texts again evoke in this context collaboration with the peoples of Vietnam, Laos and other socialist countries, while the 1980 drafts limited their language here to 'solidarity in the context of proletarian internationalism'.

These thematic changes in the constitutional preambles from 1980 to 1981 indicate on the one hand decreasing emphasis during 1980 on the Communist Party, and increasing attention to the inter-Indo-China relationships. These two modifications are in fact ideologically opposite, the first appeasing non-socialist nationalists, and the second possibly objectionable to them. Similarly, the new reference to Angkor in 1981 evokes nationalist sentiment, while the removal of reference to a 1954 victory could offend nationalists of non-revolutionary background.[19] The change from an evocation of the October Revolution and 'proletarian internationalism' to emphasis on Indo-Chinese solidarity probably reflects factional disagreement among the party leadership itself. Both are inimical to the bourgeois survivors whose co-operation the new authorities desired after January 1979.

In the very first articles, the four drafts show hesitation about the definition of the new political system. Although there was no disagreement on 'People's Republic of Kampuchea', it was at first described as a 'regime of people's democracy progressing toward socialism' (July 1980, article 2); then 'people's democracy' was dropped and the regime was simply 'progressing toward true socialism' (1980-II, article 2). The third draft modified the formulation slightly to 'progressing in accordance with pure socialism', and included 'democracy' among the regime's characteristics (March 1981, article 1); and the final solution was 'moving step by step in the direction of socialism', with 'democracy' again mentioned as one of the features of the system (July 1981, article 1).

The changes in wording may not be dismissed as mere vagaries of political scholasticism. The term 'people's democracy' has specific connotations, which were arguably inapt in the Cambodian case; and the nuances of the different ways of defining the new regime's tendency reveal both varying views on policy and also sensitivity to the possible reactions among the Cambodian population.

As defined in the *Great Soviet Encyclopedia*, a people's democracy represents the 'democratic dictatorship' of several classes—the proletariat, the peasantry, the *petit bourgeoisie*, part of the middle bourgeoisie, and based on the alliance of proletariat and peasantry under proletarian hegemony. Its political task was to strengthen the role of the working class in governing the state and remove the representatives of the bourgeoisie from power, and it is established by parliamentary means within the framework of a constitution (*Great Soviet Encyclopedia*, Vol. 17, p. 609). Obviously, the crucial features of a people's democracy were absent at the founding of the PRK.

There is even greater variety in the following prescriptions of the four drafts. In both 1980 drafts, article 3 stated that the PRK 'is ruled by the working class in alliance with the peasantry, the progressive-patriot intellectuals and the strata of other social classes with traditions of valiant revolutionary struggles against feudalism, colonialism, imperialism, expansionism', which imitates article 3 of the 1979 SRV constitution, although there are notable differences.[20] By 1981 all such wording had been eliminated, and instead we find 'The people of Kampuchea are the masters of their land' (March 1981, article 2), then 'the people of Kampuchea are the masters of their country's destiny' (July 1981, article 2), a statement included in article 3 of the July 1980 draft, but omitted from its successor of the same year.

Another common declaration of the July 1980 draft and the two texts of 1981, but omitted from the second draft of 1980, is to the effect that the people's power is exercised via elected representatives responsible to the people and whom the people may remove. In July 1980, however, it was 'assemblies at all levels' (article 3), while in 1981 it was via 'the National Assembly and other state organs' (article 2, both texts).[21] Unlike all its successors, the July 1980 draft ended its article 3 with 'the organization and activities of the assemblies at all levels and the state institutions should conform to the principle of democratic centralism. Again, as in the statements on the class character of the state, the first 1980 draft shows clear influence from the SRV constitution (article 6), which was attenuated by 1981.

In contrast, the 1981 texts include a statement that 'the party' (March 1981, article 4), later the 'People's Revolutionary Party of Kampuchea' (July 1981, article 4), is the 'leading force' in revolutionary tasks. No such statement is found in the 1980 drafts, and here it is the later texts which seem to show SRV inspiration (SRV, article 6, even more detail on party's importance).

Article 5, on minority rights, shows increasing differences among the four texts as well as in relation to the SRV constitution. In July 1980, together with remarks about the equality of all, article 5 stated specifically that the 'languages, writing, good habits and customs' of minorities were respected, a provision clearly adapted from the SRV constitution's article 5 which develops the theme in even more detail. This statement was dropped from the second 1980 draft and from that of March 1981, to be restored in the final constitution. As I shall discuss below, this clearly reflects differences within the Cambodian milieu and between Cambodia and Vietnam with respect to the rights of minorities.[22]

Article 9 of all four texts treats a matter not included in the first chapter of the SRV constitution, the armed forces, and again the second of the 1980 texts differs from its predecessor and two successors in its very laconic treatment. All four texts start off with statements about the principle of national self-defence. The earliest of 1980 and the two of 1981 then go into some detail about the duties of the armed forces in relation to the population, whereas the second 1980 draft merely states that the armed forces 'defend the nation, and the revolutionary state power, protect the achievements of the revolution and the welfare of the people'.

The final article (10) of Chapter 1 on the political system again shows obvious adaptation from the corresponding article (14) of the SRV constitution, but with interesting modifications of detail from one text to another. These articles state the broad outlines of foreign policy. The SRV constitution evokes 'militant solidarity and cooperation with the fraternal socialist countries on the basis of Marxism–Leninism and proletarian internationalism'. Both PRK drafts of 1980 repeat almost the same words, adding only Vietnam and Laos to the 'fraternal socialist countries'. Then the March 1981 draft changes the phrase to 'cooperation with Vietnam, Laos and the fraternal socialist countries', while the final text has 'with Vietnam, Laos, the *Soviet Union* [my emphasis], and other fraternal socialist countries'. Both the 1981 versions omit any reference to Marxist–Leninism or to proletarian internationalism.

Another interesting modification of detail further on in the same article is found in the list of international causes which will be supported or opposed. Among the latter, we find 'big power hegemonist expansionism' in the SRV constitution, the same in the first Cambodian draft, only 'big-power hegemonism' in the second 1980 version, 'great power expansionist hegemonism of the Peking Chinese leaders' in the March 1981 text, and 'expansionism of Peking China, racism, and all reactionary hegemonism which accompanies it' in the final PRK text. On this point the Cambodians seem to have outdone themselves in friendly socialist competition for the grand phrase.

If the purpose behind the changes in the successive drafts of the articles on the political system was not always unambiguous, in the succeeding chapter(s) on the economy, culture and social welfare, there is a move away from adherence to any SRV model towards appreciation of Cambodian realities. In part, the differences are purely formal. Thus, the first two Cambodian drafts, like the SRV text, had two chapters 2 and 3, for respectively 'the Economic System' and 'Culture and Social Welfare', but in the 1981 versions they have been combined into a single chapter, on 'the Economic System, Culture, and Social Welfare'.

There is also, throughout the four Cambodian texts, considerable reworking of the wording, and the arrangement, of provisions, even where the latter remain unaltered from one draft to the next. These changes in form, together with the changes of substance, reflect not only concern over the most effective system to apply to Cambodia, but also the debate within the Vietnamese leadership after the overly ambitious and disastrous 1976–80 plan. Within Vietnam itself, we must recall, a new constitution was promulgated in August 1979 and changes in economic policy were introduced which resemble the system actually put into effect in Cambodia after 1979.

There are in fact few substantive changes in the economic system as the constitution moved through its successive drafts. Those of 1980 called for a 'planned economy progressing toward socialism' (article 11), a statement entirely omitted in 1981, when only the initial statement, to the effect that the national economy is led by the state, was retained.

Similarly, article 11 of the 1980 drafts, 'the state controls [23] all economic activities' was replaced in 1981 by recognition of the three economic sectors, state, co-operative and family, under state leadership. Another important innovation of 1981 was recognition of hereditary rights of usufruct on family house and garden plots allotted by the state.

Also of note is a change in the rules for trading from 'domestic commerce is managed by the state' in 1980 (article 18) to 'state domestic commerce is to be developed' in 1981 (article 19). All drafts established the right to private trade in agricultural and family artisanal production, but the 1981 texts add that such private trade which is in accord with state policy is to be guaranteed by law.

Culture, Education and Social Action

These articles did not change significantly from 1980 to 1981. It is of interest that, unlike the SRV constitution, the Cambodian texts do not refer to promotion of 'the ideological and cultural revolution' (SRV, article 38), or to 'Marxism–Leninism is the ideology guiding the development of . . . society' (article 39), or 'literature and art are created from the Marxist–Leninist stand and viewpoint' (article 44).

Rights and Obligations

This chapter also varies little from 1980 to 1981. One change of potential significance relates to freedom of choice of occupation. In 1980 it was the 'right to choose an occupation according to abilities . . . and in accord with the needs of society' (article 34), but by 1981 it had become 'the citizen should receive guidance in the choice of an occupation, etc.' (article 33). Significant also is the new final article, 44, of the chapter in 1981 on minority obligations. 'Foreign minority residents of the PRK must respect PRK laws and will receive the protection of the PRK'. This was no doubt to provide a constitutional backing for action against illegal activities of Vietnamese transients, which risked becoming a social problem in Phnom Penh, and who might have tried to use their nationality to evade Cambodian regulations (Quinn-Judge, 1983, pp. 18–19).

One more interesting change in the drafts of this chapter relates to military service obligations. In 1980 this matter was the subject of article 47, the last in the chapter on rights and obligations; and it stated that 'the defense of the motherland is an obligation . . . for the citizens'. They must 'defend the motherland and serve in the army as established by law'. By 1981 this was removed to article 41, fourth from the end of the chapter, and rewritten as 'the construction and defense of the motherland are obligations'. Service in the army is still obligatory. Thus there is constitutional backing for conscription for labour service, such as clearing forests and building roads near the Thai border as part of the defence effort.[24]

Organs of State Power

In the three chapters on the National Assembly, the State Council and the Council of Ministers (titles 6–9, 1981), there are several interesting shifts in their attributions.

Two attributions of the Assembly in 1980 which were later removed were authority to decide on referendums, and authority to decide on questions of war and peace (article 51, paras. 14–15, 16–17 respectively in the two 1980 drafts). In the 1981 texts all reference to these two matters is missing, there is no authority for a referendum, and it is not certain where authority to declare war lies.

The second 1980 draft added to the Assembly's attributions the authority to establish the boundaries of provinces and municipalities under central authority (para. 140), a matter given to the State Council in the first 1980 draft (article 65, para. 17), in which the Council of Ministers fixed the boundaries of districts, sub-districts and wards, i.e. the lower-level entities. In the final text this authority was given to the Council of Ministers (article 66, para. 7).

In 1981 the State Council also lost its war powers during Assembly interims (article 65, paras. 15/14) and its authority to 'establish the principles of national defense (paras. 16/15) and to appoint the members of the National Defense Council' (para. 15, second 1980 draft only). The last undoubtedly related to crucial power plays within the PRK leadershp. The composition and appointment of such a council is not mentioned in the first 1980 draft, but the next-to-last article (68) relating to the State Council says, 'The President of the State Council is the Supreme Commander of the Armed Forces and is President of the National Defence Council'. This is identical to the final article (100) of the SRV constitution's chapter on the State Council, but there the election of a National Defence Council is a prerogative of the National Assembly (article 87).

By March 1981 this matter had been moved up to the first article on the State Council (59), where it stated that 'The President of the State Council is the Supreme Commander of the Armed Forces and is President of the National Defence Council when it is necessary to create that organ'. By July 1981 all mention of Supreme Commander and National Defence Council had been removed; and the constitutional variations in this respect were probably connected with the rise and fall of Pen Sovann.[25]

Lower-level Authorities

Between 1980 and 1981 there was a major change in the constitutional chapters on provincial and lower organs of government. The 1980 drafts had established Local Assemblies and Local People's Committees. The former were to be elected by the voting populations of the respective localities—province, district, sub-district, and ward—with the number of representatives of each assembly to be fixed by law. The committees were to be chosen by the respective assemblies, and the system was a smaller-scale copy of the national legislature and executive, with the committee at each level responsible to its assembly and to the committee of the next higher level, and the committees of province and municipality responsible to the Council of Ministers. This is also the system established by the 1979 SRV constitution (articles 110–122).

By 1981 the designated local organs had been changed to the People's Revolutionary Committees, described above. The change seems to reflect the existence of functioning Revolutionary People's Committees which had developed since 1979; and of course the system adopted in 1981 prevents a popular vote from loading a local government organ with people totally unacceptable to the central authorities.

Courts and Trials

Several interesting changes were effected in the provisions for courts and trials (Title 9 in 1980, Chapter 8 in 1981) as the constitution developed through its four versions.

First, the activities, or duties, of the court system were enumerated differently. In the first 1980 draft they were: defend state power, assure the respect and execution of the laws, maintain public order and security for society, protect state property, and protect the rights, liberties, life, and legal interests of the citizens. In the second 1980 version, defence of state power was in second place after 'provide justice', a sixth function, 'punish criminals' was added, and the other provisions were in a slightly different order. In the two 1981 drafts defence of state power was again in first place, but combined with 'defend the democratic legal system' (March) and 'defend democratic legality' (July).

The court system itself was radically altered between 1980 and 1981. The 1980 drafts provided for a Supreme People's Court, Local People's Courts, and Military Courts. This Supreme Court supervised the activities of all other courts, and was under a president elected for five years by the National Assembly and responsible to it.

By 1981 the Supreme Court had been eliminated. The court system henceforth consisted of People's Courts and Military Courts, and their hierarchy is not established by the constitution. Interestingly, the provisions for a Supreme Court in the 1980 drafts were virtually identical to those of the SRV constitution (articles 124, 131–132). The 1981 drafts represent a move away from a Vietnamese model in this respect, but perhaps not a healthy move, since a Supreme Court may have a necessary function. Thus, in its ninth session in July 1985, the National Assembly passed bills to recreate a Supreme People's Court and Supreme Public Prosecutor's Department (*SWB*, 22 July 1985).

The 1981 versions also eliminated an article prohibiting torture which had been included in both 1980 drafts (articles 97 and 94 respectively), and added a provision that members of ethnic minorities have the right to use their own languages and scripts in court proceedings (article 84, final draft), a right guaranteed in the SRV constitution (article 130).

Clearly, it was decided in 1981 to leave much more of the court organization and legal system to be established by law, as provided for by the final article of this chapter in all drafts (articles 100 and 98 in 1980, article 86 in 1981), and as was customary in pre-revolutionary Cambodian constitutions.

The changes in the PRK constitution as the text went through the drafting process show study of the SRV constitution as a model, but nothing like slavish emulation. In most respects the final 1981 text has moved farther away than its predecessors from the corresponding SRV articles; and where the opposite is true, as in the provisions on ethnic minorities, the SRV model which has been adopted is more sensitive to minority rights than the more purely Cambodian texts. Often the changes away from an SRV model show thoughtful awareness of the different PRK realities, and to that extent are encouraging signs for Cambodian national identity.

8 Government Structure

Administrative Divisions

The PRK government and administration is divided into national, provincial, district and local levels; and it has returned to the geographical-administrative divisions of the pre-1975 royalist and republican regimes, ignoring the administrative structure of DK. The country is divided into eighteen provinces (*khet*), further divided into about 122 districts (*srok*), 1,325 sub-districts (*khum*), and 9,386 villages (*phum*). There are also two municipalities (*krung*), Phnom Penh and Kompong Som, divided into wards (*sangkat*), further subdivided into groups (*krom*). Most of the *srok* and *khum* also conserve pre-revolutionary boundaries and names, although a few changes have been made. In general, the variation in number of *srok* per *khet* corresponds to population differences. Kompong Cham has the largest number of *srok*, at least thirteen, while Ratanakiri and Mondulkiri have three each.[1]

Provinces and municipalities are directly under the central government, while *srok* and *sangkat* are subdivisions of province and municipality rather than directly under the national authorities. All are nevertheless part of the state apparatus, for the authorities at each level are responsible to the next higher level as well as to their own local citizenry. This is a modification of the pre-1975 system in which *srok* were the lowest administrative unit in the national administrative hierarchy and there was no organic link between the national administration and the villages. Another difference is that provincial administration appears not to be under the Ministry of the Interior, but under the Council of Ministers as a whole.[2]

Central Government

According to the constitution, 'the people are masters of their country's fate' and they 'exercise state power via the National Assembly and the various organs of state power which they set up' (article 2). The other organs of state power are the State Council and the Council of Ministers, as well as the Front, given little attention in the constitution, but considered nevertheless as an organ of state power.[3] The constitution also states that the government of the PRK is based on a National Assembly, 'the supreme organ of state power', elected for five years in general elections, and the only body which can pass laws. From the members of the National Assembly is chosen the State Council, which is the permanent organ of the Assembly and the representative of the PRK. The government proper, the executive organ, is the Council of Ministers, which is chosen by the National Assembly and is responsible to it. There is no statement in the constitution as to whether Ministers must be members of the National Assembly, but in its first session, in February 1982, the new National Assembly passed a law on Organization and Functioning of the Council of Ministers which stipulated that 'the President of the Council of Ministers is a representative of the National Assembly' and a majority of the other ministers are to be chosen from the National Assembly.[4]

This system did not come into effect until 1981. Under the Kampuchean People's Revolutionary Council (KPRC) during 1979–81, the number of ministers gradually increased and People's Revolutionary Committees (PRC) were set up in *khet, srok, khum* and *phum*, but no information is available about the procedures adopted then for choosing government personnel, whether the first ministerial group, apparently self-appointed from among Front and Party personnel, gradually co-opted other members, or whether, for example, it was the party leadership who chose government personnel. Given the small number of leaders at that time, however, such distinctions are probably of little importance, for most wore two hats, as party and government leaders.

The KPRC system of government continued until mid-1981 when, following elections for both sub-district committees and the National Assembly, and then adoption of the constitution, a major reorganization took place.

Although the constitution was not adopted until July 1981, elections for the National Assembly had been held on 1 May. The law on National Assembly elections establishes the number of representatives as 117, chosen by province and municipality, with the number in each electoral district determined by population. It does not state, however, what population-to-representative ratio was used for calculation. The number of representatives ranges from two in the sparsely populated province of Mondulkiri to thirteen in Kompong Cham.[5]

Candidates for each district were to be nominated jointly by the Front Central Committee, central mass organizations and the Front Committees and mass organizations at the base level (article 24 of the electoral law). In each electoral district there were to be more candidates than the number of representatives to be elected.

In fact, each provincial list included one or two more candidates than the required number of representatives, and interestingly, in a complete list of candidates published before the election the one or two names which were finally not chosen were almost invariably at the bottom of each provincial list, with the only serious 'upset' occurring in Kompong Cham, where number ten of the fourteen-name slate was the odd man out (*Kampuchea*, No. 85, 30 April 1981 and No. 87, 14 May 1981).

As a result of the election, and in accordance with the constitution which was about to be promulgated, the KPRC government which had administered Cambodia since 1979 was replaced by the new structure in the opening session of the National Assembly between 24 and 27 June 1981.

By mid-1985 the PRK government was headed by a seven-member State Council under its President, Heng Samrin, who in that capacity carried out the representative function of national president. Otherwise, most of the State Council members may be more important in their party functions—Say Phouthang as Chairman of the Organizing Committee, and Heng Teav as Vice-President of the Trade Union Association.

At the same time, the Council of Ministers was up to twenty-one members, one of them, Say Phouthang, a vice-president without portfolio. The latest portfolio to be added to the government is that for Disabled Veterans and Social Affairs, obviously in relation to the severe demands placed on the PRK by the continuing military struggle.

The National Assembly meets twice a year to vote on bills proposed, as established in the constitution, by the State Council, the Council of Ministers, the Assembly's own commissions, the Presidents of the Front, the Trade Union Organization, the Youth Organization, and the Women's Organization (article 53). Probably because most Assembly members have other duties, many in the provinces, sessions may be very brief—the eighth session lasted only from 10 to 14 January 1985—leaving state business effectively in the hands of the State Council and the ministries. Thus, although the National Assembly is defined as the supreme state organ, it seems most frequently to give formal approval to measures already decided by ministries, the State Council, or the party. As an example, a National Cadres' Conference in November 1984 issued policy statements on the peasantry and on ethnic matters which were published at the time. They touched on matters which might have caused controversy, yet the role of the Assembly was to approve them without published comment in its brief session of January 1985. Elections for a new Assembly were due in 1986, but at the Front National Council on 21-22 January 1986, a resolution to postpone elections until 1991 was passed, and this was duly endorsed by the Assembly itself during its tenth session in February.[6]

Provincial and Local Government

At lower levels of government, the constitution establishes that People's Revolutionary Committees are to be directly elected in *khum* and city ward, but at the next two higher levels, district (*srok*) and province (*khet*), such committees are to be chosen directly by representatives of the next lower level.

During the KPRC period in 1979–80, lower-level officials were apparently appointed from the centre, and a Front publication of 1980 stated that during 1979 all eighteen provinces acquired their own People's Revolutionary Committees, 'or other forms of revolutionary authority', and the same was true of the *srok, khum* and *phum*.[7] Several presidents of provincial People's Revolutionary Committees were then mentioned publicly. Later, in April 1981, the names of leading provincial figures were published as candidates for the National Assembly election, in which they were all successful. In Table 6 are listed the pre-1981 names which I have found, the 1981 list, and PRC presidents in 1984–5, and early 1986.[8]

Table 6 People's Revolutionary Committee presidents, pre-1981–1986

Province	pre-1981	1981	1984–1985	1986
Battambang	Lay Samon	Lay Samon		Kai Kim Yan
Kampot		Som Chen	Som Chen	Som Chen
Kandal	Lim Thi	Hem Samin	Hem Samin	Yaem Yon
Koh Kong		Rong Chream Kaysan		
Kompong Cham	Kim Yin	Preap Pichey	Hun Neng	
Kompong Chhnang	Dok Narin	Dok Narin	Kev Sin	Kev Sin
Kompong Speu	Khieu Saroeun	Oudom Meanchey		
Kompong Thom	Nguon Nhel	Kim Yin	So Han	So Han
Kratie		Pon Ponli	Thoek Kroeun Vuttha	
Mondolkiri		Thav Ngon	Máy Soeuy	
Prey Veng		Cheam Yiep	Cheam Yiep	Touch Sak
Preah Vihear		Veng Khhuon		
Pursat		Ros Sreng	Prom Kuen	Prom Kuen
Ratanakiri		Kham Len		Bou Chuong
Siemreap		Chan Seng	Chan Seng	
Stung Treng		Thang Bai		Veng Khhuon
Svay Rieng	Heng Sam Kay	Heng Sam Kay	Heng Sam Kay	
Takeo		Pol Saroeun		Kong Lang
Municipality				
Phnom Penh	Khang Sarim	Keo Chenda	Thong Khon	Thong Khon
Kompong Som	Yem Saron	Chum Hol		

In the list for 1981 in Table 6, twelve of the province and municipality chiefs were called 'President of the People's Revolutionary Committee', while those in Koh Kong, Kompong Chhnang, Kompong Thom, Mondolkiri, Pursat, Ratanakiri, Takeo and Phnom Penh were referred to as 'Leading Cadre', which illustrates the Front publication remark quoted above about 'other forms of revolutionary leadership' in some provinces. At one time, students of the PRK were inclined to see this as a distinction between party members and non-members, and I wrote that provincial delegations to the National Assembly were led by either governors—by which I meant 'leading cadre'—or by party chiefs, the PRC presidents (Vickery, 1984, p. 242).

That distinction is not tenable, and PRC Presidents are governors, not party chiefs, although I am still not certain whether 'leading cadre' was the equivalent of local party secretary. In any case, neither title signified non-membership in the party. PRC Presidents Lay Samon, an old Vietnam veteran and Party Central Committee member Heng Sam Kay and Chan Seng, also in the Central Committee, and Kim Yin, an alternate member of the Central Committee, were certainly in the party, as were with equal certainty Koh Kong Leading Cadre Rong Chream Kaysan, a Central Committee member, and Keo Chenda, one of the more prominent Vietnam veterans. The case of Kim Yin shows, moreover, that the distinction is related to the respective provincial structure, not the individual. In Kompong Cham he was called 'PRC President', but in Kompong Thom, 'Leading Cadre'. Other such cases of apparent institutional differentiation are in Kandal where in 1981 Hem Samin was called PRC President', but during 1984–5, 'President of the Directorate of Party Affairs', and in Phnom Penh where in 1981 Keo Chenda was called 'leading cadre', but in 1984 'President of the PRC', in which post he was replaced by Thong Khon in 1985, while Nguon Nhel was given the post of Secretary of the Provisional Party Committee. Still another interesting example is in Pursat, where Leading Cadre Ros Sreng was replaced later in 1981 by Prom Kuen as President of the PRC, perhaps newly organized, while Sreng appeared in 1985 as 'Secretary of the Provisional Provincial Party Committee'. This would suggest that in early 1981 Pursat had neither a PRC nor any Party and Ros Sreng was sent as administrator from Phnom Penh. Then a PRC was formed, perhaps as a result of the elections, but there was still no party organization, which has only started to form in 1984–5. Similarly, Dok Narin, Leading Cadre in Kompong Chhnang in 1981, held the post of Provincial Party Secretary in 1985, while Kev Sin was President of the PRC.

Formally, 'leading cadre' suggests a direct central government or party appointment, while PRC 'president' implies an organization with some local participation. In some places there were also overt party officials alongside those with administrative titles. Thus, in 1979, Vann Sonn was named first as in charge of the Front organization in Phnom Penh, and then became party secretary for the capital.[9]

Of course, there *should* be separate party and administrative organizations, and this seems to be developing, but in some places they still merge. In Kampot in late 1985, for example, Som Chen, still President of the PRC, was also Deputy Secretary of the Provincial Party Committee, while So Han in Kompong Thom heads both bodies.

Elections for *khum* and *sangkat* committees were the opening move in the changes to government structure in early 1981. They were held throughout March on the basis of a Decree-Law promulgated on 16 January.[10] This law does not deal with the further choice of *srok* and *khet* committees, and I have found no published material indicating whether the indirect election of those officials as later prescribed by the constitution actually took place in 1981, or whether the terms of people already in office were simply extended, or changes effected by administrative action. The available names are inconclusive in this respect, although they indicate that some changes were made; and informal queries in Phnom Penh in 1984 brought the response that appointments to provincial leadership posts were made by the Party Organization Committee under Say Phouthang.

The provisions of this law with respect to nomination of candidates and organization of elections are worth noting. This law antedated the publication of the first 1981 constitutional draft of March, which, together with the final constitution of July, substantively revised the provisions of the 1980 drafts on organization of provincial and lower-level authorities; and although this law deals only with *khum* and *sangkat*, without reference to district or province elections, it seems nevertheless to have been designed for the situation later consecrated in the 1981 constitutional texts, according to which *khum* and *sangkat* committees would be chosen directly by their respective populations, while higher-level councils would be chosen indirectly by representatives of the lower levels.[11]

As authority, the law refers only to the Front Declaration of 2 December 1978, Front Decision of 29 December 1979, and Decision No. 32 of 29 November 1979 on the Organization and Activities of People's Revolutionary Committees.

The law states that each *khum* and *sangkat* committee would have five to seven members, candidates for which could be anyone at least 21 years old. Candidates would be nominated by 'base mass organizations' unspecified, but perhaps referring at least to the *khum* and village-level

Front organizations; and for each electoral district there were to be more candidates than the number of committee members to be elected.

People who observed or participated in these election report that they were organized and were carried out fairly, but that there were at least some local variations from the strict letter of the law.

Mr U. T., a pre-1975 teacher now in Adelaide, Australia, resided in 1979 in *khum* Saang, *srok* Choeung Prey, Kompong Cham province, where he had also spent the DK years, and he acted as President of the Election Committee of his *khum*, where the election was held on 15 March 1981. Only the President of the new People's Revolutionary Committee was elected, but there were seven candidates for the position who had been nominated by the villages within the *khum*, and their nominations then approved at *srok* level. The *khum* chief who had previously been appointed by higher authorities was not among the candidates, and after the election he withdrew properly, and, according to U. T., returned to the *srok*-level administration. U. T. believes that either the new President was expected to choose the remaining committee members, or that they were to be subsequently elected, but he left Cambodia before that next step had been carried out. Another Adelaide resident who participated in the voting in *khum* Samrong Knong, *srok* Sangkae, Battambang, said that five committee persons had been elected there.

It seems likely that local authorities interpreted the election law in various ways, that perhaps even *khum* elections were not completed for the entire country, and that further elections for *srok* and *khet* committees were indefinitely postponed.[12]

As noted, the constitution places provincial and local administration under the Council of Ministers, without specifying whether any ministry in particular should be in charge. In the article on provinces it says only that their committees are responsible to the next higher level, that is the central government. The subsequent Law on Orgahization and Activity of the Council of Ministers is also vague on this point, but seems to indicate that provincial affairs are the collective responsibility of the government.[13] This would conform to the logic of the system, in which provincial and district chiefs, unlike their pre-revolutionary predecessors, are not state officials, but chosen representatives of the populations they administer. Moreover, in 1981, all province chiefs were elected to the National Assembly, the body to which ministers are responsible, and thus they exert a direct influence on central government affairs.

Further changes have been effected in 1985, and they seem to confirm that provinces are indeed to be a collective government responsibility, and to demonstrate that PRC are being set up under the government, not by party appointees. At the same time, more names of *khet* and *srok* Party leaders appear in the press, indicating the increasing development of government and party as separate entities. On 22 February 1985 the state council met and decided on the appointments of PRC Presidents in Kompong Cham, Battambang, Kandal, and Stung Treng. No names were announced at the time, but Hun Neng in Kompong Cham was obviously one of the new appointees. The situation in Battambang is of interest in that there were persistent rumours of the removal and demotion of Lay Samon, a Vietnam veteran, who was dropped from the Party Central Committee between 1981 and 1984, and who now works in the Centre for Research in Traditional Medicine.[14]

The Front

The National Union Front for the Salvation of Kampuchea, founded on 2 December 1978, was the original organ of PRK state power; and the first PRK government, the Kampuchean People's Revolutionary Council, developed out of it with inputs from the party.[15] There have been two changes of name, to 'Front for the Construction of the Motherland of Kampuchea' at the time of the government reorganization in May–June 1981, and at the end of that year to 'Solidarity Front for the Construction and Defence of the Motherland of Kampuchea'. These names fairly accurately reflect major concerns of the central authorities, from salvation of what remained of Cambodian society in 1979, to construction once salvation had been secured, to solidarity for defence when it became clear in 1981 that military opposition to the PRK would continue with increasing foreign support.

The constitution says little about the Front, only that 'the Front for the Construction of the Motherland of Kampuchea [and] the various revolutionary mass organizations are firm supports of the state and encourage the people to fulfill all revolutionary obligations'. Nevertheless, as one of its Deputy General Secretaries explained, the Front is a political and administrative organ of the state, with the function of gathering all classes together without regard for political tendency in order to consolidate the party and state. The Front serves as a bridge between party and people in both directions.[16]

The Front Central Committee has expanded from the fourteen chosen at its First, organizing, Congress in December 1978 to thirty-five after the Second Congress at the end of September 1979, to the eighty-member National Council chosen for five years at the Third Congress held on 20–22

December 1981. Total membership in early 1986 was 120,000. Of the original Central Committee members Heng Samrin, then President, is President of an Honorary Directorate of seven, in addition to the eighty-member Council. Another of the original group, Math Ly, is also in the Honorary Directorate, and three, Ros Samay, Bun My and Long Sim, seem no longer to be politically active.

Chea Sim, Vice-President in 1979, is now Front Council President, while of the other original Central Committee members, Chan Ven is a Vice-President and Hun Sen, Mean Saman, Meas Samnang, Neou Samom, Hem Samin, Chey Kanhnha and Prach Sun are members.

Membership in the Front is open to any Khmer, within Cambodia or abroad, who accepts the Front's statutes. Like the state administration, the Front has Province and Municipality branches directly under the central organization, whereas *srok* or *sangkat* branches are established as subdivisions of the next higher level.

The Front's primary task, as noted, is to facilitate communication, i.e. the flow of information from the central authorities to the population and feedback from the people to the government. This is undertaken via Front activities proper, meetings at every level, and also by frequent trips to province centres and rural areas by central Front and state officials, an exercise termed 'going down to the base'. In principle, every cadre is supposed to make one trip monthly to get in touch with an outlying area; and much coverage of such visits is provided by the press. The Front also in principle maintains offices in each province to receive complaints from the population to pass on to the relevant National Assembly member. Although it is impossible to know whether these are mere ritual gestures, I saw some indication in Phnom Penh that cadres may be taking their visits to the base seriously.

The Front is in charge of religious affairs, which under pre-revolutionary regimes were the responsibility of a cabinet minister. Tep Vong, the PRK's most senior monk, is one of the four Front Vice-Presidents; and among the members of the National Council, in 1981, Dok Samol was listed as 'former Party Secretary for Prey Veng Province, at present in charge of religion' (Front, 1982, p. 14).

If only because of the penury of leadership in the PRK, the Front, at least at the top, has been confounded with state and party since its origin, and it would not be too inaccurate to see it as the channel through which state and party conduct public relations. Among the seven members of the Front's Honorary Directorate and the National Council's eleven officers, only three do not also hold some state or party office, and few among the remaining council members are listed exclusively as Front personnel.

Multiple Functions

Indeed, government and party are so thoroughly confounded at all levels that it would seem almost more significant to indicate those who hold only one function. To illustrate the situation, Table 7 lists all State Council, Ministry, and Party Central Committee members with their National Assembly, party, government, Front and provincial posts, plus the remaining Party Central Committee members, and other Front National Council members who are provincial PRC Presidents or Party Secretaries.[17]

Table 7 demonstrates how the Party Central Committee thoroughly permeates the government, and also that there is a cleavage between party and Front, the latter including throughout its hierarchy numerous non-party professionals and intellectuals with little or no revolutionary background who have joined the PRK since 1979. Indeed, the main reason for the prominence given to the Front in the PRK may be its function in organizing those elements who by their background might have been opposed to socialism, but who wish to work for their country and whose talents the PRK needs.

Typical of such individuals are Mme Phlek Phirun and Dr My Samedy of the Front Honorary Directorate, the former also head of the Red Cross, a post which she occupied under Sihanouk before 1970, and the latter a noted pre-war physician. One Deputy Secretary-General, Chem Snguon, while overseas during 1970–5, supported the anti-Lon Nol struggle, then returned to Cambodia after 1975 to be imprisoned by the DK authorities. Others among the Front officers are the pre-1975 intellectuals and eductors Chan Ven, trained as a teacher and the first PRK Education Minister, now Secretary-General of the State Council; Vandy Kaon, a sociologist; and Khiev Kanyarith, a pre-1975 law and economics graduate, editor of the newspaper *Kampuchea*; the monk Tep Vong; and Mme Peou Lida, also known by her original name of Sisowath Sovethvong Monivong.[18]

Another area in which the doubling of functions is apparent is the National Assembly, to which were elected in 1981 all the province chiefs, most of the top party officials, as well as most of the important non-revolutionary Front leaders. Movement among party, military and government also seems significant. The present Minister of Defence, Bou Thang, a Party Central Committee member, moved into government and military from a strictly party post, as President of the Propaganda and Education Committee. The late Chan Si also started out with the PRK in a military post, as Director of the Political Commissariat of the army, then moved to the Defence Ministry and then up to Prime Minister; and one of the ministerial

Table 7 Party Central Committee, 1985

Government	Party	Front	Province
State Council			
Heng Samrin	Sec'y Gen'l	Hon. Pres.	
Say Phouthang	Central Comm.		
Chan Ven		V.P. Council	
Men Chhan	member	V.P. Council	
Kham Len	member		Ratanakiri
Heng Teav	member	Council member	
Vandy Kaon		Dep Sec Gen'l	
Ministry			
Hun Sen	Central Comm.	Council member	
Bou Thang	Central Comm.	V.P. Council	
Chea Soth	Central Comm.		
Khang Sarin	Central Comm. (dropped 1985)		
Kong Sam Ol		Council Member	
Meas Samnang	member	Council member	
Tea Banh	Central Comm.		
Taing Sarim	member		
Chan Phin	Central Comm.		
Cha Rieng	member		
Sim Ka	Central Comm.		
Pen Navuth			
Yith Kim Seng			
Chheng Phon	Central Comm.		
Ouk Bun Chhoeun	member		
Khun Chhy	member		
	Central Comm.		
	Chey Saphon		
	Soeuy Keo		
	Lim Nay		
	Rong . . . Kaysan	Hon. Dir member	Koh Kong
	Heng Samkai		Svay Rieng
	Chan Seng		Siemreap
	Men Sam An		
	Kim Yin		Kompong Thom
	Nay Pena		Preah Vihear
Assembly Standing Comm.			
Chea Sim	Central Comm.	Pres. Council	
Math Ly	Central Comm.	Hon. Dir. member	
Tep Vong		V.P. Council	
Nou Beng	member		
Phlek Phirun		Hon. Dir. member	

Table 7 (*cont.*)

Government	Party	Front	Province
		Nat'l. Council	
		Thang Bai (Hon. Dir.)	Stung Treng
		Mây Soeuy	Mondulkiri
		Hem Samin	Kandal
		Prom Koen	Pursat

newcomers, Tea Banh, since April 1985 in charge of Communications, Transport and Postal Service, was until then Deputy Chief of General Staff.[19] If the revolutionary and DK military backgrounds of Heng Samrin, Hun Sen and Bou Thang are also taken into account, it reveals a concern to choose top government leaders with knowledge of military affairs, a concern which has no doubt been fed by the growth of foreign-backed opposition forces on the Thai border.

Mass Organizations

In addition to the Front, which is both a state organ and a mass organization, several other more strictly mass organizations have been given attention in the Cambodian press and are obviously considered important supports of the regime. Three of them are given particular prominence in the constitution as bodies whose presidents may present draft bills to the National Assembly (article 53).

Probably the most important is the Trade Union organization, which held its first National Congress on 7–9 December 1983 with 302 delegates representing 62,000 members out of a total state employee personnel of 145,000 in 'offices, factories, enterprises, hospitals, communication and transport, schools, ports, workshops, and state farms'. At the 1983 conference the name was changed from Workers' Trade Union for the Salvation of Kampuchea to Association of Kampuchean Trade Unions. It is led by two old communists from the independence struggle of the 1940s who remained in Cambodia after 1954 and who served DK until 1978. The President is Math Ly, also in the Party Central Committee and the National Assembly Standing Committee, and the Vice-President is Heng Teav, a member of the State Council.[20]

Clearly, membership in the union is not automatic with entrance into state employment, and the function of the organization seems to be to encourage more diligent work and greater output through the reward of admission to a vanguard group, although the advantages to members are not spelled out. One press account of admission of new members related that at Machine Factory number 1 in Phnom Penh, after a course on the statutes of the union, eighty workers applied to join, and seventy-five were accepted, the others being instructed to work harder and improve their qualifications. The union's task, the report said, was to encourage greater production of commodities necessary for agriculture, forestry and other productive sectors (*Kampuchea*, **36**, April 1980).

Another important mass organization is the Association of Women, with 922,628 members at the time of its first National Congress on 28–30 October 1983, attended by 265 delegates elected from *khum, srok* and *khet* branches. Its president since 1979 is Mean Saman, a relatively young woman born in 1956, who is also a member of the National Assembly from Takeo. She is said to have joined the revolution in 1970, and in November 1984 was elected an alternate member of the Party's Central Committee.[21]

A third large mass organization is the revolutionary Youth Organization, with over 40,000 members. Its first National Congress, also held in 1983, from 25 to 27 November, was attended by three hundred delegates (*Kong tap padiwat*, **109–110**, 24 November and 1 December 1983).

Laws, Tribunals and Political Dissent

The PRK constitution, in its Chapter 8 on tribunals and the office of public prosecutor, leaves the organization of a court system to be established by law, no doubt because at the time of promulgation of the constitution, in mid-1981, courts had already been functioning for over two years. Thus, with respect to the courts, the constitution just establishes certain principles which clearly relate to an already existing system. It says that People's Councillors have the same rights as judges in passing sentence, which is decided by majority of the court (article 82), all court procedure must be based on law and on the principle of equality before the law (article 81), and the accused have the right to defence (article 85).

Before the establishment of a legislative organ in 1981, Decree-Laws were issued by the KPRC. The first was concerned with the establishment of tribunals, termed 'Revolutionary People's Courts'; and the second Decree-Law, dated the same day, established penalties for various crimes. Two years later, after the adoption of the constitution and reorganization of government, the first Decree-Law on courts was replaced by another more detailed law voted by the National Assembly.[22]

According to this law, there is to be a court in each province and municipality, with a president, one or two vice-presidents, and a judge as personnel. Trials are presided over by a panel of three, or in some cases five, consisting of the above, and on occasion 'People's councillors'. The available texts indicate neither how court personnel are appointed, nor the qualifications required, nor is the position of the courts within the state apparatus clear, although they seem to be under the Ministry of Justice.

The same law adds to the right of defence of the accused that it may be conducted by the accused alone, or with the assistance of lawyers. The right of appeal to 'higher authorities' is established, as is the requirement that death sentences be sent to the State Council for approval. The first two Decree-Laws on courts and sentences were concerned first of all with treason ('betrayal of the revolution'), although they provided penalties for other crimes as well. Examples of the range of sentences established in 1979, and which seem not to have changed, is ten to twenty years imprisonment for treason, and five to fifteen years for espionage, sabotage and subversion. If a person is involved in such activities as leading a network, or uses his official position to further such activities, or if he is guilty of 'many crimes against the population in the past' (obviously aimed at former DK cadres), the sentence may range from twenty years to death. The first six articles of the law deal with such crimes against the state; then article 7 establishes sentences of ten to twenty years for murder, six months to ten years for deliberately inflicting bodily injury, two to five years for rape, and twenty years to life imprisonment, or even a death sentence, for rape followed by murder. Theft of private property may be punished by six months to fifteen years imprisonment, depending on the seriousness of the offence.

As in other areas of government activity, the PRK has called on surviving pre-revolutionary technical personnel to re-establish institutions destroyed under DK; and within the Ministry of Justice several trained lawyers have been drafting new laws. In November 1984 three volumes, totalling nearly 400 pages of various types of legal texts, had been published, and more are to come.[23] Full new criminal and civil codes had not yet been promulgated, and the Ministry of Justice lawyers said that a draft of a law on marriage and family had just been completed and would soon be presented to the National Assembly for approval.

Occasionally, trials have been covered in the press and, as would be expected, cases of treason and subversion are given most attention. In June 1980 there was the case of Hem Krisna and fifteen accomplices, given sentences of three to twenty years' imprisonment for active subversion in the service of the non-communist anti-PRK forces on the Thai border (*Kong tap padiwat*, **7**, June 1980). Just over a year later, a group of five men and a woman were tried for subversion and sabotage as 'Pol Pot mercenaries'. The five men had all been DK soldiers and cadres since the period 1970–3, and had fled in January 1979 to DK bases in western Cambodia or the Thai border where they accepted assignments to carry out sabotage in Phnom Penh. They were given sentences of eleven years to, in one case, life. The woman, who had no political background or, in contrast to the men, education, and who was only guilty of knowingly giving shelter to the saboteurs, was let off with a two-year suspended sentence (*Kampuchea*, **111**, 29 October 1981). One non-political trial which was reported involved five men accused in May 1982 of robbery and in one case murder, who were sentenced to prison for terms of eighteen years up to life for the murderer.[24]

There can be no doubt that the PRK intends to operate under a rule of law, probably difficult to re-establish after five years of wartime near-anarchy (1970–5), four more years without any legal system or even a pretence of legality (1975–9), and faced with near total loss of documents, dispersal of qualified pesonnel, and decay of institutions, in a poverty-stricken country on which war continues to be waged. Fear of arbitrary arrest does not seem to be a major concern of the people one meets, formally or casually, within Cambodia, and among refugees it is rare to meet anyone with a tale of incarceration or abuse.[25]

It would of course be fatuous to suggest that there are no defects in the system, and it would not be surprising in PRK circumstances if power to arrest has occasionally been abused and if living conditions in prisons are poor. Published remarks of the authorities indicate concern over such problems and efforts to review and improve PRK legality. Among details of the agenda of a State Council meeting in February 1985 were 'examination and decision on "Law Construction" in 1985', 'decision on the request for pardon of a convict', and 'review of the trial and conduct of the prosecution in "the Kratie Province case"', of unspecified nature. Legal matters seem to have been given particular attention in the ninth Assembly session in July. Minister of Justice Ouk Bun Chhoeun spoke on the question of 'democratic legality'; and a bill was passed establishing a Supreme People's Court and Supreme Public Prosecutor's Department, institutions eliminated from the final draft of the constitution. More recently—30 October 1985—the State Council met and decided on a Draft law on 'Arrest, Temporary Imprisonment, Release, and Search of Domicile, Possessions, and the Person'.[26]

Political Liberty and Dissent

In conformity with Cambodian tradition, and in a manner which regime leaders in most of Cambodia's neighbouring countries well understand, political dissent as familiar to the Western democracies, if not explicitly forbidden, is not encouraged. Old-line communists in the PRK and Singapore's capitalist bureaucrats would be in full accord on the 'structural weakness' of Western parliamentary democracy, its 'fatal flaw' which permits frequent changes of the team in power, and the need for a 'mainstream party' to be returned at every election for the sake of stability. Goh Chok Tong, concerned that Singapore 'might find it difficult to maintain the one-man one-vote' system would have perfectly understood Pen Sovann's declaration that where 'bad elements had been elected' in *khum* contests, 'the elections must be reorganized'.[27]

Like all previous constitutions, that of the PRK guarantees freedom of speech, press and assembly; and, as in previous constitutions, there is still a 'joker'. Such rights may not be used to 'offend good social customs or to disrupt public order or national security' (article 37). It may help put this in proper perspective by emphasizing that the two periods of greatest freedom for political dissent in Cambodian history were the last seven years of the French colonial regime (1946–53) and, to a somewhat lesser extent, the Khmer Republic of Lon Nol. Since the first belongs to a category now viewed with disapproval in all political circles, and the second is acknowledged to have been an unmitigated disaster, the present lack of opportunity for political dissent may be viewed with somewhat less concern.

As has been described elsewhere, between 1946 and 1952, there was a plurality of competing political parties contesting free elections and a large number of newspapers vigorously propounding policies at variance with one another and with the regime, whether local or colonial. As Cambodia progressed towards independence, that is, as King Sihanouk augmented his political authority, these freedoms decreased, and during the period of Sihanouk-led independence (1953–70), freedom of political dissent was more restricted than during the last French years. Dissent was not totally repressed. After 1962 no political parties other than Sihanouk's Sangkum were permitted, but newspapers representing contending views were published, so long as they did not transgress certain limits which were never explicitly defined. One such limit understood by all was that opposition to Sihanouk and his regime, the advocacy of an alternative, was forbidden. Such was tantamount to *lèse-majesté* and treason. Dissenting views had to be offered within a framework of loyalty to and support for the Sangkum and for

Sihanouk personally, in the guise of suggestions for improvement in the carrying out of policies already approved.[28]

Few Cambodians young enough to be active in politics today have ever experienced freedom of political dissent; and the rivals of the PRK show no more inclination to experiment with such freedom than the Phnom Penh authorities.[29] Moreover, greater freedom can hardly be expected with the country at war, when political dissent would ultimately, if not immediately and expressly, be in favour of the enemy. No country, it must be remembered, permits dissent in favour of the enemy in wartime; and the limits on political activity and dissent in the PRK certainly seem less onerous than those envisaged by American and British planners in the event of a war situation in those countries (Campbell, 1984).

Besides the restrictions on overt dissent there are other restrictions on personal freedom which seem strange in the affluent West, at least in peacetime. Throughout the state apparatus, circulars have been issued instructing employees not to associate with foreigners unless authorized. In particular, foreigners should not be invited into private homes. People who are not state employees seem less concerned about this restriction, and while walking about in Phnom Penh I was twice invited in for a chat and a drink by people I encountered casually in the street. Such encounters in public do not seem to be feared; and in restaurants and other public places Cambodians are not hesitant to enter into conversation with a foreigner if there is a common language, especially if the foreigner speaks Khmer. The situation is much like that during the last years of Sihanouk's Sangkum, in the late 1960s, when, even if formal regulations were not issued, it was understood that contact with foreigners was suspect, and one was often avoided by former friends, who feared harassment by the police if they were seen to spend much time with foreigners. Thus, the most restrictive features of the PRK political system already prevailed twenty years ago, under a regime in which most of the non-communist enemies of the PRK, whether of Sihanouk's FUNCINPEC or Son Sann's KPNLF, participated.

Considered in relation to the conditions in which the country exists, the PRK record on political freedom and human rights does not give cause for dismay, and with respect to previous Cambodian regimes it may be encouraging. At least, since 1979, Cambodia has seen to increase in the rule of law and concern with human rights, after a long period of erosion, starting in the mid-1960s.[30]

The Military

The PRK has always possessed a military capability, even if small; and the latter accompanied the Vietnamese forces who entered Cambodia to overthrow DK between December 1978 and January 1979. Indeed, the PRK dates the founding of its revolutionary armed forces from 19 June 1951, and regularly celebrates that anniversary. This implies a continuity throughout the DK period, although that aspect is not emphasized, and of course a number of PRK leaders served in the DK armed forces before breaking with Pol Pot.

The first Minister of National Defence in 1979 was Pen Sovann, also at the time Party Secretary and Vice-President of the Revolutionary Council government. Under him in the military hierarchy were Chan Si, Director of the Political Department; Soeuy Keo, General Staff Chief; Dy Phin, Director of Logistics; and Meas Kroch, Deputy-Chief of the Political Department.[31]

Sometime in 1980, Pen Sovann was named Supreme Commander of the Armed Forces, an apparently even higher rank, which was eliminated in the final constitution, but by July 1981 Chan Si had replaced him as Defence Minister. Sovann was no longer mentioned as being involved in military affairs, and this change may have signalled his approaching fall. The hierarchy then was, below Chan Si, Soeuy Keo, Vice-Minister and Chief of the General Staff; Dy Phin, Vice-Minister and Chief of Logistics; Meas Kroch, Vice-Minister and Chief of the Military Political Commissariat; and Tea Banh, Deputy-Chief of the General Staff.[32]

When Pen Sovann was removed from all posts in December 1981 Chan Si replaced him as President of the Council of Ministers (Prime Minister), while Bou Thang moved over from Chief of the Party Committee for Propaganda and Education to the Defence Ministry, although these shifts did not occur simultaneously.[33]

Below Bou Thang, the same men remained in the top ranks of the hierarchy, although in a slightly different order than that reported in 1979; Vice-Ministers Soeuy Keo, Meas Kroch, Dy Phin and Tea Banh, heading respectively the General Staff, the Political Commissariat, the Logistics Department, and as Deputy Chief of Staff. Here too a number of changes have been effected since the Fifth Party Congress. Soeuy Keo's position since his exclusion from the Central Committee is unknown, while Koy Buntha is a new Vice-Minister and has been reported as Chief of General Staff. Meas Kroch still held his position in December 1985, but it is his Deputy, El Vansarat, who was elected to the Party Central Committee. Ham Kit appeared as in charge of Logistics, and Chay Sang Yun is now Deputy-Chief of Staff, replacing Tea Banh, who has not fallen into disgrace but has moved over to the Ministry of Communications, Transport and Postal Service.[34]

The goal of the armed forces is obviously to develop the capability of assuming total responsibility for the country's defence, permitting the Vietnamese forces which have borne the brunt of fighting since 1979 to continue their gradual withdrawal, the completion of which is foreseen in 1990. PRK troops are already active along the north-western Thai border where the Thai army has reported that in the important sector opposite Prachinburi there is one PRK division alongside two Vietnamese.[35]

There are three categories of armed forces—main forces, regional forces and local forces. Regional forces seem to be attached to province, district and sub-district. A complete hierarchy of military ranks has apparently not been established. The five men at the top of the hierarchy carry no military title or rank at all, and when members of the field forces are mentioned by name their ranks are given as 'commander' (*bancheakar*), 'chief' (literally, 'president'/*protean*), of a unit, 'deputy chief', and 'soldier' (*yuthachon* or *senachon*).[36]

The PRK has not announced the number of persons in its armed forces, but foreign analysts estimate about 30,000.[37] Military service, and auxiliary civilian service, are obligations of citizenship established in the constitution, although officially all military personnal are 'volunteers'. Twice a year the Council of Ministers and Ministry of Defence establish a total plan for military recruitment, with totals required from lower administrative units. Then, at province and district levels, the authorities undertake a propaganda and educational campaign to encourage the requisite number of young people to volunteer. A very recent (September 1985) change has been the introduction of five years' compulsory military service for men aged 18 to 30.[38]

Occasionally, there are reports of such campaigns and their results in the press, in particular in the army newspaper. Interestingly, the reports are not uniformly positive. In November 1982 it was said that the District of Phnom Penh had previously had a rather bad record. They did not make their quota, and some of the recruits had run away or were otherwise of poor quality. The reasons alleged were fear of disability and subsequent hardship for the family. Thus, in 1982, the campaign focused on the problems of soldiers' families, and it was decided that a disabled soldier would be considered, with respect to work points and allowances, the equivalent of a full-strength worker for three years; and in addition there would be sub-district and village aid for soldiers' families. A similar story of improvement on a previously poor record was from Kompong Siem District in Kompong Cham Province. Until 1983 they had not met their quota and their recruits were undisciplined or else fled. Then, after a propaganda campaign, and pledges of public contributions for the support of soldiers' families, they had two hundred volunteers during the first half of 1983, thus exceeding their quota (*Kong tap padiwat*, **66**, 15 November 1982, and **105**, 27 October 1983).

During the first half of 1983, separate articles also announced that Takeo province had sent 550 new recruits to the army, Kien Svay District (Kandal Province) 126, and that the Province of Kandal as a whole and Bauribaur District in Kompong Chhnang Province had fulfilled their quotas. At the end of 1983 Phnom Penh city announced it was sending 414 recruits, and by mid-1984 the capital was said to have exceeded its plan by 119 per cent. Likewise, the District of Koh Thom went over its quota by 113 per cent, and the town of Takhmau, by 111 per cent, without any absolute figure being provided.[39]

Although soldiering is formally voluntary, and names are not chosen arbitrarily by the authorities, there is obviously considerable pressure on those eligible to volunteer. There is nevertheless some appreciation of the necessity for military duty in the country's present situation. When visiting the Tuol Kork textile factory, its female secretary, among their achievements, noted proudly that three of their workers had joined the army; and when on a trip to Takeo on 10 November 1984, I passed a village where new volunteers were leaving for service, they appeared to be receiving a cheerful send-off, in contrast to the atmosphere at the departure of civilian auxiliary workers which I witnessed later on the same road. With respect to quotas, Koh Thom District officials told me that in 1984 their planned semi-annual draft quotas, set for them by the province, were 117 and eighty, and that they had exceeded them, with 138 and eighty-four volunteers respectively, figures which agree precisely with their 113 per cent overfulfilment reported in the press.

Lest critical readers be inclined to dismiss such upbeat figures as propaganda, they should note the concern in anti-PRK circles that a genuinely Khmer, effective force may be developing, a concern which cuts the ground from under arguments that opposition to the PRK is for the sake of Cambodian independence. It is now clear that the prospect of a truly Khmer PRK is more worrying than the existence of a putative Vietnamese puppet.[40]

In addition to strictly military duties, troops are also given considerable attention in the press for construction and agricultural work. They are reported from time to time as having built schools, hospitals, dams, and to have prepared rice fields. They are also heavily engaged in propaganda work among the population, organizing political courses to explain policies, as well as sessions to encourage people sympathetic to the enemy to come forward, confess, and change their views. Party recruitment within the military is also an important function, and this clearly deliberate dual military and political role is reflected in the top military hierarchy, from Pen Sovann, through Chan Si, to Bou Thang, whose PRK career was in political work until after the removal of Pen Sovann in December 1981.[41]

Auxiliary National Defence Labour

Since at least 1983, the PRK has recruited groups of civilians to work along the border with Thailand, clearing brush, constructing barricades, constructing and repairing roads in the interest of defence against attacks by the DK coalition forces at the border (Wain, 1983; Vickery, 1984, pp. 297–8).

The recruitment was apparently first organized in the outer provinces, and began in Phnom Penh only last year. When I was there in November 1984 I heard remarks about people who had to 'go to Pailin to clear forest', and the task was plainly unpopular and viewed with some trepidation. The first group had left Phnom Penh just before I arrived, and they had been told that their tour of duty would be about two months. It was difficult to obtain much information about the programme, but I was told it was an obligation, like service in the army.

Since then, the position of the regime on auxiliary defence work is clear. Articles in the PRK press indicate that it is not clandestine forced labour, but viewed as a necessary patriotic task and will be given public recognition as such. At the end of January celebrations for the return of the first Phnom Penh contingent were announced, just over two months after I had been told of their departure. At the same time there was an official send-off for the second group, who apparently set out at the very end of January 1985. A rather large amount of space over three issues of *Kampuchea* was devoted to the subject, including interviews with some of the returned workers. There was also an article on their health care, which said that the Phnom Penh municipality had sent fifty-seven medical workers with the first group (*Kampuchea*, **281-283**, 31 January, 7 February, 14 February 1985). The sending of doctors to care for these workers may have prompted the special attention given to the matter in the Western press later in the year.

In July there was an announcement of the flight from Phnom Penh of the Deputy-Director of the Khmer-Soviet Hospital in Phnom Penh, who had left his post in May, which would have been just when the contingent reported as beginning duty in January would have returned. Indeed, he complained that phase three of a forced labour programme had begun, and added that there was forced resettlement towards the border provinces. His case was given more publicity in the *Far Eastern Economic Review*, which reported straight-facedly that his reason for leaving was, 'Vietnam has set up a programme to kill the Cambodian people'. Together with the Western press, the ASEAN foreign ministers also expressed concern about 'compelling citizens to work in war zones'.[42]

There can be no doubt that this work, like all defence work, is onerous and dangerous, but Cambodia has been forced into desperate measures to defend itself against attacks encouraged and supported by those same ASEAN countries. The real concern of the ASEAN governments and their press agents is probably that the Cambodians continue to fight back, and may be successfully involving the population in national defence. One of the interesting inferences from the way the Khmer–Soviet Hospital doctor was treated by the press is that few of the civilian defence workers have defected, and his was the first information about the new programme which had been revealed.

Part III The Economic System

9 The PRK Economy

When the PRK was established in January 1979 the country's economic situation was unique in modern history. Not only had Cambodia been damaged by several years of war and revolutionary transformation, the severity of which was comparable to what had occurred in parts of Eastern Europe during 1939–45,[1] but during 1975–9 the DK regime had attempted to forcibly return the country to poor peasant level with only a minimum of essential industry, primitive education, and wilful neglect of such trained pesonnel as existed. Thus, in 1979, there had been no currency or markets for four years, no taxes had been collected for at least nine—in many parts of the country for longer—such manufacture as had not been deliberately neglected or destroyed after 1975 had been run down; skilled manpower had been dispersed in agricultural communes, decimated by illness and execution; and many of the survivors had chosen to flee abroad as soon as the removal of the DK authorities permitted freedom of movement.

The economic intentions of the PRK were outlined in the eleven-point Front programme of 2 December 1978. Point 5 stated that the new regime would

> carry out a sovereign independent economic policy moving toward prosperous and authentic socialism . . . this new economy will serve the interests of the people on the basis of the development of agriculture and industry . . . it will be a planned and market economy answering the needs of progress of the society.

The DK obligations to work and eat in common would be abolished, as would the confiscation of rice and personal property. Mutual assistance and co-operation on the basis of free consent would be aided and encouraged, in order to boost production and raise the standard of living. Currency, banking and commercial transactions would be restored.[2]

Three types of economic organization were recognized, state, co-operative and family (private).[3] Under the first come all industry, finance, transport, official foreign commerce and some large-scale agriculture, especially industrial crops. The last includes most retail marketing, individual artisan, handicraft, and repair work, some agriculture, and *de facto* much commodity import trade. The co-operative sector is best described as semi-private/semi-state, and includes a significant portion of agriculture, the two highest types of Solidarity Group,[4] and certain urban enterprises such as the larger restaurants.

The markets quickly became a favourite area of work for people fleeing the fields, even for many who had not previously worked as traders, since Cambodia after DK was starved of commodities, and anything could turn over a quick profit. Buying and selling were freely allowed and, until 1983, were not even taxed. This policy gained popular support, and it also achieved a mobilization of concealed capital remaining within the country for what at the time was a productive purpose, the acquisition of essential commodities which the state could not have purchased, confiscated, or obtained through foreign aid. It represented a sort of primitive accumulation of capital via free trade; and state recognition of the necessity of the free market in spite of its violation of socialist ideals, was clear in an April 1980 KPRC order signed by Pen Sovann, which forbade checking, searching or obstructing transactions and flow of consumer goods; ordered the closure of all unnecessary checkpoints; and stated that no one, not even military or security forces, had the authority to stop trains except in emergencies due to danger.[5]

Democratic Kampuchea had not only abolished currency, but as an aspect of the millenarian peasantist trait in its revolution had held all wealth in contempt, and there had thus been little attempt to search out and confiscate cash, jewels, or precious metals held by the population prior to 1975. Many people buried their possessions as soon as they were apprised of the coming evacuation to the countryside. Others concealed them on their persons, were rarely searched carefully, and in an astonishing number of cases retained their valuables at liberation in 1979.[6]

When released from the DK constraints in 1979, the first concern of all survivors was to retrieve valuables which they had concealed, which they knew others had concealed, or which had been left by the deceased; and those who did not try to carry them in their flight across the Thai border immediately set about investing them in goods for resale inside the country. The more enterprising went themselves to the border to purchase goods from Thailand which they carried back to the markets of Battambang, Phnom Penh and other towns. Others established themselves in those markets, buying for resale the goods brought from the border and financing further trading ventures. This should not be termed 'black market', for it was not at all clandestine and there was no attempt to impede it. It was normal free trade, but carried over unusual routes—border woodlands and semi-battlefields—because Cambodia's normal routes westward were closed. The ultimate purchasers in the towns used their own pre-war hoards, where they existed, or the products which they made at home for sale, or even, where it could be spared, their government rice rations. Thus, in the beginning, the market revival was almost entirely financed by private liquid capital which had been hoarded for several years. Ultimately, this capital was exported abroad, principally to Thailand,[7] but in the meantime it had financed a necessary part of the country's reconstruction which the state alone could not have achieved. Moreover, used in this way, it did not generate severe inflationary pressure, and did not contribute to the re-emergence of wide class differences. One negative effect of this *laissez-faire* was the unrestricted sale of useless or even harmful products.[8]

Another method of primitively accumulating business capital was pillage. As the population flowed back into Phnom Penh in 1979, everything still intact was fair game. Surviving libraries were looted and their contents put on sale or, in the case of dossiers and newspapers, used for wrapping parcels. Many other articles for use or resale were available from both former government offices and private houses left untouched since 1975; and a more exotic method of appropriating old wealth was the collection of gold from the mass graves of DK victims.[9]

Since, eschewing force, the new PRK authorities had no means of extracting sufficient food from the rural areas to feed the new state sectors, foreign aid was used for that purpose, first aid from Vietnam and the Soviet Union, and later Western international aid.[10] This gave rise to the journalistic dishonesty about misappropriation of aid destined for villagers, in favour of officials, as though the inhabitants of food-producing regions should be favoured over those in the towns. This was particularly sickening in the Western press which had reviled DK for destroying towns, and who then damned the PRK for essential measures used to recreate them.

The urban market sector was left to feed itself; only state employees received government rations from food aid supplies. The market personnel, which included large numbers of spouses, relatives and friends of state employees, using hoarded valuables, loot, or commodities purchased with such, could offer adequate prices to entice surplus food from the rural areas; and some of this food also reached state employees either via their family members in the markets, or because they had their own hoard of pre-war valuables.

Money, Prices and Markets

During 1979 there was no Cambodian currency, and market prices were established by supply and demand in Vietnamese *dong*, Thai *baht*, gold, and rice, with rates of exchange determined strictly according to market forces. Thus various reports stated that 1 kg. of rice exchanged for 1.5 kg. of fish, or 1 kg. of beef was equivalent to 2.5 kg. of rice, a sarong 12 kg., and 1 oz. of gold, 2,100 kg. of rice. State employees were paid in rice, at the rate of 13 kg. per month for workers and middle-level officials, which some were able to exchange for other commodities in the market. Other purchases were made from pre-war hoards of valuables, including gold recuperated from mass graves.[11]

In March 1980 a new Cambodian *riel* was placed in circulation, at rates of 1 *riel* to 3 *dong*, and 4 *riel* to the US dollar. In domestic terms, the *riel* was at first fixed as the price of 1 kg. of milled rice. State salaries began to be paid in *riel*, and varied from 65 per month for an ordinary worker to 260 for the top three men in the state apparatus. When money salaries were introduced, payment in kind was terminated, although state employees could buy fixed amounts of rice and other essential commodities at subsidized below-market prices.[12]

The new *riel* quickly displaced other currencies from the domestic market, and was accepted in all domestic transactions. State subsidized rice was pegged at 1 *riel* per kg., and the state offered to purchase rice from farmers at 1.4–1.6 *riel*, while the free-market price of rice in 1980 varied around 2.5–3.00 *riel*. The stability of rice prices throughout 1980 surprised foreign observers, who had been sceptical about the new *riel*'s viability.[13]

Since 1980, salaries have been raised twice, I was told, and now appear to range between 140 and 500 *riel*. Examples of monthly salaries which people told me they were receiving in November 1984 were:

teachers—from 160 for a new teacher to 482 for a principal of a secondary school;

doctors—300 for an M.D.;

pharmaceutical factory employees—170–200 (specialized worker), 370 for the factory director, plus allowances (e.g. for children);

tyre factory employees—140 (unskilled worker), 400 for the director, plus allowances;

textile factory workers—140 (unskilled worker), 230 for semi-trained, 300 for a fully-qualified machine operator.

In addition to salaries, state employees still receive subsidized rice allowances of 16 kg./month for an adult and 10 kg. for a child, at 2.5 *riel* per kg. In 1984 they were also still benefiting from free housing, light and water, if only because the state still lacked the means to collect rates which had in fact been set. Light and water meters were not yet installed in most places. There are also subsidized rations of certain other commodities, and many people earn extra income by selling on the free market what they do not choose to use themselves. As an example, a person whose salary was 260 *riel*, up from 90 in 1981, could buy the following goods at subsidized prices, which I contrast with their free-market prices:

Table 8 Subsidized and free market prices for basic commodities, 1984

	controlled	free
	riel	
5 litres kerosene @	5.00	11
25 packs cigarettes, total	125.00	225
5 pieces of soap for	13.50	60
32 kg. of rice @	2.50	3
2 tins of condensed milk for	24.00	46
$\frac{1}{2}$ kg. sugar for	6.00	10

The sale of surplus rations on the free market is accepted, and non-smokers, for instance, could nearly double their disposable cash income. It is acknowledged that salaries are inadequate for a minimum basic living standard, which people with even modest demands say requires at least 30 *riel* per day in Phnom Penh; and all salaried people only survive through other expedients–selling surpluses; living together and pooling incomes, especially where one or more family members trade in the market or engage in handicraft manufacture; moonlighting in private work, such as teaching; maintaining vegetable gardens; or raising chickens, ducks or pigs.

Although salaries have more than doubled since 1980, they have only just kept pace with basic commodity prices, as the following price list in Table 9, recorded in the Phnom Penh markets, shows.

Some typical prices for prepared food in stalls and restaurants at the end of 1984 were: a dish of meat and vegetables in the simplest food shop, 2–5 *riel*; an entrée in the better restaurants, 20–50; a cup of coffee, 5, and with milk, 7; a bottle of beer, 25, and soft drinks, 6–8 *riel*.

Table 9 Price list, Phnom Penh market, 1984

	1981	1984
	riel	
pork per kg.	20	45
chicken per kg.	14	16
beef per kg.	16	40
rice per kg. (free)	2.5–3	4–6
a single egg	1	2
rubber sandals, pair	12	30+
cloth for dress, per metre	60+	120+
laundry soap, per piece	3	12

As an indication of what these prices mean for Cambodians, it may be useful to record a few prices of similar products in the best pre-war years, for example, as I noted them in 1963 (see Table 10). At that time state salaries in *riel* were roughly ten times their present levels; primary and secondary school teachers, for example, receiving 1,500–3,000 *riel* monthly.

Table 10 Price list, Phnom Penh and Siemreap markets, 1963

pork per kg.	60 (Phnom Penh)	30 (Siemreap)
beef per kg.	40	22
1 whole chicken	40–60	22
rice per kg.	3	

Thus, in terms of cash, the present regime is much more favourable for the peasants than the pre-war economy, and salaried employees must spend much more of their income on rural products than before.

State salaries have plainly been set for the most spartan subsistence level, and they offer no possibility for state employees to become a privileged stratum through salaries and legal perks. The most prosperous urban group are those who live by the market, many of whom, through family membership or association also contribute to the support of state employees. I was not able to obtain a statement of income from any traders, but their relative prosperity is apparent from their stock of goods, general notoriety, and the circumstances that the numerous eating and drinking places in Phnom Penh are heavily patronized by people who can only afford such expense by engaging in some kind of private business. In contrast to 1979–80, however, when an extreme seller's market prevailed, there is now only a minimal mark-up over prices in Thailand—no doubt the result of both competition and the very small amount of cash in circulation within Cambodia. Traders now obviously make their profit from large turnover rather than high unit margins, and all foreign goods are very expensive for the local consumer.

For certain other occupations I was able to obtain figures. One supplementary occupation whose beneficiaries are mostly state employees, because most people with the requisite qualifications have chosen to work for the state since 1979, is private tuition, particularly foreign languages, of which the most popular is English.

All over Phnom Penh small signs are posted announcing that a private language class is open, and these classes are usually conducted in the evening, after office hours. Fees are between 30 and 50 *riel* per month per person for one hour's instruction per working day. If there are twenty pupils in a class, as seems to be normal, the teacher will earn 1,000 *riel* a month for an hour's work each evening, that is four to five times his official salary; and if he conducts two or three classes per evening, his income will be very high. In contrast to the situation reported by refugees in 1980, there is now great freedom to open such classes, even if they are not formally authorized (Vickery, 1985).

Artisanal or small-scale technical work, manufacture of small commodities, repair work and photography constitute a lucrative sector. Most people engage in such work as full-time self-employment, but I met one woman who told me that she worked as a teacher during the day and she and other members of her family made joss sticks at home in the evening for sale in the market. One establishment from which I was able to obtain information was a group of workers making moulded concrete Buddha images for installation in temples. Once a mould has been made it does not take long to turn out images, each of which, depending on pose and size, sells for 400–700 *riel*. Although sales are seasonal, and turnover was particularly good during the month of *kathen* (October–November), the artisans considered that the work provided a good living for the group of thirteen workers and their families.

Another such profitable task is home weaving. Just outside Phnom Penh I found a woman who worked full time at her own loom, turning out a type of sarong; and her monthly income over expenditure for material was 1,800 *riel*, the equivalent of three top salaries and worth 360 kg. of rice, or enough to feed twenty-four people for a month, or 40 kg. of beef. In addition, she kept a few chickens and a couple of pigs, and so was indeed well-off.

Throughout 1982 all private economic activities and indeed all income generation, was free from taxation, for the first tax laws were only passed in November 1982, and applied beginning in 1983.[14]

The first law established the principle that all private businesses should pay tax on gross income, and some general rules about the modalities for tax collection, but details of precisely who should pay and at what rates were left to the Finance Ministry to determine. The principles enunciated in the law appear to tend towards leniency. Article 3 states that low income-earners might be temporarily exempt. I have not seen the Finance Ministry documents establishing rates of taxation, but several traders in one of the large Phnom Penh markets told me what their monthly assessments were. They ranged from 90–130 *riel* for book stalls, to 180 for a retail rice vendor, to 320 and 1,000 respectively for silver and gold shops. In addition, each stall paid a daily 2-*riel* market upkeep fee to the municipality. On one occasion, I was present in the market when the tax collectors—young men and women in neat dark uniforms—were making their rounds, and I observed that taxes were paid in cash on the spot against a receipt, and could ascertain that the tax receipt was for the amount which the vendor had told me he paid. Although none of the vendors would tell me his income, none complained about their tax rates, which appear quite low compared with the visible volume of trade. Presumably taxes are based on some serious assessment of income, since the tax law requires detailed bookkeeping and affidavits on stock.

The Buddha-image makers also revealed their tax obligations—130–160 *riel* per month, per shop, i.e. 40 per cent or less of the price of one of their cheaper products; and at the top end of the private scale, an employee in one of the largest and most popular Phnom Penh restaurants said their monthly tax was about 10,000 *riel*, on a gross income of 8,000 on ordinary days and 20–30,000 on Sundays.

The law on import taxes, obviously devised for the overland commodity trade from Thailand, addresses in its first article one of the main problems of the *laissez-faire* market since 1979—'the import of unnecessary commodities' which 'should be slowed down'. Taxation would also, it said, encourage local production and contribute to the state budget. The law established three broad categories of imports and the rates at which they should be taxed, although final details were again left to the Finance Ministry.

Category I, articles of family and ordinary daily use, and raw materials used in domestic production such as all types of cloth, thread, cigarette papers, and dyes are subject to a tax rate of 5–10 per cent; the second category includes goods of limited necessity and high price, such as bicycles and motorcycles, radios, tape recorders and cassettes, which are subject to a 15–25 per cent rate. Category III, taxed at 30–50 per cent, comprises unnecessary goods, such as cigarettes, luxuries and canned goods. These rates are also very modest, reflecting both the continuing real need for this sort of trade, and the state's reluctance to risk resentment over interference in private activities. It is interesting that medicines, which are badly needed and often cannot be obtained other than on the free market, but which require more regulation than at present to prevent the sale of impure or harmful products, are not mentioned in any of the taxable categories.

There was also clearly a desire to bring foreign retail trade under some kind of overall supervision, for article 7, the first in Title 2 on 'Modalities of Commodity Import', states that traders must use established routes and present their goods for inspection at established points where they will be issued with receipts for tax payment, permitting them to transport their goods onward.

There is no independent assessment of the efficacy of the Import Tax regulations, which may remain largely theoretical, if only because of the very troubled conditions along the routes from the Thai border. At least, at the end of 1984, there was no sign that they had hindered trade, for the markets were well supplied with both necessities and luxuries straight out of Thailand.[15]

Financial Organization

In 1980, together with the introduction of currency, a national bank was established. Within the state organization, it occupies the place of a ministry and provides funds for state commerce and loans to producers. By the end of 1984, in addition to the national bank, there were a bank for foreign trade and over thirty branch banks at province, district and municipality level (*Kampuchea*, **278**, 7 January 1985). Inflation since the new *riel* was introduced in 1980 has been surprisingly low. Obviously, the authorities have not resorted incontinently to the printing press. There may also be a currency support aid programme organized by the Soviet Union, a matter on which I have discovered no information.

Both the foreign aid and market capital from hoards and loot were obviously temporary expedients. The PRK, like its predecessor, recognized that the country's economy must ultimately depend on its agricultural sector, which is potentially capable of producing substantial food surpluses for export as well as certain industrial products such as cotton, jute and rubber, either for export or for local processing in the few industries to which the country is suited. The key then, to both Cambodia's economic recovery and its cohesion as an independent state, depends on agricultural recovery and development.

State domestic commerce is financed with cash loaned by the national bank to provincial and district trading offices for the purchase of agricultural produce, such as rice. The same branch offices are also responsible for selling commodities to the rural areas, and out of these sales they repay their loans. For the first two years of the bank's existence, it was reported that 450 million *riel* had been loaned for the purchase of agricultural produce. I have not found an equivalent statistic for subsequent years, but a report in early 1985 said that state purchase of rice had increased from 16,000 tons in 1980–1 to over 440,000 tons in 1983–4, an amount which was 50 per cent over plan.[16] Most of the recent trade statistics are expressed in percentages of the plan, which are difficult to use in the absence of either the plan targets or earlier base figures. It is of interest, however, that for 1983–4 state purchases had been more than planned, state sales to the populace had been only about 60 per cent of plan, and 76 per cent of the money advanced to the lower levels for agricultural purchases had been repaid. This would seem to indicate that farmers are earning more from the state than they return in the form of purchases from the state, and are using the cash in the private market.[17]

The state, via its banks, also loans money to the agricultural sector for purchase of animals and equipment. For 1984 the national bank provincial office in Kandal (where Phnom Penh is located) announced that it had loaned 2 million *riel* to local fishing groups, over 17 million to handicrafts (family-size manufacturing enterprises, such as weaving), and 18 million to the province commercial office for the purchase of rice. In the same period, the fisheries repaid 1.4 million, handicraft enterprises over 12 million, and the commercial branch 8 million. The loans were described as short- and long-term, but without specific details. Neither is it clear whether the difference between lending and repayment represented defaults, extended credit, or loans not yet due. Here also, though, as with state commerce, it appears that more cash is going out to the rural areas than is coming into the treasury (*Kampuchea*, **277**, 3 January 1985).

PRK Agriculture

The initial policy for agriculture was recovery through almost total *laissez-faire*, without taxation, compulsory deliveries or any large measure of state control; likewise, if only because of insufficient resources, without significant state aid either.

State control and guidance was exercised from the beginning through state appropriation of all land and real estate, a situation officially established in article 14 of the constitution. Thus, the state was able from the beginning to influence the reorganization of agriculture, and to guide it towards a form of socialization.

The change of regime from DK to PRK in 1979 occurred during what would normally have been the rice harvest season, and because of the battle situation and the sudden end of the DK state discipline, all normal work was interrupted. Where conditions permitted, rice was harvested and consumed. Fowl, pigs and even draft animals were also consumed heedlessly; and wherever the population reached them before the new authorities took control, former DK stores of food were appropriated and consumed. Thus, in most parts of the countryside during the first half of 1979, at least, people who stayed where they were suddenly had adequate food after months or years of malnutrition or starvation. They ate well, however, without sufficient concern for the future, depleting both potential seed stocks and the draft animals necessary for agricultural production in Cambodian conditions.

Although former private property in land was not recognized by the new PRK, peasants who had remained on their own land during DK, or who were able to return to it immediately after January 1979, were allowed to continue working it as though it were their own property. Conflict arose when displaced peasants returned to their former homes to find that others had appropriated their land in their absence. In such cases the state refused to intervene in favour of the former owners, and urged that the matter be settled amicably through discussion between the parties and mediated by the local authorities.[18]

The anarchy resulting from the sudden release from DK discipline, the weakness of the new authorities, and the movement of large numbers of the population who had no intention of participating further in agricultural work augured poorly for the next planting season; and measures taken either by Vietnamese or PRK authorities to secure seed supplies or build up food stores were often wilfully misinterpreted (Vickery, 1984, pp. 219–20).

In 1979 the government immediately announced that, in line with the policy of moving towards socialism, agricultural producers should be organized in 'Solidarity Groups' (*krom samakki*) of ideally ten to fifteen families in order to co-operatively produce and share in the rewards.

I have not obtained a precise official statement on the organization of Solidarity Groups in 1979, but in basic outline the groups were probably very similar, if not identical, to those in the circular of August 1980. There, ten to fifteen families per group was considered to be the ideal, but this could vary according to local conditions. In mountainous or sparsely settled areas the number might be as low as five to seven families; and in the thickly settled areas there were up to sixty or seventy families per group. The amount of land allotted to each person in the group should be calculated according to the normal size of a farm in that area, with the proviso that each worker should have from 1 to 2 hectares. Thus, arrangements should be made to redistribute land from groups which had it in excess to groups which had insufficient land.[19]

This circular referred to land distribution to groups during 'the past year', 1979–80, acknowledging that there had been dissatisfaction in some places. Where land from the previous distribution was insufficient, additional land should be given to the group, and excess land not in use should be loaned to group members to increase their family production. The circular also commented on the necessity to ensure that each group had sufficient animals for ploughing and breeding. It is clear that there were both collectively-owned and privately-owned animals, as well as animals whose status, private or collective, was unclear. The latter, it stated, should be used in collective work first, and then privately after collective work was finished. Collectively-owned animals would be allotted to families who owned none in order to accomplish the necessary work.

From this circular it is clear that there were various categories of land possession and administration. There was Solidarity Group land, and land belonging to higher administrative units such as village and *khum* which could be loaned to groups and families as needed. The original distinction is not clear. At one point it was stated that all *khum* and villages should give all farms in their regions to the groups, but in other sections we see that some land still remained outside the groups under control of the higher units; and within the groups some people were favoured in being allowed to remain in possession of their former private land, even if this exceeded the group norm. It is likewise unclear how some animals were neither definitely private nor collective. In this 1980 circular there is no reference to different levels of collectivization as appeared in later policy statements.

Because of the lack of means of production and the very rudimentary potential for state control, what in fact emerged in the 1979 planting season was traditional family production, with solidarity groups more or less effective where lack of draft animals and other means of production would have in any case imposed co-operative labour (Vickery, 1984, p. 222).

By the end of 1979, in the harvest season, state policy on the division and distribution of agricultural produce was outlined as follows:[20]

1. No taxes on agricultural produce, and no obligatory contribution to the state.

2. Each Solidarity Group should set aside sufficient seed for the next planting season, and such seed was not to be placed in village or *khum* stock.
3. One part of each groups's produce was to be given to village and *khum* for support of (a) crippled resident war veterans; (b) state employees without salary such as the village and *khum* committee members, the permanent local military (not to exceed one platoon), teachers, infirmary staff. The amount set aside for such personnel was the ration given to heavy workers, but if any of them had received state support, additional local support was not required.
4. The remaining produce was to be retained by the group and divided as follows:

   (a) Workers on heavy tasks, such as ploughing, harrowing, and digging ditches, should receive more than those on light tasks; remuneration should vary according to time worked; everyone in the group should receive enough for a livelihood; and the aged, infirm, children, and women whose husbands were absent, should receive enough even if they did little work.
   (b) Owners of cattle, buffalo and seed (i.e. private ownership of such was acknowledged) who used them in group work should receive extra remuneration as agreed within the group. The circular emphasized that collective agreement was required, and that the group leader could not arbitrarily decide on such matters.
   (c) The village and *khum* were forbidden to seize any produce for application to any kind of budget, or to stock and hoard produce; after harvest, all produce should be redistributed according to the norms outlined above.
   (d) Farmers who insisted on working privately should be encouraged, but *not forced* to join Solidarity Groups; all production outside the group, on unoccupied land, was the property of the producers, and sugar palms could be owned by individuals; and finally, producers were free to trade their produce in the market, without 'anyone having the right or authority to forbid them'.

In general, the policies laid down in this circular were carried out, and individual rights were observed (Vickery, 1984, pp. 222–4). Nevertheless, objective conditions—lack of seed, of draft animals, of food for the working population—meant that nothing like a normal area could be planted, or harvested.

However difficult the objective conditions, the PRK authorities seem to have felt in 1980 that more could be done to increase production incentives in agriculture, and this was reflected in another circular, issued on 30 August 1980, that is, at the end of the 1980 planting season.[21]

This circular announced that even though development of a collective economy was the goal, family (i.e. individual private) economy should be encouraged and expanded in order to aid the collective economy. So far, the circular continued, the measures for expansion of the family economy had not greatly increased peasant incentives, increases in agricultural production were slow, and living standards too low.

One of the problems raised was that of effective possession of land. Depending on the availability of land and agricultural conditions, it was established that each family was entitled to a private plot of between 1,500 and 2,000 square metres of land for their house and production of their own food. New families in an agricultural area should have a plot designated for them by the authorities, and old families whose own traditional plot was smaller should be given additional land. Because of this problem of land possession, an important principle established in the new circular was that families still living on land which they had formerly owned should be allowed to continue in occupation of that land even if it was a larger area than the norm. Probably a majority of peasant families in some parts of the country were in that situation and they may have been disturbed by attempts to 'collectivize' parcels of their land during 1979. The circular reaffirmed that trees on family land belonged to the family, an important point if the trees included sugar palms or other valuable fruit. After harvest, all produce from the family plot would be the exclusive property of the producers, free of tax or contribution to the state, and available to the producers to use or sell privately on the open market.

Besides the family plot, which is in fact a very small area, barely sufficient for a nuclear family's support, each peasant family worked in a Solidarity Group, and the August 1980 circular laid down the principles for division of the production from group land.

As in 1979, all production by a group should be divided among the members of the group and not given to the villages or *khum* for other purposes. It was emphasized, however, that before division among group members, adequate seed for the next season's crop must be subtracted, and apparently, although this is not explicit, the seed would be stored by the group rather than by the village. The amounts of seed per hectare necessary for the main varieties of rice and for corn were listed, and it was recommended that an additional 10 per cent be kept to assure adequacy.

After provision for seed, everything else was to be divided among group members, according to a work point system. That is, if the main workforce of healthy adults received 1 point for a normal day's work, the less healthy, the aged, or the very young whose work capacity was less would receive 7–8/10 of the points of a full worker, with percentages established for dependants, the ill, village nurses or teachers who do not actually perform field work, as well as allowances for those performing essential clerical and administrative tasks. There were also work point allowances for the group use of privately-owned buffaloes or cows, and for the private family care of collectively-owned animals. One difference in emphasis from the 1979 circular concerned the relations between the Solidarity Group and the state.

The latter circular stated that some goods *should be sold* to the state, even though this was still not compulsory. In particular, a portion of the food produced by the Solidarity Group should be sold to the state 'in order to buy implements from the state', and people who grew the industrial crops, such as jute, cotton and tobacco, which the state has encouraged people to grow and which they cannot use themselves, should be sold to the state for use as raw material in industrial production. It is clear that in 1980 there was a problem of insufficient production of an agricultural surplus for feeding the urban population and for industrial use, and the state was trying to encourage increased voluntary production and sale of surpluses for the secondary and tertiary sectors.

Although the above-cited circulars of 1979 and 1980 did not describe them, state plans for agriculture had apparently always envisaged a basic three-tier structure of increasingly collectivized groups. This appeared in a study by a French agronomist in 1983 and identically in information about recent government decisions on agricultural policy published in the press in late 1984.[22]

In the first, and highest or most collective type of Solidarity group, all labour, from preparation of the fields through harvesting, is performed in common, with animals remaining family property. At the end of the season remuneration is in kind or in cash according to the work point system. According to official figures, this type had increased from 3 per cent of the national total of groups in 1979 to 38 per cent in 1982, with a planned increase to 50 per cent in 1983. Grunewald estimated that the actual 1983 total was about 35 per cent.

In the second type, land allocations are made to families at the beginning of the season, according to the number of persons per family. Then ploughing, harrowing and transplanting (for rice) are carried out in common, but thereafter each family is responsible for its allotment, and exchanges of labour or equipment are made by private agreement. Officially, this type expanded during 1979–81, from 27 to 57 per cent of the total, then decreased to 53 per cent in 1982, and a further decrease to 45 per cent was planned for 1983; but Grunewald estimated the total in that year at about 55 per cent.

The third and lowest type is little more than family economy on allotments of land made at the beginning of the season; and, ideally, contracts with state purchasing agencies should be arranged for the disposition of surplus. This type was said, credibly, to have represented 70 per cent of the total in 1979, and to have decreased to 9 per cent in 1982, with a further decrease to 5 per cent planned for 1983, although the true figure then, according to Grunewald, was more likely around 10 per cent.

In view of Grunewald's figures, which represented the official position plus informed estimates of an outside expert in 1983, the figures released in November 1984 following a National Cadres Conference are surprising. Solidarity Groups of the first category, 'the primary factor for the advance to socialism', were said to comprise only 10 per cent of the total, while the third category, 'private in nature' and requiring efforts 'by the revolutionary authorities to upgrade it to the second category', still contained 35 per cent of the rural population. Only the second category, at 55 per cent was in line with the 1983 figures.[23]

The reality behind these figures is that 'collectivization', or socialization, of the agricultural sector has hardly begun, since the majority category 2 Solidarity Groups are in fact little more than family farming units with the minimum amount of co-operative work imposed by the objective situation (lack of animals, tools), and which would prevail even in the absence of all state intervention.

The significant difference between the real conditions of the PRK peasant economy and the same under a capitalist regime is that land ownership is nationalized. Land thus cannot be bought and sold, pawned or otherwise used as security for debt with the risk of capitalist expropriation by usurers if the debt is unpaid. A consequence of this is that in the absence of other constraints there is no way of forcing peasants to produce for the non-productive sector of society, and Cambodian peasants since 1979 have had a greater freedom of choice in the consumption and disposition of their produce than ever before.

This freedom may be one reason why agricultural recovery in terms of total area planted and total production has been disappointing. In 1984 the country had not yet reached food self-sufficiency, particularly in rice, the traditional Cambodian staple. During the 1960s, over 2 million hectares were planted annually in rice and produced over 2 million tons of paddy, adequate for feeding the population and for a sizeable export surplus. In contrast, only 774,000 hectares were planted in 1979, and just over 1.4 million hectares, producing at best 1.5 million tons, in each of the following three years. This was plainly not enough to allow for seed and to adequately feed the population, not to speak of an export surplus. In 1983 there was an increase to 1.66 million tons of paddy, which still left a small shortfall, but in 1984 disastrous floods cut the harvest down to perhaps just over 1 million tons.[24]

Since 1979, in particular during 1981 and 1984, Cambodia has been plagued by unusually severe floods which destroyed tens of thousands of hectares of crops and negated predictions of rice self-sufficiency. There is a possibility that poorly-designed dams and water channels constructed during 1975–9 have contributed to the flooding by allowing overflow into areas which had not been so vulnerable under natural conditions. Foreign technicians working on irrigation indicate that this is to some extent possible, but perhaps not as widespread as imagined.

In some places new high-yield rice strains have been introduced, and some farmers claim success, with up to 3 to 4 tons per hectare. It is well known, however, that these rice varieties require the use of modern fertilizers, which means that, unless Cambodia can construct its own fertilizer industry, the new strains are unlikely to have wide application.

Agricultural expansion has also been delayed by the lack of draft animals, buffaloes and cattle, without which fields cannot be prepared for cultivation. The crucial variable is not manpower, for the population today is approximately what it was in the late 1960s when over 2 million hectares were planted, but animals. Thus it is estimated that in 1967, when 2.5 million hectares were planted, there were over 1.2 million head of draft animals, which by 1979 had decreased to only 768,000 head. In 1982 the number of animals had increased to 981,000, and 1.4 million hectares were planted. Even if the animals were used as efficiently as before the war, that is if the same ratio of land planted per animal were achieved, the total would still not suffice to feed the population. Thus current conditions therefore prevent large accumulations of surplus, either for trade or for state use, whatever the economic organization.[25]

Even if objective conditions prevent the rapid attainment of pre-war levels of production, productive relations in agriculture between 1979 and 1983 were such as to encourage farmers to produce mainly for their own consumption and only such surplus as could easily be sold at high prices on the free market, not surpluses for Cambodia's state sector. If the official line in 1979 was that farmers had total freedom to either eat or sell their product on the free market, and in 1980 declared hopefully that a portion of the food produced 'should be sold to the state', by November 1984 the party was saying that 'the peasants must deliver part of their produce to the state'.[26]

The state's intention is to acquire agricultural produce by exchanging locally-made industrial products of use to farmers. An example is from an *SPK* (PRK bulletin) news item of October 1984, which stated that in the Oraing Auv district of Kompong Cham province 1,400 metres of cloth, 577 sarongs, 1,560 school notebooks, and other household articles had been sold to the population in exchange for the purchase of over 4 tons of beans, soya and sesame (*SPK*, in French, 29 October 1984, p. 1).

The November 1984 National Cadres Conference decisions on agriculture which stated that 'the peasants must deliver part of their produce to the state' also contained prohibitions on the exploitation of the peasantry, 'activities of traders competing with the state in the purchase of agricultural and industrial products', and the sale of 'state goods on the free market', for 'state goods . . . must be sold directly to the peasants and solidarity production groups' (*SPK*, 16 November 1984).

These statements clearly show the tension existing between private and state marketing, as private traders apparently try to acquire state products and resell them to farmers at a profit, thereby channelling agricultural produce into the private sector. Apparently, no fixed amounts of compulsory sale to the state had yet been established and the authorities were still trying to rely on exhortation and group pressure in the countryside to acquire produce. Moreover, the products which the state was prepared to buy in 1984 were still quite limited.

Among written answers to questions which I asked the Ministry of Agriculture was an admission that the state could then only buy such important products as paddy, maize, beans, tobacco and sugar, while other things, such as sugar cane, poultry, ducks, shrimps, baskets, sarongs, mosquito nets could be sold freely on the market. This distinction was confirmed wherever I had the opportunity to speak to producers. A Cham family on Chrui Changvar told me that the state took very little of the fruit and fish which they produced or raised in artificial ponds, and they sold nearly all of it on the free market for a total monthly income of between 1,200 and 2,700 *riel*. Another example was a village between Phnom Penh and Neak Luong, where they grew peanuts for sale to the state, kept most of their rice for their own consumption, and grew water melons for the free market.

Since 1983 a form of taxation, though not called such, has been imposed on agriculture. I have not obtained a complete schedule of these voluntary 'patriotic contributions', but the Ministry of Agriculture, in their written replies to my questions, stated that the contributions from rice land depended on productivity. Land producing over 2 tons per hectare should contribute 120 kg. of paddy to the state, land producing between 1 and 2 tons,

100 kg., and where productivity was less than 1 ton, 80 kg. The villagers on the road to Neak Luong told me that they paid 100 kg.; or in cash 160 *riel*, but claimed that they used a new rice strain yielding 3–4 tons per hectare. The Cham family whom I cited above said their 'tax' on orchard land was 100 *riel* per year per 100 square metres—which they did not find oppressive.

These figures suggest that the intended rate of agricultural taxation is about 8–10 per cent of gross product, fairly heavy as tax, but as total forcible appropriation less than pre-war peasants paid in tax plus usurious debt repayment plus the odd 'voluntary contribution' for national development.[27]

Industry

Industrial development since 1979 has been disappointingly slow, but in large part this has been for reasons beyond the control of PRK authorities. The latter are very frank in discussing the weaknesses of their industry, but have unfortunately sometimes resorted to the explanation that all industry was destroyed 'by Pol Pot', which is plainly not true, and which has given some anti-Cambodian news media the opportunity to allege PRK–Vietnamese incompetence or malevolence, or even to contrast the PRK unfavourably with DK (Becker, 1983).

As discussed earlier, essential industries were maintained to some degree under DK, and during 1975–6 numerous technicians were called back from evacuation to run them (Vickery, 1984, pp. 80, 109–10, 159–61). Most of the latter were either returned to agriculture or executed during the purges in 1977, and the lack of competent personnel and proper maintenance meant that by 1979 much of the industrial plant had been allowed to deteriorate to far below its pre-war standard. The reason, however, was obtuse social policy, rather than the deliberate destruction of industry.

In the anarchy immediately following the overthrow of DK, moveables such as books and newspapers from libraries, wooden fixtures from houses, and pumps used in irrigation were often looted by the returning population, or in some cases by departing DK forces to prevent their use, so that when new technicians turned to the renewal of industrial production many factories had in fact been ransacked. Much of this, however, had occurred early in 1979, and not under DK.[28] Many factories, as surviving personnel willingly attest, operated right up to a few days before 7 January 1979.

When the DK authorities evacuated the city just ahead of the Vietnamese–PRK troops, surviving factory personnel in their thousands were included in the movement towards the Thai border (Picq, 1984, p. 168); and when order was restored under the new government industry, like everything else, had to start from scratch with the workers who had avoided the DK evacuation and technically qualified personnel from among the 'new' people who were now invited to return and resume work in their areas of specialization.

For the year 1984 the present Industry Minister, Meas Samnang, and his staff presented me with a statement representing the official view of the industrial situation, which I was only able to check on the ground to a limited extent, owing to lack of time, for there seems to be no difficulty arranging visits to industrial establishments.

According to their statement dated 28 November 1984, there were fifty-seven industrial plants with 154,000 workers under the control of the Ministry; and these included electricity, vehicular transport, construction, textiles, metal, chemicals, food products, tobacco, soft drinks, soap, paper, tyres and rubber sandals. Production totals were also supplied and I consider the figures reliable since, in nearly every case, Meas Samnang admitted that production was qualitatively and quantitatively inadequate for the country's needs, and that plans were unfulfilled. Perhaps the only industries satisfying both demand and plan are the cigarette and soft drink factories.[29]

The two main reasons given for the inadequate production, both in the ministry's statement and according to personnel at the three factories I visited, were insufficient raw materials and insufficient power. For example, both Meas Samnang and the administrator of the Tuol Kork textile factory said that much more cotton cloth could be produced by existing plant if larger supplies of raw cotton were available, that is, if the country's cotton-growing potential were realized. Current (1984) production of cloth is only about 75–85 per cent of plan and is insufficient for the country's needs. Likewise, the jute bag factory in Battambang operates well under capacity because of insufficient supplies of raw jute, which before the war had been grown by farmers in the surrounding area.

As for rubber, one industry for which Cambodia was well endowed with the basic raw material, both the Minister for Industry and the tyre factory personnel averred that raw rubber production had been restored sufficiently to satisfy the requirements of existing plant, but that they nevertheless operated under capacity because chemicals required in production which had to be obtained from abroad were insufficient. It is nevertheless claimed that tyre production is at present adequate for the number of vehicles in operation within the country.

Rubber production comes under a General Directorate for Rubber Plantations, with a total complement of 14,635 personnel, up from 2,028 in 1980, the first year in which production was resumed under the PRK. According to a 1982 FAO report, rubber production in that year was 7,500 tons from 14,000 hectares, against 53,000 tons from 64,000 hectares in 1967. By the end of 1984, 19,500 hectares were said to have produced 55 million litres of liquid latex, 110 per cent of plan, which was converted into 13,300 tons of raw rubber—only 84 per cent of plan. The figures for area planted and final production sound reasonable in comparison with the 1982 FAO report, but apparently there are still problems with refinement of the latex.[30]

The official view on the position of industry in the present and near future is that Cambodia's major economic sector is agriculture and that the tasks of the small industrial base are to satisfy the demand for agricultural implements, means of communication, and articles of daily use, where agricultural products may be transformed into objects of consumption. Thus, industry is to be based first on the country's own agricultural products for the satisfaction of further agricultural production; and of course industrial goods are essential to increase agricultural output. Among the pre-war industries not yet functioning, there are definite plans to reopen the plywood factory in 1985; and as soon as possible the cement factory in Kampot; the phosphate plant in Tuk Meas, required for fertilizer production; and the brewery in Kompong Som are to be put back into production.

Foreign Aid and Trade

Obviously Cambodia in 1979 was a disaster situation requiring aid from the international community; and much has been given, but less than required, largely because of the efforts of the United States and ASEAN to prevent the successful development of the PRK. The largest amounts of aid have come from the Soviet Union, Vietnam and then from other socialist countries. Western aid is from international organizations such as UNICEF, the International Committee of the Red Cross, FAO and Private groups.

As far as I know, no complete report on all foreign aid exists. In early 1980 the PRK published a list of donor countries and organizations with types and amounts of aid to that date. In the lead was the Soviet Union which up to January 1980 had given aid worth 134 million dollars, which included 150,000 tons of food, 4.6 million metres of cloth, 660 trucks and cars, and several other types of commodities. In addition, Soviet personnel had come to assist in the reconstruction of the Kompong Som port, a hospital, educational facilities, rubber plantations, roads and factories. The report seems accurate, for Soviet personnel are still visibly engaged in all these areas of work, and the dollar total is not out of line with that given by Western sources for 1982 and which incensed the Western powers trying to exert an economic squeeze on Cambodia. Among the noticeable Soviet aid projects in 1984 were the Technical Institute which they support and staff, and a new electricity plant, opened in November. In contrast to one journalist's efforts to show the Soviets reneging on a deal to repair Phnom Penh's water supply system, this was not mentioned at all in the 1980 PRK list of aid projects, and a Western European team working in Phnom Penh in 1984, to investigate ways to repair the water system could find no evidence that the Soviets had ever been involved in that area.[31]

In terms of cash value, the second largest donor during 1979 was Vietnam, whose aid of various kinds was said to have totalled $56 million, and aid in 1980 was expected to be about $62 million. The totals are approximate, for nearly all the Vietnamese aid was in kind or in the form of work by Vietnamese technical personnel. There was food aid, especially rice and rice seed; medical aid, including personnel, medicine and construction of medical facilities; personnel and equipment for transport; school supplies and teachers; factory repair work; and household commodities. Vietnamese aid still continues, particularly in the form of technical experts and training of Khmers in Vietnam.[32]

The same 1980 list included descriptions of aid to date from Laos (500 tons of rice, and other products), Hungary, Bulgaria, Mongolia, Poland, Czechoslovakia, Germany, and India, who variously supplied medicine, cloth, vehicles, and school supplies. Since then, Germany and Czechoslovakia have sent medical teams, the latter which I saw in Takeo where they operate a hospital. Aid totals from international and private Western organizations were also listed, which argues for the accuracy of the report, since they can easily be checked.

A number of the private Western groups are still active: as examples, Oxfam and American Friends Service Committee continue with medical work and a well-drilling project; Church World Service has irrigation and animal vaccination projects; and World Vision operates a paediatric hospital.

One joint Vietnamese-Cambodian programme which began as part of the Vietnamese aid effort in 1979 and has expanded to cover much trade between the two countries is the establishment of 'paired provinces'. This means that each of the Cambodian provinces and two municipalities of Phnom Penh and Kompong Som are paired with one, or occasionally more than one, Vietnamese province or city, for the purpose of co-operation in aid and trade. The complete list of pairs is as follows:

Phnom Penh—Ho Chi Minh City and Hanoi
Battambang—Quang Nam-Da Nang

Kampot—Kien Giang
Kandal—Ben Tre
Koh Kong—Minh Hai
Kompong Cham—Tay Ninh
Kompong Chhnang—Hau Giang
Kompong Som—Haiphong
Kompong Speu—Cuu Long
Kompong Thom—Dong Nai
Kratie—Song Be
Mondolkiri—Dac Lac
Preah Vihear—Thuan Hai
Prey Veng—Dong Thap
Pursat—Tien Giang
Ratanakiri—Nghia Binh, Gia Lai-Cong Tum
Siemreap—Binh Tri Thien
Stung Treng—Phu Khanh
Svay Rieng—Long An
Takeo—An Giang[33]

All the Vietnamese units, except Hanoi and Haiphong, are in the south, the nearest part of Vietnam to Cambodia, and further geographical logic is seen in the pairing of border provinces with those adjoining on the other side. This also means that Cambodia's ethnic minority provinces, Ratanakiri and Mondolkiri, are paired with Vietnamese provinces where many of the same minorities live, and where minority cadres have been trained in Vietnamese socialist methods. Hanoi, paired with Phnom Penh in addition to Ho Chi Minh City, may be chiefly symbolic, but the link between Haiphong, the only other northern Vietnamese centre involved, with Kompong Som, is certainly related to the port function of both, and the ability of Haiphong to provide aid in that area.

A recent published description of what province pairing involves concerns Kratie and Song Be. Firstly, in early 1979, Song Be sent 4,000 tons of food aid, including 400 tons of rice. Vietnamese technicians also came to help in the construction of irrigation installations. Construction aid continued through 1982, and there was also medical aid in the form of medicines and training of Cambodian personnel. More recently, the two provinces have engaged in direct, possibly barter, trade. Song Be has sold cement and other construction materials and seed rice to Kratie, and the latter has sold tobacco and sesame to Song Be (*Kampuchea*, **283**, 14 February 1985).

Foreign trade is an area in which little precise information is available. Dollar figures for exports (rubber, beans, timber, kapok, tobacco) and imports (virtually all other commodities) range from the official KAMPEXIM (state trading agency) $1.2 million and rbl. 6.07 million to $3 million and $175 million, or $4–5 million and $200 million of other sources.[34] The official figures do not cover the paired-province trade with Vietnam, nor the private cross-border trade with Vietnam and Thailand.

One new development was the first measure taken since 1979 to impose state control of foreign exchange. In September 1985 PRK authorities announced that Vietnamese *dong* in private hands had to be exchanged for Cambodian *riel*. The immediate reason was obviously the demonetization in Vietnam of the old *dong* and its replacement by new currency with ten times the unit value. Interestingly enough, the PRK, in recognition of the *de facto* legitimacy of private market trade, took up the old worthless *dong* at a rate of 1 *riel* for 5, protecting the Cambodian traders from loss, perhaps even at a rate better than that finally prevailing on the market. It will be interesting to see if free private accumulation of new *dong* will be permitted, or if the state intends the currency exchange to be a first step in centralizing all foreign trade. The latter would no doubt be preferred, given industrial growth in Ho Chi Minh City, and the possibility for exchanges with resource-rich but industry-poor Cambodia.[35]

New Developments Since the Fifth Party Congress

In his Political Report to the Fifth Party Congress, Heng Samrin announced the PRK's first five-year plan, a 'programme of socio-economic restoration and development (1986–90). The emphasis in this plan, in line with Cambodia's natural advantages, is to be on agriculture, and the four 'economic spearheads' are food supplies, rubber, timber, and aquatic products. By 1990 rubber production is to be restored to 50,000 hectares, with a production of 50,000 metric tons of latex, very nearly the 1967 output, compared with 26,000 hectares and 20,000 tons, to the end of November in 1985.[36] Other proclaimed planning goals are shown in Table 11.

Plans for industry are still modest, 'the selective restoration of existing industrial production capacity' and the gradual construction of 'small and medium industrial bases appropriate to the country's situation.

Another important point is the expansion of 'the socialist trade network in the localities'. The state 'should organize purchasing, collection and delivery', with the motto, 'for the peasantry, selling rice and agricultural products to the state is patriotism; for the state, selling goods and delivering them directly to the people is being responsible towards the people'.

Table 11 Additional goals in 1986–90 Five-Year Plan

		1985 production[37]
timber	200,000 cu.m.	95,000 cu.m.
fish	130,000 metric tons	66,000 tons
hemp	15,000 metric tons	60% of plan, no quantitative figure
electricity	300 million kw	107% of plan, 4% increase over previous year, no absolute figure
food	7% annual increase rate	

This certainly gets at the crux of a serious problem—how to bring the essentially agricultural economy into a close relationship with the state rather than orientating the peasantry towards a market dependent on supplies from overseas. Unless the state wishes to extract agricultural supplies by force, there must be local production of goods required by the agricultural producers, and so far industry has lagged behind agriculture.

If this part of the plan shows an intention to move closer to 'socialism', another economic intiative represents a step away. Heng Samrin also announced that in order 'to mitigate the weaknesses of the state-run sector, we advocate the development of our economy encompassing four components': state, collective, family and private. This innovation requires a constitutional amendment, and in fact means that part of the light manufacturing sector which the state wanted to be under direct control has had to be given over to private investment.[38]

An example of what this means in practice comes from a press article about handicraft production in Phnom Penh, where

> private persons may engage in handicraft production . . . as regulated by law, so long as their products do not compete with state products; and so long as the state lacks raw materials, it may not impose a production plan nor an agreement to sell all produce to the state.

In one section of Phnom Penh the article reported eighty-nine groups with 1,270 workers, producing articles of metal, glass, bamboo, wood, rattan and cloth; and each worker was said to earn about 950 *riel* per month—or more than twice the salary of a state industrial worker in 1984 (*Pracheachon*, **22**, 31 December 1985, p. 2).

Taxation on agriculture ('patriotic contributions') is being tightened. Instead of three categories of land, there are now five, adjusted with respect to location in terrain of varying productivity, from rich riverine plains to less productive forest and hill tracts. This assures a higher gross income for the state. In addition, there is fiscal tinkering to promote specific economic goals. For example, double-cropped land is taxed less than single-cropped, newly-cleared land is exempt from tax for five years, people in the highest-level co-operatives receive a 5 per cent tax exemption, those in the second level a 3 per cent exemption, while the lowest level—in fact, family agriculture—pays the full tax.[39]

Part IV
PRK Policies

10 Domestic Policies

Education and Culture

Among the first promises of the new Salvation Front at the end of 1978 was the re-creation of a modern educational system which, if not deliberately destroyed during 1975–9, had disappeared as a result of neglect and contempt.[1] As soon as security permitted in 1979, former teachers were encouraged to report for assignment, and throughout the country efforts were made to set up new schools, even in very primitive conditions.

PRK educational policy started from the general principle that the state should develop an educational programme in conformity with the pedagogical principle of 'linking general knowledge to practice, learning to production, and school to society'.[2] The goal was to ensure school attendance by all children of school age, and to eradicate illiteracy.

State education in Cambodia extends from pre-school to tertiary level, and includes teacher training and adult literacy programmes. Pre-schools, for children from the age of 3, are of two types—those which are separate schools with teachers paid by the state, and those which are for children of factory or production group personnel, with teachers paid by those enterprises. Such schools are admittedly available to only a minority of the population, for official statistics give the number of pre-schools in 1984 as 500, with 30,366 pupils. The functioning of pre-schools in enterprises was confirmed during visits to textile and tyre factories where employees mentioned this as an advantage of working there.

The really significant educational sector is of course the general educational stream which children enter at the age of 6, and which combines primary and secondary schooling in a ten-year programme, divided into three levels, from lowest to highest, of four, three, and three years respectively.

Tertiary education is still limited. Of previously existing institutions, the Faculty of Medicine and Pharmacy was reopened at the end of 1979, and the Kampuchea-Soviet Technological Institute in 1981. Other branches which combine secondary and tertiary level training are teacher training institutions and the Language School. Aside from this, tertiary education depends on sending students abroad and nearly three thousand have been sent since 1979, most to the Soviet Union and Eastern Europe.

The deficiencies faced in 1979 included dilapidated buildings and missing books, but the most serious was lack of teachers, for of the approximately 25,000 active before 1975, only 7,000 reappeared in 1979, and in 1984, only 5,000 of those worked for the Ministry of Education.

Beside the fact that teachers may have suffered disproportionately under DK, many fled abroad immediately in 1979 without trying to work for the new government, while still others found different and more personally rewarding work in the PRK after 1979. Education Minister Pen Navuth acknowledged that all PRK ministries sought to employ former teachers because of the general penury of educated personnel; and among my own former teacher acquaintances who survive, most are now in other occupations.

According to the Ministry of Education, the numbers of schools, pupils and teachers in general stream institutions in the first PRK school year and in 1984 were as shown in Table 12.

Table 12 Schools, pupils and teachers in general stream institutions, 1979–1980 and 1983–1984

	1979–80	1983–84
Level 1 (years 1–4)		
Schools	5,290	3,005
Pupils	947,317	1,542,825
Teachers	21,605	33,479
Level 2 (years 5–7)		
Schools	14	200
Pupils	5,104	146,865
Teachers	206	4,329
Level 3 (years 8–10)		
Schools	1	13
Pupils	301	6,969
Teachers	20	277

Level 1 enrolment is thus slightly higher than the equivalent level in the last pre-war year (1969), but the two higher levels have not reached pre-war numbers, and in particular Level 3 has far fewer schools and pupils than pre-war secondary education.

As Education Minister Pen Navuth explained some of these statistics, in 1979 efforts were made to begin basic schooling immediately with whatever personnel and material was available, using people with any degree of literacy to instruct others. Thus, a 'school' was wherever any instruction was taking place, even if it was just one teacher with a group of students beneath a tree. Later, as organization improved, these *ad hoc* 'schools' were consolidated and formalized, which explains the higher total of Level 1 schools in 1979 than in later years.

Similarly, most of the 'teachers' in 1979 were not professionals, but anyone with some literacy which they could pass on. Lack of trained teachers has been one of the main impediments to rebuilding a school system, and teacher shortage is the explanation for the slow growth of secondary schooling. Thus, a major effort is being made to train new teachers, and expansion of this sector, as in 1954–64, may again provide opportunities for mobility from peasant to 'middle-class' status, although the level of teachers' salaries—160–500 *riel* per month—is less of an economic incentive than pre-1970 salaries were.

Since 1979 there have been regular training sessions for old teachers who have resumed work and for new personnel. In 1979, before the first school year opened in the fall, teachers were assembled for study sessions of from one week to three months to learn about the new government's policies and teaching methods. By 1984 over 40,000 people had completed such courses. In addition, all teachers study for one or two months during summer vacations.

In addition to this supplementary training, there are also regular courses to form new teachers from among school graduates. A Level 2 graduate may become a Level 1 teacher after one year of training, or with an additional three years of teacher training, a Level 2 teacher. New teachers for Level 3 must complete level 3 and then go on for three to four years of teacher training; and the first new teachers formed in this way were expected to be ready in 1985. Up through 1984, all Level 3 teachers were survivors from those trained before 1975.

Each province has a school for training Level 1 teachers, and there are seven regional pedagogical centres for more advanced teacher training in Phnom Penh and in the provinces of Battambang, Kandal, Kompong Cham, Prey Veng, Takeo and Stung Treng, the last destined in particular for members of the north-eastern ethnic minorities.[3] At the top of the teacher training system is a Higher Pedagogical Institute in Phnom Penh.

The creation of new school textbooks and teaching materials has posed special problems. Not only did new books have to be written and printed, but they had to reflect the ideology and political orientation of the PRK, unfamiliar to, if not unpopular with, surviving intellectuals who were called upon to compose the new textbooks. Firstly the royal bias of pre-war education had to be eliminated, socialism inculcated as a positive ideal, and inter-Indo-China friendship and co-operation taught in place of the traditional suspicion, or the 'hereditary enemy' view of Vietnam. The problem was least acute in Level 1 books, designed to teach basic skills, and aside from the absence of lessons praising royalty and the inclusion of a selection on 'traditional friendship with Laos and Vietnam', there is virtually no difference between primary readers today and those of the 1960s.

Obviously such problems increase in the higher grades, and a reflection of the problem has been the delay in producing new history textbooks and the absence of any instruction in history, although I was told by Pen Navuth that they hoped to begin history instruction in Level 1 in 1985 and in Level 2 in 1986.

One new subject resulting from the change of political orientation is 'political morality', which combines the type of material found in traditional civics study with some history lessons, particularly on the history of the Cambodian revolutionary movement and the left-wing struggle against the French—matters totally without precedent in the pre-war syllabus.

Otherwise, the syllabus is quite traditional, with perhaps more time devoted to Khmer language and literature than previously, and until the 1984–5 school year at least, *no foreign language instruction*. The last point requires emphasis because of the persistent propaganda line about the Vietnamization of Cambodian schools and the imposition of that language on Khmer students. Information elicited at all levels, from Pen Navuth, to schoolteachers at work, and in private from students and parents met in chance encounters, confirmed the total falsity of this charge. The Level 3 syllabus, as would be expected, calls for four hours of foreign language instruction per week, in Russian, German, or Vietnamese—in that order—but it has not been implemented because of lack of teachers. It was hoped that the first classes might begin in the 1984–5 school year.

The choices of foreign language for school instruction are in relation to those countries which are politically important for the PRK, and also those which have provided aid in its development, including aid for the reconstruction of the educational system. Vietnamese aid was particularly important in the Medical Faculty, because of the common French language which the older generation of Vietnamese doctors shared with surviving Khmer medical students, and Vietnamese influence there was apparently crucial in reorientating Cambodian medicine in accordance with modern principles.[4]

Vietnamese aid has also been important in higher-level teacher training, and there again their co-operation was favoured because of the French language which they shared with Khmer personnel educated before 1970. Vietnam also provided textbook specialists, and until a new Khmer printing press was ready all textbooks had to be printed in Vietnam. In the Higher Pedagogical School there are some Vietnamese directly engaged in teaching, and preparatory courses in Vietnamese are offered there because with each year the numbers of French-speaking Vietnamese teachers and Khmer students are diminishing. According to Pen Navuth, they will be able to start phasing out these foreign specialists from 1987, and by 1995 all personnel will be Khmer.

The other main source of foreign aid in education has been the Soviet Union, both through the Kampuchea-Soviet Higher Technical Institute and in the places given to Cambodian students for secondary technical and tertiary study in the Soviet Union.

At the Technical Institute, re-opened in 1981, over eighty Soviet teachers instruct some seven hundred students in the specialities of construction, electricity, irrigation and mining, and from 1985, in industrial chemistry. The students enrol for either a technical diploma or an engineering degree course, of four and five years' duration respectively, and after completing the eighth year, for the technical diploma course, or the tenth year of secondary school. At the beginning of the first year, one-quarter of this time is devoted to intensive Russian language study, after which all course instruction is given in that language. Students receive state scholarships of 120–150 *riel* per month, and at graduation are required to work for the state for one or two years, after which they may have an opportunity for further study abroad. The first graduates were in 1983. Present plans call for the gradual Khmerization of instruction, and between 1986 and 1990 they hope to replace most Soviet instructors with their own graduates and other Khmer trained in the Soviet Union.

The importance of the Soviet Union in the second area—Khmer students abroad—is seen in the figures. Of over 2,800 at the end of 1984, 1,500 were in the Soviet Union. Most of the others were spread among the Eastern European countries, predominantly Germany. They are distributed at three levels—university, middle technical, and skilled worker; and at the university level about 24 per cent are on industrial courses, 18 per cent on agricultural, 18 per cent on economics, and 18 per cent on pedagogy. Except for skilled workers, few of these students had finished their courses and returned in 1984, and the first university graduates were expected back in 1985.

In conclusion, it is worth noting a remark of Pen Navuth's in relation to foreign language instruction and the use of foreign expertise. Obviously, he said, Cambodia needed foreign aid in 1979, and Vietnamese experts were most useful, both because of a common cultural language and previous experience, and because the Vietnamese, even more than Soviet or Eastern European personnel, could live under Cambodian conditions without special facilities, such as air-conditioned quarters, refrigeration, and special foods. The Vietnamese language, however, in contrast to Russian or German, was not a world language, and while it would continue in importance as a vehicle for communication with a neighbour, it would not assume as much importance as the European languages, including eventually perhaps English and French, in the Cambodian curriculum.

At present, except for special courses of immediate practical necessity, such as Russian at the Technical Institute and Vietnamese where the latter personnel are employed, language instruction is provided at the Language School, an institution midway between secondary and tertiary level which prepares students for study abroad and trains interpreters for government departments. Languages taught are Russian, German, Vietnamese and Spanish, the last because of a Cuban aid programme, which also provides the Spanish instructors.

Most of those preparing for study abroad are Level 3 graduates who do one year of language and then go on to their country of destination. The interpreters are not new school graduates, but personnel chosen by their ministries. After two years at the Language School, they go abroad for an intensive course, in the Soviet Union for ten months, in Germany for five months, and in Vietnam for three months, which again illustrates the relative importance of the languages in Cambodian objectives.

The general impression from talking to Cambodian educational personnel, visiting schools, and examining textbooks, is of the intelligent use of foreign aid and exiguous resources left in 1979 to construct a new modern, national school system orientated to the country's needs and realistic potentialities.

Cultural Preservation

Cambodia's rich heritage in art, dance and music is again receiving support from the state, and individuals again have leisure to devote to such cultural pursuits. A classical ballet corps is being trained under the instruction of the few teachers and dancers who survived and remained in Cambodia after 1979. Although it is not difficult for the visitor to gain access to their rehearsals, in the same Sala Chanchhaya at the old Royal Palace where their predecessors trained under royal patronage before 1970, they do not seem to perform frequently in public.

The almost weekly official theatre evenings at the Bassac Hall favour more modern types of entertainment, dance sketches with political themes, and stylized folkloric performances based on the culture and rituals of Cambodia's different regions and ethnic groups. Although the quality of the performances is high, not all of them are strictly traditional, and much of the work reflects the Chinese training of Chheng Phon and his colleagues of the 1960s when this type of 'folklore' took its place as a genre in Cambodian Fine Arts education.

The most important part of Cambodia's cultural heritage is the architecture and sculpture of the Angkor period. Here the PRK is doing what is possible with very limited resources. Funds and expertise are not available for the large-scale reconstruction and preservation such as were undertaken by the French. At present it is hardly possible to do more than clear the undergrowth from the more important edifices and to station guards to prevent theft. I must insist that there is no evidence for the charge that the PRK wilfully neglects the ancient temples, or that PRK and Vietnamese forces are free to engage in looting. I have visited Angkor Wat in 1981 and 1984 and found it well cared for and little the worse for wear since my last pre-war visit in 1965.

The PRK has also begun to form a conservation corps for the temples. Some of the personnel trained by the French before 1975 have resumed work, and the head of this service, whom I met at Angkor in 1981, went to the Soviet Union in 1984 for training in conservation techniques. More significant as evidence of PRK interest in the Angkor heritage was my meeting with one of the new young curators on an excursion to visit the pre-Angkor temple at Phnom Da in southern Cambodia. He had been one of the first group of new cadre trained to work as curators at the ancient temples; and his notebook from the three-month course demonstrated that he had received an intelligent introduction to the standard views on Angkor political and art history. He seemed interested in his work, and if representative of his department, his example shows the seriousness of the new government in this area.

Religion

When the Salvation Front was established in December 1978, point 4 of its 11-point programme included 'the right to freedom of opinion, association, and belief'; and among the fourteen-member original Front Central Committee was a representative of the Buddhist clergy, Long Sim.

As subsequent practice has shown, this was not to be interpreted as total freedom to propagate any doctrine whatsoever, or to freely organize religious groups. What was intended was to permit the re-establishment, under state supervision, of Cambodia's major indigenous religions—Buddhism, the faith of over 90 per cent of the population, and Islam, for the most important ethnic minority population, the Cham, constituting perhaps 3 per cent of the total. Christianity, as a foreign religion closely associated with both the French colonialists and the American aggressors, has had a much harder time.

Buddhism

Like every South-east Asian regime since the beginning of historical records, the PRK intends to integrate religion into the service of the state, and to prevent religious practices contrary to state policy.[5] Thus, religious policy was further elaborated in a Circular of 19 August 1979 on 'the provisional policy line on Buddhism'. There was to be freedom to believe or not to believe in Buddhism. Adherence to Buddhism was a voluntary act of each individual, and both believers and non-believers would have the same rights in society. According to this policy statement, the rights and duties of monks are the same as for others. Monks are to be issued with identification documents by local authorities, and they must respect government regulations. Buddhism will be of the traditional Khmer variety; and the state recognizes traditional ordination practices. Dogmas from other countries will not be permitted.[6]

Since all monks had been defrocked under DK, the first step in reviving Buddhism was to renew ordination procedures, for which specific ceremonies conducted by a traditionally defined group of monks are required. No one, even if previously a monk, may simply put on robes and declare himself ordained; and this is a universally-recognized requirement of traditional Buddhism, unrelated to the politics of any state. Apparently in 1979 there were a number of such private resumptions of monk status,[7] but their continued toleration would not only have undermined the policy of having religion serve national interests, but would also have discredited Cambodian Buddhism among the Buddhists of other Asian countries.[8]

Although there was one monk among the original Front Central Committee, it is not clear where he spent the DK years, but even if he had never been defrocked, he could not alone have reordained others. Thus, an initial proper ordination was organized by the Front and the KPRC on 19

September 1979, with a delegation sent from the Buddhist community of Vietnam, possibly from the Cambodian community in southern Vietnam whose temples had not been closed by the Vietnamese authorities after 1975. Seven Cambodians, all former monks of twenty to sixty years service, were reordained.[9]

Religious affairs are now under the direction of the Front rather than a government Minister of Cults, as in pre-revolutionary Cambodia. The division into two orders, the majority Mohanihay and aristocratic Thommayuth, no longer exists, and Cambodian Buddhism is considered as simply Theravada. This in fact means that the Thommayuth has not been revived.[10]

The Sangha organization has been simplified. There is no longer a *sangharaja*, but a *protean* (president) of the Sangha, at present Tep Vong, who is also a member of the Front Council, and a Sangha *protean* in each province.[11]

Cambodian informants often state that only men over 50 years old may be ordained, because of the need for youth in productive activities; but in fact young monks may occasionally be seen, and officials explain this relaxation of the rules by a disinclination to offend local feelings on a sensitive issue when there is a strong demand for a young man's ordination. A monk must also be ordained in his own place of residence, and by the local ordination committee.[12]

Each *wat* is administered by a lay committee varying in size according to the wat's importance. The president of a *wat* committee in function, as well as in dress, corresponds to the *achar* of pre-war times. At Wat Niroatraingsey, in Chbar Ampeou, Kien Svay District, just across the Bassac river from Phnom Penh, the committee president, who before 1975 had been a ward chief (*cau sangkat*), confirmed that his committee consisted of seven members chosen by written ballot from among eleven candidates proposed by the Municipal Front organization, and that if there was local objection to any candidate in such elections that person's name would be withdrawn.[13]

Most *wats* now only have between two and four monks. Wat Niroatraingsey has four, as does Wat Svay Poper, a large, well-preserved temple facing the Bassac river south of Central Phnom Penh,[14] and in the eleven *khum* of Koh Thom district, 60 km. due south of Phnom Penh, there are twenty-five *wats*, with a total of forty-five monks.

The reopening of *wats* at random in all their traditional locations has not been permitted. Communities desiring a *wat* apply to their local Front organization, and applications are approved in sufficient number to satisfy local needs. Thus, in formerly wealthy areas with several *wats* close together, only one functions at present; and those who might call this 'suppresion of religion' should remember that *wats* and monks are privately supported and that the resources to support the pre-war number do not exist today.[15]

Wat Chbar Ampeou, in excellent shape but very close to Wat Niroatraingsey, has no monks and functions only as a school; Wat Svay Poper, in a formerly wealthy and upper-class, even royal, neighbourhood where four large *wats* almost adjoined one another along the river-front, is now the only one of the four functioning. One of the others, Wat Preah Yuravongs, badly damaged, is under reconstruction, another, Wat Nuon Moniram, or Wat Than, appears undamaged but is used as housing for military personnel; and the fourth, Wat Keo Preah Phloeung, suffered extensive damage. Its site was just being cleared in November 1984 to be used, I was told, by nearby residents, as an office for the Ministry of Interior. In one of Phnom Penh's northern suburbs Wat Srah Chok, where clearing had just begun in 1981, has now reopened, with four monks and a primary school, while the nearby Wat Pipheatraingsey houses over a hundred personnel of the Trade Union Office. In the centre of town, Wat Saravan, surrounded by state offices and residential buildings, and still totally overgrown in 1981, has been cleared and also houses state employees, from the Defence Ministry.[16]

Reconstruction and maintenance of *wats* is by private donation, as was customary in the past, and of course the monks are fed, as was traditional, by their congregations. In addition, where the grounds of the *wat* are suitable, as at Wat Svay Poper, the monks, like most other state employees, cultivate small vegetable gardens for their own use. Before 1970, a number of *wats* were directly supported by the royal family, and there was also, until 1975, a state budget for the Ministry of Cults. This type of direct support by the state and its leading figures has been discontinued although, as the president of the Wat Niroatraingsey committee told me, the state may help *wat* committees obtain materials for reconstruction.

The private support for *wats* is supplied through traditional channels. I arrived in Phnom Penh at the end of October 1984, right in the middle of the *Kathen* season, a month during which private groups organize the major annual donations of robes and other articles of daily use to each *wat*. Usually, the *wat* which is the object of each group's support is chosen by virtue of some connection with the chief organizer—it is located for example, in his birthplace or where he once worked. Colourful stands are set up along the street in town or on country roads where passers-by may give cash contributions; and during my stay in Phnom Penh the *Kathen* booths could be seen in virtually every block of the city centre. At one of them, the organizers told me their *Kathen* was for a *wat* in Takeo province where their relatives lived, and they expected to collect 1–2,000 *riel* to finance supplies for its two monks.

Permission has to be sought to open a *Kathen* collection, but apparently it is always given when the *Kathen* is for an authorized *wat*. Interestingly enough, the request should be for permission to finance the construction of a school at the *wat*, for in most areas outside the cities primary schools are located at *wats*, and education, rather than purely religious activities, is more in line with state policy. In fact, the 'school-building' *Kathen* may be purely conventional, as I saw the day after my arrival when I visited a *Kathen* at Wat Phnom Prasith, 35 km. north-west of Phnom Penh. The local Front president, either because he was a loyal party man, or because he mistook me for a Russian, tried to convince me that the *Kathen* was not for the *wat* itself, but for the school. The crowd of local celebrants, however, in this traditional, and even in the best of pre-war days, poor peasant area, obviously considered it a religious occasion, and the important donation was the pile of bright yellow new monks' robes.

This does not indicate any rural disapproval of the state's emphasis on a useful social role for religious institutions, for *wats* have always housed schools, both traditional and modern; and after the DK experience everyone, even the most faithful, recognizes that rebuilding the educational system is at least as important as reopening *wats*.

An ancillary religious activity, which was traditional before 1975, but which persists with additional vigour because of the damage done to *wats* in 1970–9, is the artisanal manufacture of Buddha images, as mentioned earlier. In Phnom Penh the main pre-war centre of the trade was behind the palace, but it has now been transferred to the grounds of Wat Preah Yuravongs. There, thirteen small shops, some run by the pre-war artisans, turn out moulded cement Buddha images in various sizes and in all traditional poses.[17]

Islam

Islam, the second major world religion in Cambodia, has been accorded the same freedom as Buddhism. The Muslim population, most of whom are of Cham ethnicity, number about 185,000 and the number of functioning religious centres is probably about what it was before 1975. A Cham elder on Chrui Changvar told me that eighty of the 150 Cham families living there before 1975 had returned and that the same three mosques are again functioning, although children have little time for formal religious instruction in addition to the Khmer school programme which they follow.

Ethnic Minorities

As has been noted above, the PRK constitution recognizes the equality of all national minorities, the right to maintain their own culture, literature and language, and the right to use the latter in court. Likewise, the most important minority religion, Islam, seems clearly to enjoy the same freedom as Buddhism. Certainly there is no support for ethnic prejudice and discrimination in PRK laws or official statements.

Minorities constitute a smaller proportion of Cambodia's population than before 1975. If any problem arises in this area, it is likely to be based on the question of defining an ethnic minority. In pre-war census records the only indigenous minorities recognized were the Chinese and the Vietnamese. Under the Khmer Republic and DK, the Vietnamese, who had constituted about 6 per cent of the total population, were all expelled or killed, and a smaller number have so far returned. The Chinese, another 6 per cent of the population before 1975, were not especially disadvantaged under any regime, but may have emigrated in disproportionate numbers since 1979. Both of these groups, to the extent they remain in the PRK, inhabit the same areas and engage in the same occupations as before.[18]

The return, and the size, of the Vietnamese minority has occasioned much comment in Western news media, with the PRK receiving more censure for humane treatment of these former inhabitants of Cambodia than Pol Pot's Democratic Kampuchea, particularly since 1979, has received for murdering them in an excess of chauvinism. In apparent ignorance of the fact that their figures belie their claims, the anti-PRK propagandists worry that an alleged figure of 150–200,000 Vietnamese raises 'serious questions about Hanoi's long-term intentions towards Kampuchea', or, two years later, voice concern about 'the spectre of massive Vietnamese resettlement', while still unwilling to name any figure higher than 200,000—less than half the pre-war Vietnamese population who in the majority knew no other home.[19]

As the PRK sees it, 'like Kampuchean and other survivors of the Khmer Rouge genocide, Vietnamese residents . . . were authorized . . . to return to their former places of residence'; and the PRK also 'authorized Vietnamese people with relatives in Kampuchea to join them and live and work here in accordance with Kampuchean law.' 'By mid-1983 about 56,000 Vietnamese' had returned (PRK, 1983, p. 7).

Of course, none of the figures is verifiable, but the only point which needs to be made here is that even the largest serious totals which have been suggested by Western enemies of the PRK are still within an acceptable range, given the pre-war population and proclaimed PRK policies.

Despite the fact that no foreign observer can go out and count Vietnamese in Cambodia, some impressions are not without value. In 1983 a Vietnamese-speaking scholar-journalist found that large numbers of the Vietnamese in Phnom Penh were not settlers, but had come as individuals for a variety of personal reasons, and would probably return home (Quinn-Judge, 1983, pp. 18–19). When I visited Phnom Penh in 1984 after an absence of three years, my impression was that there were fewer Vietnamese evident around the city centre, but many in traditional Vietnamese neighbourhoods northwards along the river. This would seem to support both the PRK argument that the Vietnamese who come are returning residents, and Quinn-Judge's feeling that the casuals would not remain. Moreover, with respect to the latter, there is no hesitation within Cambodia, either by PRK personnel or Vietnamese diplomats, in stating that they are unwanted and when caught are sent back to Vietnam. Another impressionistic assessment was at Neak Luong, a river port on the Mekong south-east of Phnom Penh. It was traditionally a centre of Vietnamese population, to the extent that journalists during 1970–2 were calling it 'New Saigon'; and anti-PRK propagandists who have never visited post-1979 Cambodia like to evoke it as an example of Vietnamese encroachment (Eiland, 1985, pp. 106–13). On a visit there in November 1984, I found it less active than before 1970, with the market apparently divided between Khmer and Vietnamese, and many of the latter thoroughly assimilated into Khmer life, both in language and dress.

In one area it was possible to accomplish some quantitative research. At the end of November 1984 I drove south of Phnom Penh through Saang to Koh Thom, and while making what started out as little more than a social call I was able to take a careful look at the latest district (*srok*) statistics, which included an ethnic breakdown of the population in the district's eleven *khum*. This was particularly interesting since Koh Thom lies right on the Vietnamese border, and contained numerous Vietnamese before 1970, although I have not found the total. The 1984 Koh Thom population of 113,880 included 14,840 Vietnamese, of whom 10,803 lived in the *khum* of Prek Chrei where they were in the majority (out of 12,335). This is not unexpected, since Prek Chrei is a finger of land almost totally enclosed by Vietnamese territory, geographically and economically more a part of Vietnam than of Cambodia. In the ten other *khum* the remaining 4,000 Vietnamese were spread evenly, thus in small minorities wherever they lived.

Of equal interest as a comparison is that during Ben Kiernan's visit to Koh Thom in 1980 he was told that the population was 86,342, and that there were no Vietnamese—that they had not been permitted to return. Thus

Cambodian authorities, perhaps only the local ones, were still influenced by DK chauvinism, which has been replaced by a more humane attitude towards former non-Khmer residents; and except for one *khum* with geographical peculiarities, the Vietnamese influx has been exiguous–in the realm of 3.6–3.7 per cent. If this proportion were extrapolated to the entire country, as might seem reasonable, since a district like Koh Thom should have more Vietnamese than districts within the country or far from the border, and exceptional *khum* like Prek Chrei would be cancelled out by areas unlikely to have Vietnamese at all, the result would be around 260,000, in a population of 7 million. Even if this is higher than official PRK figures, it is not something about which foreigners need show concern.

In fact, the total is probably much lower. During a trip to Cambodia in January 1986, Ben Kiernan found reliable statistics indicating that Prey Veng had only 8,650 Vietnamese, and Svay Rieng less than 1,000. In the district of Chrang Chamres, just north of Phnom Penh, and a heavy minority area before 1970, of 8,000 families making up the population of 30,000, 1,882 families were Cham, 1,300 Vietnamese, and 204 Chinese.

The third important minority group, the Cham, were defined before 1975 as 'Islamic Khmer', while the name 'Upland Khmer' (*khmer loeu*) was given to Mon-Khmer and Chamic hill and forest groups who were a majority in the two north-eastern provinces of Ratanakiri and Mondulkiri, and who also populated much of the south-western mountains, and parts of the north. If such definitions implied equality, as they were intended to, they also, by assimilating the designated peoples to the majority Khmer, removed any need for special consideration for their culture and language.

Today the Cham are the group in which the state takes the greatest interest as a *national minority*. Their religion, Islam, is the only religion other than Buddhism to be expressly tolerated, and it is clear from press and public pronouncements that a greater effort than under any previous regime is being made to integrate the Cham into Cambodian society, and to make them feel that they are first-class citizens.

With respect to the other minorities, the official view today may be similar to that prevailing before 1975, at least in so far as it concerns their integration into Khmer society and transformation of their own cultures to conform to it. There is little detailed information available about these groups since 1975, but policy towards them was stated in a resolution of the National Cadres Conference in November 1984 entitled 'Policy toward Ethnic Minorities', which was mainly related to the north-eastern groups.[20]

This resolution began with 'the minorities are always considered as an integral part of the Kampuchean nation', and the first concern expressed was the solidarity of the minorities with the rest of the population in the interests of national defence. Point 2 continued the theme of 'promoting the solidarity between ethnic minorities and the majority through making them all into a single community of brothers and sisters'. This involved 'suppression of all differentiation and inequality which still existed and the end of "majoritism" and chauvinism . . . and opposition to any act of discrimination against the minorities'.

As part of the effort to achieve equality and solidarity, the minorities should be 'encouraged to participate in collectivization . . . to join solidarity groups'; and the state should give them facilities for adopting a 'sedentary way of life'. Gradually, 'monoculture and individual production' should give way to collective organization of 'more stable and modern' agriculture; and the resolution expressed an intention to modernize communications in the minority regions in order to facilitate their integration into the rest of the country and its markets.

An important aspect of state policy, therefore, is the transformation of the minorities into good Khmers, and this is to be facilitated by the movement of Khmer settlers to the minority areas. The resolution speaks of granting 'facilities for settlement and production to all who volunteer to live in the Northeast region for the first five years of their life [there]'; and 'all state employees appointed to the Northeast for a long term are authorized to take their families' and to receive special aid and a 'salary worthy of their merits'.

Point 5 of the resolution calls for the elimination of illiteracy and training of teachers from among the minority groups. 'The language and the literature of each minority, if such exists', are to be respected, so that these groups may 'write, speak, and teach in their own languages'. 'The use of the minority languages is equal with the Khmer language'. It is not clear from this, however, whether new writing systems are to be developed and taught where none existed previously, or whether it refers only to those minority groups in which literacy already exists.

Depending on the interpretation, the last point may represent a new development in state policy. When, shortly before the Cadres Conference resolution had been published, I asked Education Minister Pen Navuth about the development of literacy and educational materials in minority languages, he said that it might be possible in the future to support education in Cham and Thai, which already possess their own scripts and literature, but there was no plan to develop literacy in any of the other minority languages. Members of those groups, that is the 'Upland Khmer', would be expected, he said, to learn Khmer in school and to use it wherever literacy was required. As an example of that policy, it had been reliably reported to me in Phnom Penh that Vietnam had offered to train north-eastern minority medical personnel in their own languages, for some of which Vietnam has already developed scripts and trained personnel, but this was rejected by the PRK authorities.

There is thus no question of any systematic official discrimination, nor any doubt of PRK sincerity in treating all such groups equally, but there is an assumption that all minorities will gradually be transformed into 'modern' agriculturally-settled Khmer, retaining only those features of their traditional cultures which are not in conflict with the transformation. There is also, no doubt, an assumption that such development is what the minority groups themselves desire. Assimilation of the minorities to the mainstream Khmer may not in fact cause any problems. We do not know how the events of the past twenty years have already transformed those regions, nor what is left of traditional cultures. It is clear from the examples of South-East Asian minorities which are accessible, as in northern Thailand, that they want lowland commodities, that their cultures may be modified in the acquisition of new products, and that their integration with lowland markets, in particular via such products as opium and timber, may transform them as much as benevolent state intervention would. Certainly, if the Cambodian minorities have cause for grievance, they, in contrast to similar groups in Thailand, have powerful representatives to whom they can turn. Members of local minorities are appointed to responsible administrative positions—in 1981 they were province chiefs in Mondulkiri, Ratanakiri, Stung Treng and Preah Vihear; and they occupy some of the top positions in the armed forces.[21] Certainly the PRK has a better record than any previous Cambodian regime in giving responsible positions to non-Khmers.

11 Foreign Policy

The first outline of PRK foreign policy was in points 9 to 11 of the Declaration of 2 December 1978. The new government intended to follow a policy of 'peace, friendship, and non-alignment with all countries without regard for political and social regimes, on the basis of peaceful coexistence and mutual respect'. They intended to 'resolve all differences with neighbouring countries by peaceful negotiation', and in particular they hoped to 'end the border conflict with Vietnam'. They further desired to re-establish relations of friendship and co-operation with the countries of South-east Asia; and Cambodia 'will not participate in any military alliance, and will not permit any country to establish military bases or to introduce military equipment onto its territory'. Finally, they would 'reinforce solidarity with the revolutionary and progressive forces in the whole world' (Service d'Information du FUNSK, 1979, pp. 15–16).

It is ironical that the point against foreign bases and military equipment is very much like the one that Sihanouk's government refused to accept at Geneva in 1954, in order to be able to request American aid against the Cambodian revolutionary forces represented by some of the present PRK leaders, and that the latter have had to modify it in order to utilize foreign military aid against opponents backed by Sihanouk and the United States. Whether or not that part of the 1978 declaration was intended as a serious policy statement, probably no one among the emergent PRK leadership, or their Vietnamese supporters, foresaw in 1978 the extent of foreign support for Pol Pot and his crowd who had been reviled in the West for nearly four years.

After the new government was established, its first act towards putting the principles of 1978 into effect was the 'Treaty of Peace, Friendship and Co-operation', signed with Vietnam on 18 February 1979. The treaty, which covered friendship, co-operation, mutual aid and support in various ways, managed to stay within the terms of the 1978 declaration. Military aid was covered by article 2, which spoke of mutual assistance in order 'to strengthen the capacity to defend the independence, sovereignty, unity, territorial integrity, of each country against imperialists and reactionary forces. Article 4 dealt with the peaceful negotiations of problems between the two countries, in particular the border question; article 5 reiterated the desire to pursue a 'policy of friendship and good neighbourliness with Thailand and the other countries of Southeast Asia'; and article 7 stated that the treaty was not aimed at opposing any third country.[1]

Two years later, the documents emanating from the Fourth Party Congress and the new constitution reiterated the principles of 'independence, peace and neutrality', but there was a more particular commitment to tightening 'the bonds of solidarity and co-operation with Vietnam, Laos, the Soviet Union and other fraternal socialist countries'.[2] Whether or not this narrowing of foreign policy interests was inevitable, international response to the establishment of the PRK forced them to rely on Vietnam, the Soviet Union, and the international socialist community for support. To date, in 1985, India is the only major non-socialist country to recognize the PRK, Vietnam provides troops for its defence, and its main economic support comes from the Soviet Union.

As of November 1984, full diplomatic relations had been established with twenty-seven nations, eleven of them in Africa, and including all the East European socialist group except Romania and Yugoslavia. In Asia, besides its Indo-China neighbours and India, only the Soviet allies Mongolia and Afghanistan recognize the PRK, and among Latin American countries only Nicaragua and Panama. The Cambodian seat in the United Nations, and in a number of other international organizations, is still held by Democratic Kampuchea—now the Coalition Government of Democratic Kampuchea—since the Sihanouk and Son Sann groups joined with the Pol Pot remnants on the Thai border in 1982.

This is indeed diplomatic isolation, but not self-imposed, and the excuse given by the enemies of the PRK has been the imposition and maintenance of the regime by foreign armed force, continuing foreign occupation, and lack of a democratic political process. These reasons appear increasingly disingenuous with each year. The PRK has now lasted longer than its two immediate predecesors, Pol Pot's Democratic Kampuchea and Lon Nol's Khmer Republic, both of which were given wide recognition and the United Nations seat after forcibly overthrowing internationally-recognized predecessors. The Khmer Republic would not have lasted as long as it did without foreign military support; and in the early phase of their struggle, Pol Pot's forces may only have survived with *their* foreign aid, from Vietnam. In 1981 the PRK held National Assembly elections, which, if not in conformity with the highest standards in the advanced West, may stand comparison with electoral exercises in a number of non-communist Asian countries; and it is ludicrous to insist on international electoral supervision for the PRK alone. The PRK government and administration are indigenous, not Vietnamese, and the Vietnamese troops in Cambodia have a clearly defined function in defence of the country against enemies who are themselves dependent on other foreign support.

The motives of the leading opponents of the PRK must be more complex than those stated. Their Cambodian rivals of course wish to return to power—the Sihanouk and Son Sann groups to restore a semblance of pre-1970 society. Among the main foreign backers of the latter, China probably views Indo-China in relation to Sino-Soviet affairs, and as relations with the Soviet Union improve, Chinese interest in the Democratic Kampuchea Coalition is likely to cool. The ASEAN countries have varying interests in Indo-China, somewhat disguised by their joint action for reasons of principle. The position of Thailand, the most insistent on an anti-Vietnamese stand, is conditioned by past history in which the Thai played a dominant role in Cambodian affairs. Indonesia is much more moderate, and would probably accept a settlement with Vietnam and the PRK.

The present United States government has apparently not accepted the American defeat in Indo-China of 1975, and would like to roll back socialism, at least to the Cambodia-Vietnam border. For five years after 1979 the United States insisted that it was only following ASEAN leads in Indo-China, but as some hopes for a negotiated settlement appeared during the past year, American statements have revealed that, if necessary they will keep pushing ASEAN from behind while following. In Kuala Lumpur in July 1985, Secretary of State George Shultz warned ASEAN against formulating peace proposals which Vietnam might accept (*Bangkok Post*, 13 July 1985, p. 1).

Settlement nevertheless seems closer this year than previously, unless foreign support for the Democratic Kampuchea Coalition increases—an area in which the United States is also taking initiatives.[3] The PRK and Vietnamese have offered a five-point proposal, under which Vietnamese forces, ostensibly the main foreign concern, could be entirely withdrawn. The essence of the five points is:

1. exclusion of the Pol Pot clique from Cambodian politics;
2. recognition of the PRK;
3. free elections to which foreign observers would be invited, but which does not imply international *supervision*;
4. formation of a zone of peace in South-east Asia, apparently to involve pledges of non-interference in Indo-China by ASEAN; and
5. international guarantees of the negotiated agreements (*The Economist*, Intelligence Unit, No. 2, 1985, p. 18).

Within Cambodia's area of diplomatic recognition, economic and political ties are becoming increasingly close, in particular with Vietnam and the Soviet Union. The formation of an Indo-Chinese economic bloc is certainly under way. Moreover, this makes considerable sense, with Cambodia's agriculture and Vietnam's industry; and no Western power ever objected to such integration until it began to be undertaken by the Indo-Chinese peoples themselves.

The Soviet Union supplies the bulk of direct economic aid, although details of aid agreements are not available. There has been much speculation as to whether the Cambodians might play a Russian card against Vietnam, some of it, I believe, misplaced, as in the case of Pen Sovann's removal.[4] There can be no doubt, however, that the PRK welcomes the widest possible Western contacts, both because of the greater possibilities for economic aid and to maintain genuine independence. Russian and German are planned as the major foreign languages for study in schools, most tertiary students are sent to the Soviet Union and Eastern Europe, and the freedom allowed for private instruction in English indicates a hope that relations with other Western, or English-speaking countries, will improve.

There must be factional differences among the PRK leadership connected with the country's foreign relations, but care must be exercised in analysing them and drawing conclusions. One recent *Far Eastern Economic Review* article asserted that different treatments in the Vietnamese and Cambodian press of Heng Samrin's speech on the thirty-third anniversary of the Cambodian Party showed lack of Cambodian enthusiasm for the relationship with Vietnam. Thus, the 'official Khmer newsagency' omitted most of Samrin's eulogy of Ho Chi Minh, mention of Vietnamese volunteers, and the expression of gratitude to the Vietnamese forces in Cambodia, and relegated the speech to page four. The problem with this analysis is that it is based on the French version of the *SPK* news bulletin, which as I have earlier indicated is sometimes inaccurate. In the newspaper *Kampuchea*, the real official news organ of the Cambodian people, Samrin's speech was on page one, with much fanfare and none of the omissions in question.[5]

Notes

Chapter 1

1. See *Encyclopaedia Brittanica*, (1985, Vol. 6, p. 707, 'Kampuchea'), and *Encyclopaedia Universalis* (1986, Vol. 3, pp. 808–10, 'Cambodge').
2. This is the apparently official figure given to Ben Kiernan by a Cham official in a community near Phnom Penh in January 1986. Cambodian authorities before 1975, like the traditional Vietnamese, always tried to assimilate Cham, calling them 'Khmer Islam', and did not keep census statistics for the Cham as a separate group. For pre-war figures I accept the most serious demographic study of pre-war Cambodia, Jacques Migozzi, *Cambodge faits et problèmes de population* (1973, p. 42), where the total 'Islamic' minority, which included more than the Cham, was 150,000 in 1970; and if they increased at the annual rate of 2.9 per cent, which Migozzi deduced for the popualtion as a whole, their numbers in 1975 would have been around 173,000. Since I do not believe that the Cham, country-wide, suffered more than the Khmer under Democratic Kampuchea (DK) (see Vickery, 1984, pp. 181–2), they, like the Cambodian population as a whole, should by now have recovered or even exceeded their pre-war numbers.
3. Nothing more than a guess is possible for their numbers. The PRK does not have census figures for them (interview with Mme Peou Lida, Deputy Secretary-General of the Solidarity Front for Construction and Defence of the Motherland of Kampuchea, in November 1984). The total of such groups is probably not over 200,000. The 1983 population estimates for the entire country grouped the outlying provinces Koh Kong, Preah Vihear, Stung Treng, Kratie, Ratanakiri and Mondulkiri together with 424,484 population (Grunewald, 1983, with statistics from PRK government estimates).
4. For discussion of the Vietnamese population, see pp. 165–7. I have not found any estimate of the present Chinese population.
5. See discussion in Vickery (1984), pp. 184–8.
6. I saw an example at district (*srok*) level in Koh Thom in November 1984.

Chapter 2

1. The main sources on Thiounn have been Hess (1901); *Nagaravatta*, No. 301, 21 September 1941, on the occasion of his retirement; and *Kampuchea*, No. 436, 24 September 1946 and No. 441, 2 October 1946 on the occasions of Thiounn's death (23 September 1946) and funeral. See also Chandler (1983a, pp. 163, 168); and Kiernan (1984, p. 31).

2. They represent the exception to David Chandler's view that 'at no point in the chain of command was initiative rewarded' (Chandler, 1983a, p. 148).
3. The tradition of this incident, however, handed down orally, remained vivid in the popular memory.

Chapter 3

1. For example, Poc Khun, scion of an old Thai-orientated aristocratic family, and grandson of Palace Minister Thiounn (see above, p. 5). By this time the Poc and Thiounn were interrelated in a network of aristocratic and commercial families (see Kiernan, 1984, p. 31), with members in the forefront of the independence struggle (see Bunchhan Mol, 1972 and 1973); and a Poc was the wife of Prince Sisowath Monireth, uncle of Sihanouk, eldest son of Sihanouk's predecessor King Monivong, and an important political figure in his own right.
2. See Kiernan (1984, pp. 63–4), but there were thirteen, not seven, who invaded the palace and were subsequently sentenced. Their names and sentences were published in *Cambodge* (a Phnom Penh newspaper which began publishing daily in French with some Khmer pages on 20 March 1945), 23 December 1947.
3. All of the above is from *Cambodge*, respectively from No. 94, 17 July 1945; No. 87, 6 July; No. 96, 17 July; No. 116, 11 August; No. 9, 30 March; No. 110, 4 August; No. 121, 17 August; No. 79, 27 June; No. 124, 21 August; No. 126, 23 August; No. 127, 24 August; see also Kiernan (1984, p. 51).
4. *Cambodge*, Nos. 140, 8 September and 144, 13 September on allied arrival; No. 149, 19 September, on status of Vietnamese; Nos. 172–3, 18–19 October, Murray's communiqué; Kiernan (1984), p. 50–2).
5. Details of cabinet membership from Université Bouddhique Preah Sihanouk Raj (1965), based on a doctoral thesis by Phouk Chhay.
6. See Kiernan (1984, pp. 44–5, 50, 52–3); and p. 66, on the name 'Son Ngoc Minh', and its similarity to 'Son Ngoc Thanh'.
7. See Kiernan (1984, p. 75). All the leading members of this group calling for an Indo-Chinese Front were Khmer, a point deserving emphasis in the present political climate.
8. See Kiernan (1984, pp. 79–80), where the Front name in Khmer is given as Samakhum Khmer Issarak. At least, that is how a participant related it thirty years later. A near contemporary document, 'Khmer Armed Resistance', dated October 1952, states that the new Front was called 'Nekhum Issarak Khmer', and that its chairman was Tou Samouth, while Son Ngoc Minh was chairman of the Provisional National Liberation Government. See Chapter 6 below on 'The Party', where I note conflicting information about these events in different sources. No detail may be accepted with complete confidence.
9. See Kiernan (1984, p. 110), where he opts for a September date for the founding of the Cambodian party. See discussion of this in Chapter 6, 'The Party', below.

10. See Vickery (1982b, p. 94), from the contemporary press. Dap Chhuon had joined Sihanouk in 1949. See also Kiernan (1984, p. 99). Proof of the expanding area of revolutionary control in the Cambodian countryside is given in maps prepared by the French authorities and found by David Chandler and Ben Kiernan in the Phnom Penh National Archives in 1981 (see Kiernan, 1984, p. 126).
11. See Kiernan (1984, pp. 122–3). Unless otherwise noted, all further information about the activities of the Cambodian communists in the 1950s and 1960s may be found in greater detail in Kiernan.
12. See Kiernan (1984, pp. 173, 187) for examples of conflicting information to which Kiernan neglects to give attention.
13. See Kiernan (1984, p. 170) on the change of Vietnamese and KPRP positions to pro-Sihanouk, just when the latter signed an accord with China in February 1956.
14. Kiernan (1984, pp. 174–5) has information on continuing conflict between the rural left and Sihanouk's government, and he provides evidence (p. 152) that the KPRP policy of restraint after Geneva was unpopular among rural cadres, that it was not only Pol Pot who was coming 'to regard this restrained KPRP stand as a betrayal of the revolution'. It seems unlikely that So Phim, later an opponent of Pol Pot, continued to feel 'restrained' after his post-Geneva experiences (noted by Kiernan on pp. 174–5).
15. See Kiernan (1984, p. 187). Kiernan rejects this interpretation, arguing that since Samouth is alleged to have said, '"if we do not struggle, we would be serving US imperialism"', he 'did not accept the view that the Sihanouk regime was the primary enemy'. It was always clear, however, that for many of the Cambodian left the United States *and* Sihanouk were the main enemies and if Tou Samouth had not held such an opinion, he would have seen no need to call the meeting which Kiernan describes. See further the remarks by Pen Sovann, below, Chapter 6, p. 72.
16. Kiernan (1984, p. 190); Vickery (1984, p. 119).
17. See Kiernan (1984, p. 241, n. 135). The PRK now explicitly accuses the Pol Pot clique of Tou Samouth's murder; for example, Pen Sovann in his Political Report to the Fourth Party Congress, said that Pol Pot and his 'partisans from France' assassinated Tou Samouth on 27 May 1962, a date two months earlier than previously reported (Kiernan, 1984, p. 197). For a description and analysis of Sovann's report see Chapter 6.
18. Speech in Norodom Sihanouk (1962, pp. 147–8), where little detail is given. For the selections from the allegedly full text which I have reproduced, see Kiernan (1984, p. 196 and p. 241, n. 127). It is at least unlikely that Setha was Tou Samouth (Vickery, 1984, pp. 200–1), and all other records of Samouth suggest that he was continuously in Cambodia during that time.
19. Laura Summers, 'Translator's Note' to Khieu Samphan (1979) and Vickery (1982b, pp. 104–5).

20. There is some confusion in details reported from different sources. See Kiernan (1984, pp. 200–2), and comment in Vickery (1984, p. 200).
21. Details from the contemporary press. See also Vickery (1984, p. 22, and notes); Vickery (1982b, p. 105). It was not surprising that Khieu Samphan criticized the reforms (Kiernan, 1984, p. 205). It was not that he was trying to undermine his own reforms in order to follow a 'Pol Pot line', but that he realized the way in which the nationalizations could be misused for reactionary interests. Neither does Samphan's resignation merit the remark that he was possibly 'instructed to abandon attempts at reform by Pol Pot' (Kiernan, 1984, p. 204)—a misuse of the evidence. Even as Minister he had no power to enforce decisions on his enemies; had he stayed on he would only have been presiding over measures which he opposed, and, in the political climate of the time, which I followed on the spot, Samphan would have risked his life remaining in the government against Sihanouk's wishes.
22. See Kiernan (1984, p. 208). This unusual interpretation contrasts with most statistical evidence and all earlier syntheses of that evidence. The 'record rice harvest' and 'rice exports [which] soared' were only slightly more than a return to normal conditions after the slump year of 1962; and rice production in any case was determined more by natural conditions that by state policy. For figures, see Rémy Prud'homme (1969, pp. 254–5). Neither does a temporary improvement in balance of payments, particularly when they depended on exports of agricultural products, argue for the success of reforms. Moreover, as Prud'homme indicated (pp. 273–5), the figures themselves were '*douteuses*'. Certainly, within Cambodia at the time no one thought things were going well. By the end of 1964, Sihanouk was on the air with long speeches about the huge budget deficit, in itself an admission of failure (an example was broadcast on 5 December 1964). Kiernan seems to have been misled by the upbeat published remarks of Hou Yuon, who could not have said anything different, and may well have written with tongue in cheek (Kiernan, 1984, p. 208, n. 188).
23. See Kiernan (1984, pp. 231–2) for an example of the extreme leftist line. Kiernan does not recognize, however, that such a line could be attractive to large numbers of peasants, and was not just irrational Pol Potism.
24. For detailed treatment of the events, see Kiernan, 'The Samlaut Rebellion 1967–68', in Kiernan and Boua (1982); and Kiernan (1984, pp. 249–55). In the two treatments there are differences of interpretation to which the reader should give attention.
25. For further details and names, see Kiernan (1984, pp. 256–68). Note that one of the targets of the first peasant revolt was an enterprise organized by an urban communist intellectual, and moreover one who appeared to by sympathetic to the Chinese Cultural Revolution. This must have influenced the Cambodian intellectual left, forcing them to realize that to make a revolution they would have to adopt peasant goals.

26. Kiernan (1984, pp. 300–2), provides some reminiscences of American involvement with Cambodian plotters in southern Vietnam.
27. Hang Thun Hak was a Thanhist student activist and guerrilla in the 1950s (see Kiernan, 1984, pp. 130–1, photo 9), studied drama in France and China, then became Director of the Fine Arts University, and eventually Minister and briefly Prime Minister (1972–3) under Lon Nol. He was believed, both by friends and enemies, to be the leader of a Marxist intellectual group which favoured a pro-Soviet line. Although they have been left out of discussions of Cambodian politics, perhaps simply because they have nearly all disappeared without leaving written records, they at least deserve a footnote.
28. On the factories given to Cambodia as part of the Chinese aid programme, see *Far Eastern Economic Review*, 9 May 1963, pp. 319–22. Kiernan (1984, p. 149), notes how Zhou Enlai at Geneva in 1954 wished to recognize the Cambodian and Lao governments at a time when even the Colombo powers refused to recognize Sihanouk; on p. 204, Kiernan also shows that in mid-1963 neither China nor Vietnam were 'interested in supporting an underground struggle in Kampuchea'; and on p. 263 he records Chinese support for Sihanouk and limited interest in Pol Pot as late as 1967.
29. See Vickery (1984, p. 197), and references there.
30. The standard document is Pol Pot's 'Black Book' Kampuchea Démocratique (1978). For an accessible interpretation, see Stephen R. Heder (1980a, p. 13 and n. 25).
31. See sources listed in Kiernan (1984, Chap. 5, n. 8).
32. For example, the allegation that 'Zhou Enlai went as far as encouraging Sihanouk to lay claim to what was then undisputed Vietnamese territory' (Kiernan, 1984, p. 182, with Sihanouk and Wilfred Burchett cited as sources). This is not Sihanouk's version of an event which occurred in 1960, when Burchett was not in Cambodia; and in 1956—Burchett's date—the event did not occur.
33. Quotations from Kiernan (1984, p. 223). The Vietnamese–Chinese co-operation in training and utilizing Cambodian cadres is recorded by Kiernan (p. 179), who notes that among the Cambodians who moved between Vietnam and China 'none went to the Soviet Union, however'. This co-operation is also apparent in an interesting Tuol Sleng prison dossier, that of Lach Dara, daughter of Lach Saren, a Khmer who had gone to Hanoi in 1954, and then to China, where he worked for Peking radio. In 1961, Lach Dara, her mother, brother and sister left Cambodia to join Saren in Peking, where she studied medicine in a programme arranged by Son Ngoc Minh. After graduation in 1970, she left China to proceed via Hanoi to Cambodia to join the revolutionary struggle.

Chapter 4

1. Their ethnic status is mentioned in People's Republic of Kampuchea, 'List of Names of Candidates for Election', Phnom Penh, mimeo. 1981, English translation from Khmer original. See 'Bibliography' 'National Assembly Biographies (trans.)' for description of this source.
2. *Far Eastern Economic Review*, 9 May 1985, last page [no. p.n.], Jim Laurie, 'Letter from Phnom Penh'; *Phnom Penh*, Khmer-language newspaper, No. 214–215, 13 April 1985, p. 2.
3. This is expressed, for example, in Chea Sim's opening address and Pen Sovann's Political Report to the Fourth Party Congress in 1981. See Chapter 6 on the Party, below.
4. On this point, see Michael Vickery (1984, Chap. 5, n. 111); and for more on Hou Yuon, see Kiernan and Boua (1982, Chaps. 1 and 6).
5. See Vickery 1984, pp. 144–7) for details of factional analysis. I neglected there to mention Phurissara, whose visit to Bangkok was reported in *Far Eastern Economic Review*, 14 November 1975, p. 16, and who was also mentioned as Minister of Justice in *Summary of World Broadcasts*, 27 February 1976.
6. See Vickery (1984, Chap. 3, n. 49); and Henry Kamm, *New York Times*, 1 March 1980, interview with Ieng Sary, quoted in Shawcross (1984b, pp. 333–5). See also Chomsky & Herman (1979, Vol. 2, p. 351, n. 80).
7. See Snepp (1977, pp. 339–40) for reported American espionage networks left in Cambodia.
8. Shawcross (1980, p. 370) cites American government sources which estimated a ten-day supply of food in Phnom Penh. He also notes François Ponchaud's estimate of a one-month supply; the *New York Times* of 9 May 1975 reported only eight days' rice on hand in Phnom Penh on 17 April; and an American AID official estimated only six days' rice: see Chomsky & Herman (1979, Vol. 2, p. 160).
9. See Vickery (1984, pp. 66–9, map p. vi). Roughly, the North-West Zone comprised the provinces of Battambang and Pursat; the West Zone, Kompong Chhnang, Koh Kong and part of Kompong Speu; the South-West Zone, Kampot, Takeo, Kandal and part of Kompong Speu; the East Zone, part of Kompong Cham, Prey Veng, Svay Rieng; the North Zone Siemreap, Oddar Meanchey, Preah Vihear; the Central Zone part of Kompong Cham, Kompong Thom, and part of Kratie; the North-East Zone, Stung Treng, Ratanakiri and Mondulkiri. Most of Kratie province was a special zone by itself.
10. See Vickery (1984, p. 146). Since then, in November 1984, I have discovered reference in a Tuol Sleng prison dossier to Poc Deuskoma's death from illness in 1971 (Dossier M.182 of Men Tol aka Sat, a Vietnam-trained DK doctor).
11. See Y Phandara (1982, p. 106), 'Chuon Mom [sic], ministre de l'Energie'. In Vickery (1984, p. 147), I said the Energy Minister had not been identified; but Phandara should have known this kind of information. If so, Mum's story of pig-tending (Vickery, 1984, p. 165) may be false.

12. If it seems that I am giving undue attention to socialist theory in this discussion, I should emphasize that it is only in those terms that the Cambodia–Vietnam conflict poses a problem. Bourgeois social science would happily explain that conflict as the natural result of 'ancient hostility' between the two peoples.
13. See Kiernan (1984) for the history of this development, and Vickery (1984, Chap. 5) for the 'peasant populist' analysis.
14. See Nayan Chanda, *Far Eastern Economic Review*, 21 April 1978, p. 18; Kiernan (1984, pp. 267–8, 270–1, 280–1); Vickery (1984, pp. 265, 268); and for the official DK view, Kampuchea Démocratique 1978).
15. See above, Chap. 3, on Son Ngoc Thanh. The Thanhists also eventually became anti-Vietnamese, perhaps reflecting their class background, similar to that of the DK leadership, but this was not so clear in the 1940s to early 1950s, when the Thanhists were still seen as part of the left.
16. See references in n, 14 above.
17. See *Asiaweek*, 22 September 1978, p. 10; 15 September 1978, p. 15; Heder (1978, p. 18); and for more detail, Vickery (1984, pp. 193–5).
18. See Carney (1982, p. 34). In his oral presentation at the conference, Carney made the point more forcefully than in the draft paper.
19. See Front (1980) and below, Chapter 6, 'The Party'.
20. See PRK (1979a), members are also listed in *Summary of World Broadcasts (SWB)*, 10 January 1979.
21. Most biographical information is from the biographies of National Assembly candidates cited in note 1, above.
22. KPRC Order No. 06, 14 October 1979; *SWB*, 24 November 1979; and *SWB*, 2 June 1979.
23. *Kampuchea*, No. 94, 2 July 1981, p. 2, for lists of names in the new structures.
24. *Kampuchea*, No. 117, 10 December 1981, on replacement of Pen Sovann; *Kampuchea*, No. 119, 24 December 1981, with mention of Bou Thang, still as chief of Propaganda Committee; *Kampuchea*, No. 120, 31 December 1981, report on Phnom Penh meeting about the Third Front Congress, with mention of prominent personalities, but no Prime Minister; *Kampuchea*, No. 122, 14 January 1982, mention of Chan Si as Prime Minister and Defence Minister; *Kong Tap Padiwat*, No. 43, 10 February 1982, Chan Si still Prime Minister and Defence Minister; *Kampuchea*, No. 127, 18 February 1982 announced the appointments of Chan Si as Prime Minister and Bou Thang as Defence Minister.
25. *Asiaweek*, 18 December 1981, pp. 13–14; *Far Eastern Economic Review*, 11 December 1981, pp. 8–9 and 18 December, pp. 16–17.
26. Ibid.; and Chanda (1981a, pp. 24–6); and see below, Chapter 6, 'The Party'.
27. One contribution in that vein was Ben Kiernan (1981, pp. 1–9).
28. See 'The Military', in Chapter 8, 'Government Structure', below.
29. Hun Sen's promotion was announced in *Kampuchea*, No. 279, 17 January 1985; and in *Kampuchea*, No. 285, 28 February 1985, following a State Council meeting, he announced further changes, but without giving names.

30. The full names of some ministries which may be unclear in abbreviation are: 'Comm./Post'—Communications, Transport and Postal Service; 'Home & For. Trade'—Home and Foreign Trade, sometimes translated as Domestic and Foreign Commerce; 'Econ. Co-op w. Soc. Bloc.'—Economic and Cultural Co-operation with Socialist Countries; 'State Affairs'—Inspection of State Affairs, the function of which I am uncertain; 'Disabled & Soc. Affairs'—Disabled Veterans and Social Affairs; 'Pres. Office'—in charge of the President's Office. The 1985 changes were reported in: *Kampuchea*, No. 284, 21 February (Taing Sarim); *Kampuchea*, No. 285, 28 February (Disabled Veterans); *Kampuchea*, No. 287, 14 March (Khun Chhy); *Kampuchea*, No. 290, 4 April (Tea Banh); *Summary of World Broadcasts*, 27 August 1985 (Chan Phin); ibid., 29 August 1985 (Say Phouthang).
31. Former DK names in the latest structure are Heng Samrin, Men Chhan, Chea Sim, Math Ly, Hun Sen, Sim Ka, Ouk Bun Chhoeun and Ung Phan. Vietnam veterans are Say Phouthang, Nou Beng, Chan Si, Bou Thang, Chea Soth, Khang Sarin, Meas Samnang, Khun Chhy, Taing Sarim and Chan Phin. See further below, Chapter 6, 'The Party'. Removal of the 'Minister of Interior' [Khang Sarin] was reported in *The Economist* Intelligence Unit (1984–5), and was rumoured to Ben Kiernan in Phnom Penh in January 1985.
32. I.e. agents of enemy factions cannot be recognized by their appearance or their language before they act.
33. In the communiqué of the tenth conference of Indo-Chinese Foreign Ministers in Ho Chi Minh City, January 1985, it was stated that 'within five to ten years' time the so-called Kampuchea problem will of itself be settled ('Australian Foreign Affairs Backgrounder', No. 466, 20 February 1985). The *Far Eastern Economic Review* (4 July 1985, p. 37), noted that 'The Vietnamese have set themselves a time frame of two years to wrap up the Cambodia problem'; and Hun Sen, in an interview with a Thai publication, said they hoped for total withdrawal of Vietnamese troops within five years. See *SWB* (22 July 1985). Reports both within Cambodia and from refugees at the border show that numbers and authority of Vietnamese civilian advisers have diminished over the past two to three years.

Chapter 5

1. For further remarks on these matters, see Thion & Vickery (1982, pp. 395–419); and Vickery (1984, Chap. 1).
2. See Vickery (1984, pp. 81–2) for an outline of DK class theory.
3. See below, Chapter 9, 'The Economy'.
4. See below, 'The Economy'.
5. See below, 'The Military', in Chapter 8.

Chapter 6

1. See *Kong tap padiwat*, 27 June 1981. On Third Congress, January 1979, see below. See also Vickery (1984, pp. 196–202). To avoid confusion with the name of the Khmer People's Revolutionary Party (KPRP) of the 1950s, I have chosen to render the name of the present party as PRPK.
2. Or, as Kiernan (1984, p. 109, n. 111) put it, a 'translated captured document declassified by the US Government in 1978'. On Pol Pot's party history, see Kiernan (1984, pp. 364–7), and Chandler (1983b, pp. 288–300).
3. This interpretation has been accepted in Heder (1979, pp. 2–23), Kiernan (1984), Chandler (1983b), Vickery (1984, p. 197). Heder does not indicate where he obtained the September 1951 date, but it was probably from the same document as that used by Kiernan.
4. See discussion below.
5. See discussion below.
6. See Kiernan (1984, pp. 78–85) on the founding of the Cambodian party.
7. See Kiernan (1984, pp. 79–80, 82). The Vietnamese source is Tân Huyên and Pham Thành (1980, pp. 119–20). It must be emphasized that this work places the information at the end of 1950, before noting the events of 1951.
8. Kiernan (1984, p. 82). The second Vietnamese work cited above is Pham Nguyên Long, Thành Dú'c Tân Huyên (1980, p. 67), thus published in the same year as Kiernan's *Dat Nu'o'c*. The third Vietnamese compilation is *Tim hieu dat nu'o'c Campuchia nah hung*, with articles by eleven authors and published by the same house as the second work, in 1979. Unlike the other two books, its material is footnoted to early or apparently original sources. Thus, the material on the Issarak Front and Son Ngoc Minh's declaration of independence is sourced to a work of 1952, while the information on the party's founding date as well as the details on ICP branches in Cambodia which Kiernan incorporated in his study are sourced to 'Materials of the Committee for the Study of the History of the Party' (Tu' lieu su'u tam cua Ban Nghien cu'u lich su' Dang). *Campuchia dat nu'o'c* cites *Tim hieu* as source for ICP branches in Cambodia, but does not footnote the other details, while *Dat nu'o'c*, Kiernan's source, provides no references at all, but the passages in question are nearly verbatim copies of the more thorough document.
9. *Kampuchea*, **92**, 18 June 1981; and the organization is called *Kana cheat mutkaha machim nokor khmer*—slightly different from the term picked up by Kiernan.
10. See below, pp. 65–73. More controversial evidence is to be found in a pamphlet, 'Khmer Armed Resistance', published in English by the Khmer Peace Committee in October 1952, and thus a document of rare contemporaneity, at least outside the Vietnamese archives (in the Bibliothèque Nationale, Paris, catalogue No. 16°0²1.1287). It records the 200-member Congress of early 1950, the formation of the Issarak Front with Tou Samouth as chairman, the formation of a Provisional Government with Son Ngoc Minh as chairman, the

March 1951 conference to form an 'Alliance Bloc' of the three Indo-China peoples, the assassination of the French commissioner in Phnom Penh in November 1951, an attack on a Battambang train in February 1952, and other military victories; and in conclusion it refers to the Khmer leadership: Chairman Son Ngoc Minh, Tou Samouth and Sieu Heng. On all these points it is very close to the other standard sources, but there is *no mention* of the founding of a party at all. This suggests that there may be no precise answer to the question about the party's founding date, that there may have been no formal founding in 1951, or that it was known only to a very restricted group, or that it simply grew informally around the Front and Provisional Government leadership, with everyone else assuming its existence. Some PRK sources seem to share this view. A supplementary issue of *Phnom Penh*, 10 October 1985, on the occasion of the Fifth Party Congress, published an article from the Party's Central Committee for Propaganda and Education, entitled 'From One Congress to Another'. There the date of the first Congress is given, in a subtitle, as 28 June 1951, but the text states that, following the February 1951 decision of the Indo-China Party to split into three national parties, the 'Directorates [*khana aphibal*] in charge of regional party affairs called a cadres' conference to decide on the founding of the party ... that cadres' conference [date unspecified] has been taken as the First Congress, the Party's founding Congress'.

11. Interview in Hanoi with AFP, reported in *Summary of World Broadcasts* (*SWB*), 16 January 1979.
12. *Summary of World Broadcasts*, 16 January and 7 February 1979, interviews in Hanoi and Berlin.
13. 'Front d'Union Nationale pour le Salut du Kampuchea', Phnom Penh, 1979. For the use of 'zone' and 'region', see Vickery (1984, Chap. 3, n. 5).
14. *SWB*, 5 July 1979. The last name was published in *SWB* as 'Chan Kiri', but it must be an error for 'Chan Si'. Note that when a Finnish party delegation visited in January 1980, they were announced as having visited Chea Sim and Heng Samrin, and as making connections with the Front, the Revolutionary People's Council, and the Cambodian People (*SWB*, 29 January 1980). I wish to thank Stephen Heder for suggesting the significance of the announcement about the Japanese delegation. Retrospectively, the only name in the list which surprises is Keo Prasath, then only second man in the Foreign Ministry, later in 1979 ambassador to the Soviet Union, now working in the central party organization.According to *Far Eastern Economic Review Yearbook 1980*, pp. 205–6, he is the son of the revolutionary veteran, Keo Moni, who studied in Moscow and Hanoi, and lived in Vietnam before returning to Cambodia.
15. See Chapter 7 below, on draft texts of the Constitution.
16. Decisions Nos. 85 s.r.m.chh., undated; 84 s.r.m.chh., 9 May 1980; 60 s.r.m.chh., 21 April 1980; 87 s.r.m.chh., 22 April 1980; published in PRK (1984, Vol. 1, pp. 97–104).
17. *Kampuchea*, **34**, April 1980. The celebration was on 13 april.

18. Throughout the years 1955–70, the date of independence, 1953, when it was granted to Sihanouk by the French, or 1954 after the Geneva Conference, was a sore point which divided Sihanouk from his rivals of both left and right. It is interesting that Chea Sim wished to avoid that question.
19. *Kampuchea*, **91**, 11 June 1981, p. 4. The Congress resolutions added that midway through 1960 Pol Pot and Ieng Sary began to take control of the party to make it into an organ for betrayal of the revolution.
20. Kathleen Gough (1982, p. 57, n. 2) reported seeing a photograph of forty-four members at the Third Congress, 'early in 1979'.
21. Chea Sim's speech, apparently entire, in *Kampuchea*, **89**, 28 May 1981.
22. An outline of the report was given in *Kong tap padiwat*, **27**, June 1981. I have seen only a French translation of the full report, apparently an official one done in Phnom Penh, and which was kindly lent to me by Ben Kiernan. Page citations here are to this French typescript.
23. Yukanthor undertook his anti-French campaign while in France, and then went into comfortable exile in Siam without ever returning to Cambodia. See above, p. 5.
24. Kiernan (1984, p. 114, n. 130) quotes a long passage from a 'Viet Minh' document which illustrates this view.
25. This line and the Vietnamese documentary source, is quoted in Stephen R. Heder (1979, pp. 2–23) and in Kiernan (1984, p. 113, n. 129). Further illustrations of the complexity, and I would say insolubility, of this problem, are Kiernan's statements, taken from apparently contemporary sources and participants, that a 'provisional central committee for liberation' was formed in April 1950, and that, according to a contemporary Vietnamese source, on 8 February 1951, i.e. the next-to-last day of the ICP Congress, Le Duc Tho called nine 'Cadre Committees' (admittedly an unclear formulation) of the ICP in Cambodia to a plenary session to form the new Cambodian party right after the ICP Second Congress (Kiernan, 1984, p. 130). Thus, the Vietnamese as well as the Khmer lines on this subject have varied and I find the arbitrary choice of one of them as 'the truth' to be an unconvincing procedure.
26. *Kampuchea*, **90**, 4 June 1981, p. 8, from which all citations from Le Duan's speech are taken.
27. Pen Sovann's Political Report, p. 64. According to Stephen Heder's interviews in 1980, the PRK authorities were already discomfited to find that there was a danger of *khum* organization being taken over by Sihanouk and Lon Nol-regime officials. See Heder (1980c, pp. 12–16 and 'From Pol Pot to Pen Sovan [sic]', pp. 21–31).
28. See below, pp. 167–71.
29. See Chapter 3, above, n. 22; and see Vickery (1984, Chap. 5) for similar suggestions I made there about the path of the Cambodian revolution.
30. *Kong tap padiwat*, **27**, June 1981. There was also an official French translation, a copy of which Ben Kiernan has provided me.

31. Names from *Kampuchea*, **90**, 4 June 1981, and standard romanizations, in so far as listed, from PRK, Ministère des Affaires Etrangères, Départment de Protocole, 'Liste des dirigeants kampuchéens', 1984. Not all of the 1981 names figure in the 1984 list, as I shall comment below; and one, Rong Chream Kaysan, seems to have been rebaptized—Rong Thomea Kaysan. In 'National Assembly Biographies' (trans.) he is named 'Rong Chreamkesan' (Rong Prhamkesan?), indicating difficulties in reading Khmer script, but in the list of Central Committee members published after the Fifth Party Congress (*Pracheachon*, **3**, 16 October 1985, p. 2), he is called 'Rong Phlam Kaysan'. The confusion is real and not restricted to foreign translators. The other explanation, that there are three Rong . . . Kaysans, one in the Central Committee in 1981, another in 1984, and a third in 1985, seems unlikely.
32. The information here has been taken from 'National Assembly biographies', since all but Sim Ka were also elected to the Assembly in May 1981. Ben Kiernan has information that Sim Ka was an East Zone DK official.
33. The report of the cadre conference was in *Kampuchea* **270**, 15 November 1984, the Khmer text of which clearly said eight *alternate* members, without naming them. Unfortunately, the English and French versions of the daily SPK news bulletins said 'eight new members' (10 November)/'huit nouveaux membres' (14 November), which probably misled Paul Quinn-Judge (1985b, pp. 18–19). Men Sam An's elevation to full membership was noted in *Kampuchea*, **256**, 9 August 1984, p. 6; and reference to Chheng Phon as alternate member is in *SWB*, 21 May 1985. Say Chhum was named in *Kampuchea*, **282**, 7 February 1985. Nay Pena was quickly promoted to full membership in February 1985, according to *Kampuchea*, **286**, 7 March 1985.
34. Information on Chheng Phon in China is from an interview with Ben Kiernan on 28 August 1981.
35. On Hang Thun Hak, see above, p. 20. The information here on Hang Thun Hak and associates is admittedly heresay. No such reports could have been published under Sihanouk, and under Lon Nol it was inexpedient to call attention to their leftist background. It was nevertheless current oral tradition among intellectuals, and I heard it as early as 1964 from Kong Orn, a sympathizer of the group and during 1972–5 a close collaborator of Hang Thun Hak.
36. Nay Pena's promotion to Full Member was reported in *Kampuchea*, **286**, 7 March 1985; and his position in Preah Vihear, in *SWB*, 30 April 1985, further information in personal communication from Ben Kiernan.
37. According to information obtained by Ben Kiernan in Phnom Penh in January 1986, Sar Kheng and Say Chhum worked closely with veteran communist Nay Sarann until the latter was arrested in 1976, after which they went into dissidence.
38. See Pen Sovann (1981, pp. 77–8), the French version. Later figures from Chanda (1981b) and Quinn-Judge (1984).

39. See Quinn-Judge (1985c, p. 32): '95% of [Ho Chi Minh] city's party and mass-organization membership had joined up after 30 April 1975'; and 'by the late 1970s the party organization, at least in Ho Chi Minh City, was re-assessing all members who had joined after 1974'.
40. Keo Chenda, cited in *SWB*, 4 January 1984; August report in *SWB*, 5 August 1984.
41. Advance announcements about the Fifth Congress were reported in *Summary of World Broadcasts*, 1 July, 9 August, 29 August 1985. The last described a Kompong Speu provincial congress chaired by Say Phouthang, chief of the Party's Organizing Committee. See also Quinn-Judge (1985d, pp. 42–3).
42. *Pracheachon*, **3**, 16 October 1985, pp. 1–2. The Central Committee list cannot possibly be in order of rank, and it seems to have been put together quite randomly. The same lists were published in *SWB*, 17 October 1985. The information on Ros Chhun is from Quinn-Judge (1985d), who was mistaken there about Neou Samom whom he confused with Neou Sam.
43. This was shown by the list of leading personalities attending a seventh anniversary celebration of the Front (*Pracheachon*, **14**, 3 December 1985, p. 4).
44. The increase in military personnel in the Central Committee indicates that the elimination of Soeuy Keo had more to do with his Vietnam background than with party dissatisfaction with the military, as speculated by Quinn-Judge (1985d, pp. 42–3). The list here ignores the different types of provincial party organizations, which I discuss below.
45. Quinn-Judge (1985d), plus the research of Ben Kiernan who has supplied the detail on Kong Korm's, Nguon Nhel's and Yos Sons's backgrounds. Quinn-Judge mistakenly attributed Chheng Phon's theatre background to Pen Navuth.
46. See above, p. 47. Two whose photos in *Pracheachon* (**4**, 18 October 1985, p. 2) suggest relative youth are Kai Kim Yan and Khoy Khhun Huor.
47. *Far Eastern Economic Review* (26 September 1985, p. 7) predicted that Hun Sen would become the new Secretary-General.
48. Personal communication from Ben Kiernan who will give the evidence in detail in a forthcoming publication. He was also informed that 'core' group membership was over 70,000, to be compared with the 4,000 claimed by Pen Sovann in his Political Report to the Fourth Congress in 1981. One article in the PRK press which indicated rapid party expansion revealed that Kandal Province had eighty party branches, twenty-eight of them at *khum* level, as well as some party members in ninety-six *khum*, out of a total of over 160 *khum* in the province. The 10,000 party membership was confirmed for me by Central Committee member Kong Korm on 19 May 1986.
49. Published in *Pracheachon*, **2**, 14 October 1985. An English translation appeared in *SWB*, 17 October 1985.
50. The economic provisions of the plan as outlined in the Political Report are discussed below in Chapter 9.
51. See below, Chapter 11, on Foreign Policy.

Chapter 7

1. The Brazzaville Conference of January 1944 established the policy for the first post-war agreements between France and the colonies. It was decided that representative assemblies should be set up in the colonies on the basis of universal suffrage, but that self-government should not be allowed. This was concretized for Cambodia in the *Modus Vivendi* signed on 7 January 1946, which made Cambodia an autonomous state within the French Union.
2. A detailed study is Gour (1965). See also discussions of party politics in Vickery (1982b) and in Kiernan (1984, Chap. 3).
3. République Khmère, Ministère de l'Information (1970), 'Projet de Constitution soumis au referendum le 30 Avril 1972', 'Bulletin d'Information République khmère', Paris, Nos. 29/72, 21 August 1972; *Far Eastern Economic Review*, 23 October 1971 and 18 March 1972.
4. Text of the constitution in Ponchaud (1976, pp. 217–26).
5. Front Central Committee, 'Documents of the Second Congress of the Solidarity Front for the Salvation of Kampuchea' [in Khmer], Phnom Penh, September 1979, p. 28.
6. Ibid., p. 39.
7. Kampuchean People's Revolutionary Council order No. 06, 14 October 1979, in *SWB*, 24 November 1979.
8. *Kampuchea*, **49**, mid-August 1980. The other fifteen members were: Vandy Kaon, Mat Ly, Nu Beng, Chan Ven, Sun Hong, Minh Kosany, Nhim Vanda, Sau Phan, Chhuor Leang Huot, Yit Sovann, Uk Sokon, Thu Somuni, Cha Sim, Meas Samnang, Kev Samut.
9. *Kong tap padiwat* (Revolutionary Army), **11**, October 1980.
10. I have only seen a French version. The preceding acts were Front declaration of 2 December 1978; Kampuchean People's Revolutionary Council decision No. 32 of 29 November 1979; Constitutional Council meeting, 11 April 1980; Party Central Committee meeting, 18 April 1980.
11. That is, Pen Sovann, Deputy Chairman and probably dominant personality on one committee, and Say Phouthang, chairman of the other committee, clearly represented different factions.
12. My Khmer version of this text is dated only '1980'. It was not mentioned in the press and no names are attached.
13. *Kong tap padiwat*, **20**, February 1981; *Kampuchea*, **76**, 26 February 1981.
14. *Kampuchea*, **78-9**, 12 and 19 March 1981. Text in No. 78.
15. *Kong tap padiwat*, **29**, end June 1981, on first Assembly sitting; and *Kampuchea*, **95**, 9 July 1981 for the final text. In the following discussion this will be referred to as the July 1981, or final, text.
16. See Chapter 4 above, and Chapter 8 below.
17. Angkor Wat has one central tower and four corner towers on the next lower level of the temple edifice. When viewed directly from east or west, a three-

tower silhouette appears, but when seen from an angle, all five towers are visible.

18. Translated from the second, Khmer, version of 1980. The French text of July 1980 has somewhat different wording, but it may be a vagary of translation.
19. A persistent subject of contention between Sihanouk and his leftist and anti-monarchist opposition during 1955–70 was whether independence had come via Sihanouk's dealings with the French in 1953, or after Geneva in 1954.
20. Text of Socialist Republic of Vietnam Constitution in *SWB*, 27 August 1979.
21. See below on National Assembly.
22. See Chapter 10 below, 'Ethnic Minorities'.
23. To use the Khmer wording of the second 1980 draft here, probably more faithful to the intent of the time than the earlier French version.
24. See Chapter 8 pp. 123–6, 'The Military'.
25. See above, p. 46. I wish to thank Stephen Heder for calling my attention to this matter.

Chapter 8

1. Two pre-1975 provinces have been combined into Siemreap-Oudar Meanchey. The number of sub-provincial units is taken from Front (1980) and may not be entirely accurate since changes at this level are made from time to time. A 1979 school geography text, from which I have taken the number of *srok* per *khet*, gave totals of 118 *srok*, 1,080 *khum*, and only 3,500 *phum*. In early 1986 Phnom Penh was reorganized and a new administrative unit, the *Khaud*, created.
2. Constitution, article 66, section 5; articles 71 and 74.
3. Constitution, article 3.
4. Constitution, Chapter 6 treats the Council of Ministers; and see PRK (1984, Vol. 2, pp. 15–31).
5. This election was authorized by Decree-Law No. 03 kr. c. 81 of 3 March 1981 (PRK, 1984, Vol. 1, pp. 31–54), which referred for its authority to the Front Declaration of 2 December 1978, Front Decision of 29 September 1979, and Decision No. 32 of 29 November 1979.
6. *Kampuchea*, **297**, 17 January 1985; and see below, 'Ariculture', p. 147, and 'Ethnic Affairs', p. 170. Information on the extension of the Assembly is from Ben Kiernan and *SWB*, 10 February 1986.
7. *Kampuchea*, **43**, June 1980; *Summary of World Broadcasts, Part 3, The Far East*, 11 July 1979; 1 March 1979; 24 May 1979; 8 September 1979; 6 June 1979; 20 August 1979; and quotation from Front (1980, p. 28).
8. The 1981 list is in *Kampuchea*, **85**, 30 April 1981. Where no names are listed for 1984–5 there is uncertainty. Some of the 1981 incumbents are no doubt holding the same posts, but an announcement in *Kampuchea*, **285**, 28 February 1985

indicated that changes were being made in Kompong Cham. Battambang, Kandal and Stung Treng.

9. Information on Central Committee membership is from *Kampuchea*, **90**, 4 June 1981. Kim Yin in Kompong Cham was in *Kampuchea*, **36**, April 1980. Keo Chenda as President of the Phnom Penh PRC is in Ministère des Affaires Étrangères, Départment de Protocole, 'Liste des dirigeants kampuchéens', 1984; and the information on Thong Khon is from *Summary of World Broadcasts*, 3 June 1985. Vann Sonn was in *Summary of World Broadcasts*, 6 June 1979 and 20 August 1979. Appointments later than the 1981 list are from Front (1982) (Prom Kuen, Mây Soeuy, Hem Samin); *Kampuchea*, **277**, 3 January 1985 (Hem Samin), *Kampuchea*, **283**, 14 February 1985 (Thoek Kroeun Vuttha), *Kampuchea*, **287**, 14 March 1985 (Kev Sin); *Summary of World Broadcasts*, 1 July 1985 (Hun Neng). By 1985, in Kompong Chhnang, Dok Narin had taken the post of Secretary of the Provincial Party Committee, while Kev Sin had become President of the PRC (*Kampuchea*, **279**, 17 January 1985).
10. Decree-Law (*kret-chbap*) No. 01 kr. c. 81, 16 January 1981, concerning Elections to Choose Members of Revolutionary Peoples Committees for sub-district (*khum*) and ward (*sangkat*), published in PRK (1984, Vol. 1, pp. 17–30). Two wards of Phnom Penh had held their elections in January. The Phnom Penh elections were reported in *Kampuchea*, **80-81**, 26 March and 2 April, 1981; and results for the entire country began to be reported in *Kampuchea*, **83**, 16 April 1981, which listed the electoral turnouts for only twenty-nine *khum* in five provinces, plus the city of Phnom Penh; and publication of those elections results was not resumed in later issues.
11. See Chapter 7 above, 'The Constitution'.
12. Thus, not only were results for most of the country not reported (see note 10 above), but Pen Sovann, in his political report to the Fourth Party Congress, complained about poor results.
13. PRK (1984): see note 4, above.
14. *Kampuchea*, **285**, 28 February 1985. Kai Kim Yan in Battambang, Yaem Yon in Kandal, and Veng Khhuon in Stung Treng, have been revealed in *Pracheachon*, Lay Samon's whereabouts discovered in Phnom Penh May 1986.
15. See Chapter 4, above.
16. This and further information below is from Front (1982), and interview with Mme Peou Lida, Deputy General Secretary of the Front National Council, in November 1984. The figure for total Front membership was obtained by Ben Kiernan in January 1986.
17. The situation displayed is that of 1984–5. For provincial posts held by Central Committee members and other changes see Chapter 6 above.
18. The last, a member of royalty, daughter of Sisowath Monipong, a brother of Sihanouk's mother (*Cambodge*, a Phnom Penh newspaper, announced her birth in its issue No. 149, 19 September 1945). She is thus a granddaughter of King Monivong (1927–41) and a first cousin of Sihanouk.

19. See 'The Military', below.
20. *Kong tap padiwat*, **111-12**, 8 and 12 December 1983; quotation from No. 112.
21. *Kong tap padiwat*, **105-106**, 27 October and 3 November 1983; and see above, 'The Party'.
22. Decree-Law No. 01 k.c. on the organization of Revolutionary People's Courts; and Decree-Law No. 02 k.c., on sentences, both dated 15 May 1980, and published in PRK (1984, Vol. 1, pp. 3–15). 'Law on the organization of tribunals and the office of prosecutor', dated 10 February 1982, published in ibid., Vol. 2, pp. 1–10.
23. PRK (1984); and Information from interview with Ministry of Justice lawyers, Phnom Penh, November 1984.
24. *Kampuchea*, **142**, 3 June 1982. Prisons are operated by the Ministry of Interior rather than the Justice Ministry, and are not open to objective investigation by foreign scholars.
25. A New York based 'Lawyers' Committee for International Human Rights' (1984) alleged that there was no respect for the rule of law in the PRK. The claim was made without any examination, apparently without any knowledge of, laws in force in the PRK, or of courts which function. Their witnesses who claimed arbitrary arrest and brutal prison treatment were few in number and mostly from the conflict-stricken north-west. As Ben Kiernan's analysis of the lawyers' report showed, their own material revealed more instances of capricious arrest, prison brutality and prisoner deaths in the small DK-controlled camps on the Thai border than in all the rest of Cambodia under the PRK.
26. *Summary of World Broadcasts*, 22 July 1985; *Pracheachon*, 10, 19 November 1985, p. 1; and see Chapter 7, 'The Constitution', above.
27. See 1 August speech by Singapore First Deputy Prime Minister Goh Chok Tong to university students, cited from *The Age* (5 August 1985, p. 9), also reported in *Far Eastern Economic Review* (15 August 19895, p. 10); and on Pen Sovann, see above, p. 70.
28. Vickery (1982b); in Chapter 3 above.
29. See, for examples, *Bangkok Post* (28 January 1985) on mistreatment of prisoners and refugees by Son Sann's KPNLF; Quinn-Judge (1985d, pp. 28–9); Bekaert (1985) on abuses of human rights by the KPNLF.
30. Although intellectuals in the advanced democracies should always strive towards an ideal, it is intellectually dishonest to single out any poor, war-torn nation for criticism against that ideal without giving equal consideration to the total situation, including local traditions, developments in the recent past, and conditions prevailing in other comparable countries. The Lawyers' Committee deny that the relativity argument should be used in relation to the PRK, but in their report they performed veritable intellectual contortions to give relative respectability to Pol Pot and his DK remnants. Their report was indeed 'political propaganda', as I wrote, and to which charge they took exception in *The Washington Post* (23 August 1985). In fact, assuming the stories to be true in

outline, their witnesses, who had been released after a period of imprisonment without trial, provide evidence which could be interpreted as intervention by PRK authorities to rectify illegal acts committed during a period of tension in 1981. The pattern is evidence of an improved situation which all concerned with the development of a rule of law should welcome.

31. This list is from *Summary of World Broadcasts* 16 May 1979. No such list should be assumed complete; and the first public mention of any person does not necessarily signify recent appointment.
32. Pen Sovann was named Supreme Commander in *Kampuchea* (**34**, July 1980), and still later in the report of a Military Congress in *Kong tap padiwat* (**23**, April 1981). As noted above, in Chapter 7, the post of Supreme Commander was deleted from the 1981 constitution. Sovann was last mentioned as Defence Minister in June 1981 when he gave an address on the thirtieth anniversary of the army's founding (*Kong tap padiwat*, **28**, June 1981), and by 24 June, at the opening of the first Assembly, and the installation of the new government, he was already no longer Defence Minister (*Kong tap padiwat*, **29**, July 1981). The new military hierarchy was reported in *Kong tap padiwat*, (**30**, July 1981).
33. See Chapter 4, p. 46, and n. 26.
34. The pre-Fifth Congress ranking occurs in local press reports and in a Foreign Ministry Protocol Department booklet, 'liste des dirigeants kampuchéens', 1984. In 1984 Tea Banh, still Vice-Minister, was also mentioned as Chief of Civil Aviation (*Summary of World Broadcasts*, 5 April 1984), and in 1985 he became Minister of Communications, Transport and the Postal Service. Paul Quinn-Judge (1985e) was apparently misinformed about Koy Buntha replacing Lay Samon in Battambang. The new appointments are mentioned in *Pracheachon*.
35. United States government sources implicitly recognized the truth of the first announced withdrawals in 1982 (Vickery, 1984, p. 291), and there is no reason to doubt that subsequent withdrawals have been real, even if numbers are difficult to ascertain. In September 1985, a Vietnamese Central Committee member, Hoang Tung, said there were 'about 100,000' Vietnamese troops in Cambodia, which seems credible (*Summary of World Broadcasts*, 3 September 1985).
36. In a press conference in Hanoi in 1980, Pen Sovann said that officers were not given ranks, but that this might be done later when conditions were right (*Summary of World Broadcasts*, 3 January 1980). All information here on military organization has been pieced together from diverse reports, mainly the army newspaper, *Kong tap padiwat*. I have not seen any complete table of military organization. Three particularly useful lists of units and individuals were in *Kong tap padiwat* (**52**, 25 June 1982; **55**, 25 July 1982; and **88**, 25 June 1983).
37. A figure of 30,000, supported by careful research, was offered by Timothy Carney (1982, p. 37), and 30,000 continues to be repeated in the media, for example, *Far Eastern Economic Review* (21 January 1985, p. 7). The total is probably higher, for in a recent article an American military figure involved

with Cambodia, while showing concern that the PRK army might become effective, was unwilling to offer an estimate of their strength (Eiland, 1985, pp. 106–13).

38. *Kong tap padiwat* (**136**, 31 May 1984), on setting of plan by Council of Ministers and Ministry of Defence; semi-annual drafts reported to me by Koh Thom District officials. The new State Council decree on conscription was reported in *Summary of World Broadcasts* (25 September 1985).
39. Respectively, *Kong tap padiwat*, **76**, 25 February; **79**, 25 March; **80**, 5 April; **85**, 29 May; **108**, 17 November 1983; and **136**, 31 May 1984. A year earlier it had been claimed, in *Kong tap padiwat* (**74**, 5 February 1983), that total recruitment was 5.6 per cent over plan.
40. This was brought out of the closet by Eiland (1985).
41. Although Bou Thang reportedly had a military role in the revolution before breaking with Pol Pot.
42. First announcement in *Summary of World Broadcasts*, (27 July 1985); McBeth (1985, pp. 38–9), including report of the ASEAN foreign ministers' reaction.

Chapter 9

1. Vickery (1984, Chap. 5), for comparison with Yugoslavia.
2. 'Front d'Union Nationale pour le Salut du *Kampuchea*', (1979). The following paragraph is from the same source.
3. Constitution of the People's Republic of Kampuchea, article 12.
4. See below, pp. 138–43.
5. This was recorded in *SWB*, 4 April 1980.
6. For one published example, see Pin Yathay (1980) and references to it in Vickery (1984, pp. 89, 115, 158). The most striking case of which I have heard was of a family which succeeded in carrying about 10 kg. of gold out of Phnom Penh and retaining over 5 kg. until fleeing to Khao I Dang in 1979. Needless to say, they lost most of it there.
7. The amount of Cambodian wealth exported to Thailand has been enormous. Chanda (1980) reported an estimate that 87.5 lb. of gold per day crossed the border from Sisophon; and on the Thai side it was estimated in 1980 that 'about 50 million baht [$2.5 million] of goods in the black market is daily transacted [with Cambodians on the border] and in the banks in Aranyaprathet, about 30–40 million baht of money is deposited every day . . . mostly from the black market operation' (*The Nation Review*, 12 September 1980).
8. In Phnom Penh in November 1984 a doctor at the 7 January Hospital told me of patients becoming ill, and on occasion dying, after using defective drugs purchased in the market.
9. The major destruction of libraries, of which the outside world was made aware in 1979, may no longer be imputed exclusively, or even principally, to DK.

There is ample eye-witness testimony to looting and resale during 1979; and the remnants of old libraries and archives are still on sale in Phnom Penh. See Vickery (1984, p. 227), for one example; and note the declarations of the new PRK government: a memo by Heng Samrin, 24 February 1979, on protection of state property and property abandoned by private owners admitted much looting (*SWB*, 7 March 1979); and another memo from the Information Ministry urged people to hand over to the authorities antiques dumped by DK, saying over one thousand items had already been recovered (*SWB*, 12 July 1979). On gold from mass graves, see Chanda (1980).

10. In a response to a letter from Hans Luther, Nayan Chanda reported observing such Vietnamese and Soviet aid, saying that while it was impossible to verify the amounts that had been claimed, such as 200,000 tons of food from the Soviet Union, he had seen 'large amounts' of Thai rice bought by the Soviet Union from Thailand, American corn also sent by the Soviet Union, and Vietnamese rice during 1979 (*Far Eastern Economic Review*, 25 April 1980, p. 5).
11. See *Far Eastern Economic Review Yearbook 1980*, for July 1979, p. 208; *Asiaweek*, 12 October 1979, p. 19; and Vickery (1984, pp. 228–29).
12. See Vickery (1984, p. 229), where I was in error in stating that the change occurred in April. *Far Eastern Economic Review* (4 April 1980) reported the first cash salary payments to state employees on 25 March. Locally, the change was reported in *Kampuchea* (No. 32, end of March), with details of the Proclamation of 20 March 1980 on the printing of new money, and detailed descriptions of each of the new bills, without, however, any information on prices, salary levels, or rates of exchange. The original authorization to introduce a new *riel* had apparently been a Circular of 10 October 1979 of the People's Revolutionary Council indicating a plan to effect the change even earlier. Also reported in *SWB* (**12**, 22 March 1980); and see *Far Eastern Economic Review Yearbook 1980*, p. 170.
13. Corrèze & Forrest avec Vu Can (1984, pp. 156–7) for the state purchase price figure; Vickery (1984, pp. 229–31); and *Far Eastern Economic Review Yearbook 1981*, p. 170; see also Barry Wain, *Asian Wall Street Journal* (29 January 1981). Shawcross (1984b, pp. 264–5) characteristically muddles the story of the new *riel*, claiming that it favoured state employees to the disadvantage of everyone else, by forcing a devaluation of the *dong* which had hitherto been a market currency. Whatever was decreed, the *riel–dong* rate stabilized at 1 to 3, and later 1 to 4, though the effect of supply and demand, and even if there had been an effort by the state to call in *dong* in private hands, it could have had no effect, as the foreign currency still in private hands testifies. Private *dong*, then as now, would cross the border for purchases in Vietnam. As for the peasants, who had been selling rice at 1 kg. for 1 *dong*, after April 1980 they could sell 1 kg. for 1 *riel*, equivalent to 3 *dong*, and thus purchase more foreign commodities than before. As explained further below, PRK currency policies, whatever their defects, have favoured the peasants relative to other economic sectors. Measures

to collect Vietnamese *dong* from the public only began in late 1985 (*SWB*, 16 and 24 September 1985).

14. 'Decree-Law on Income Taxes' and 'Decree-Law on Import Taxes' both passed 27 November 1982 by the State Council, published in PRK (1984, Vol. 3, pp. 27–44).
15. New Decree-Laws Nos. 22, 23 and 24, dated 14 June 1985, and reported in *SWB* (30 July 1985), but it is too early to know anything of their implementation.
16. *Kampuchea*, (**127**, 18 February 1982) and *Kampuchea* (**278**, 7 January 1985).
17. Ibid.
18. This is apparent from the 30 August 1980 decision on 'Increasing the family Economy'—English translation by Chantou Boua (1980). Given the total destruction of land records, and the imprecise titles held by many peasants at the best of times, state adjudication of such disputes in favour of alleged former owners would have been an administrative nightmare, and the decision taken was the only rational one, quite aside from any question of 'socialist' vs. free enterprise principles.
19. Report on agriculture for 1979 and early 1980 in *Kampuchea* (**36**, April 1980).
20. Circular No. 47 k-p, 20 December 1979, reproduced in PRK (1980).
21. See note 18 above.
22. Grunewald (1983, p. 16), and a new resolution regarding the peasantry adopted by a National Cadres Conference in November 1984 and published in SPK (16 November 1984).
23. PRK news bulletin, SPK [in English] (16 November 1984, pp. 1–4).
24. Data on 1979–82 and 1983–84 figures are in Quinn-Judge (1985a, p. 66). The planned hectarage, an estimate (64 per cent) of fulfilment, and discussion of the situation by Agriculture Minister Kong Samol was in SPK [in Khmer] (5 November 1984). A new, slightly higher, figure for 1984 production was published in *Kampuchea* (**278**, 7 January 1985). At productivity of 1 ton per hectare, just over 10 per cent of total paddy production is required for seed; and if consumption is based on a daily ration of 400 g. of milled rice, annual per capita consumption is 227 kg. of paddy (paddy › rice conversion faction is 0.64). Thus, the 1982 production of 1,563,000 tons minus 156,300 tons for seed would leave enough for a population of 6.2 million, whereas the population was estimated to be 6.8 million. Even if allowance is made for the large number of small children who do not require 400 g., hardworking adults may require more, and the national average does not reveal the differences between areas of surplus and deficit, equalization of which the country's inadequate transport system does not permit.
25. Grunewald (1983) comments on this deficiency; and the figures I have used here are from his study, taken in turn from the Ministry of Agriculture and from Tichit (1981). The 1967 figures show a ratio of 2.08 hectares planted per animal, and the 1982 figures only 1.5; but the 1967 ratio with the 1982 total of animals would result in 2.04 million hectares planted, producing at 1982 yields 2.16

million tons of paddy, which, if distribution was perfect, might be enough for the population of just over 7 million. Of course, distribution of both animals and product is uneven, and it has been well known since 1979 that some provinces, such as Mondolkiri, far from the urban centres, are over-supplied, while others are perennially in deficit.

26. Boua translation (1980), KPRC Decision of 30 August 1980 (note 18 above), p. 12; and *SPK*, 16 November 1984, p. 3.
27. Official taxes on agriculture after 1954 were low and collection was lax, but in 1965 there was an attempt to increase tax by the expedient of reclassifying land (See Vickery, 1984, p. 264, and n. 24). Peasants were perennially in debt, pledging their crops in advance for supplies at rates of often up to 100 per cent; and throughout the 1960s *ad hoc* 'voluntary contributions' were assessed by officials at all levels for various constructive or decorative purposes. Thus, I noted in October 1962, in Siemreap, announcements about the collection of money for the repair of the town's market. Hamlet chiefs were called to a meeting and told that they were to collect 50 *riel* per person, plus 1,000 *riel* from owners of houses made of concrete brick, 500 for a wooden house with a tile roof, 300 for large thatched houses, and 100 for very small houses. These sums were very high for all but the wealthy.
28. Hermann Schwember, a Chilean engineer working with a Dutch aid project in Phnom Penh, told me of the discovery of pumps and pump parts which had been taken by individuals after January 1979.
29. An article in the Bangkok *Nation Review* (25 January 1985) called 'Finally, something "good" from Phnom Penh', commented on the popularity of PRK cigarettes along the Cambodian–Thai border.
30. The rubber production center at Chup, in Kompong Cham Province, started by the French and now a state enterprise, was officially opened again on 8 April 1980, according to *Kampuchea* (**36**, April 1980). The 1984 figures are from *Kampuchea* (**281**, 31 January 1985).
31. *Kampuchea* (**40**, May 1980) for the PRK report on foreign aid; *Far Eastern Economic Review* (10 February 1983, p. 12) and Vickery (1984, p. 292) for the 1982 statement on Soviet aid. The rumour about Soviet aid and the Phnom Penh water supply is taken from Becker (1983); other information from personal observation in Phnom Penh, November 1984.
32. Although there have been propaganda attempts to deny any real Vietnamese aid, large amounts of food and transport were observed in 1979 by one of the most reliable Western correspondents. See note 10 above.
33. *Kampuchea* (**283**, 14 February 1985). Kompong Thom was missing from that list, but had been mentioned in a PRK news agency (*SPK*) bulletin on 6 November 1984 [in Khmer].
34. Official figures in *Far Eastern Economic Review Asia Yearbook 1985*, p. 132; other figures from *The Economist Intelligence Unit* (No. 2, 1985, Appendix 2 and p. 3 respectively). rbl. = rouble

35. The new regulations on Vietnamese *dong* in the PRK were reported in *SWB*, 16 September and 24 September 1985. The relationship to Ho Chi Minh City industry is suggested by a report in *The Economist Intelligence Unit* (No. 2, 1985, p. 20). Free *riel-dong* exchange still prevails (May 1986).
36. Figure for 1985 from *Kampuchea* (**328**, 2 January 1986, pp. 8–9).
37. ibid., and *Pracheachon* (**24**, 7 January 1986, p. 4).
38. Article 12 of the constitution defines the economy as comprising three sectors—state, co-operative and family. A report on the necessary amendment was made to the tenth session of the National Assembly, reported in *SWB* (6 February 1986).
39. The new tax regulations were outlined in *Pracheachon* Nos. **18**, 17 December 1985 to **21**, 27 December 1985.

Chapter 10

1. On the situation of education under previous regimes, see figures in *Annuaire statistique retrospectif du Cambodge (1937–1957)* (Phnom Penh, June 1985); and commentary in Vickery (1984, pp. 18–26, 101–2, 112, 171–4).
2. 'Education in the People's Republic of Kampuchea', pamphlet published by the Ministry of Education, Phnom Penh, December 1983. Information here is from this pamphlet, from an interview with Education Minister Pen Navuth on 24 November 1984, and from visits to Phnom Penh primary and secondary schools, the Language School and the Kampuchean–Soviet Higher Technical Institute.
3. See below, 'Ethnic Minorities'.
4. See Panaritis (1985, particularly pp. 2–3).
5. For Thailand, see Suksamran (1977, p. 27), on the duties and responsibilities of the Department of Religious Affairs, and p. 28, 'Primary Aims'.
6. Circular No. 1 s.c., PRK (1980, pp. 96–100). For Thai similarities, see Suksamran (1977, p. 32).
7. The problem of private, unorthodox resumption of monk status was evoked in the PRK regulations on ordination. See note 9, below.
8. For similar official Thai concern with 'unworthy candidates' for ordination, see Suksamran (1977, p. 28), 'Specific Aims', No. 9.
9. PRK (1980, p. 125) and Circular No. 24–81, s.1, of the Central Committee of the Front for Solidarity and Salvation of Kampuchea, dated 5 June 1981, on the subject of 'Ordination' (PRK, 1984, pp. 173–7). See also *SWB* (21 and 28 September 1979), where the arrival of a Vietnamese Theravada delegation was reported, but not the fact that it was involved in the reordination. There is some sensitivity within the Cambodian leadership to the fact of Vietnamese aid in this domain. When I enquired about this of Mme Peou Lida, Vice-President of the Front, and in charge of religious affairs, she vehemently denied the Vietnamese

role, affirming that reordination had started with Long Sim, 'a revolutionary monk for over 50 years', in the liberated zone; although she avoided answering a query about where he had been during DK, and when his 'liberated zone' activities had begun.

10. Suksamran (1977, p. 28), 'Specific Aims', Nos. 7 and 8, suggests that Thai authorities would also view this as desirable.
11. As in Thailand, the 'Sangha administrative structure . . . parallels and copies that of the civil government'—Suksamran (1977, pp. 38–9, 41–5).
12. Ordination regulations are in Circular No. 24–81, cited in note 9 above.
13. In a response to Elizabeth Becker's articles on Cambodia (Becker, 1983), I suggested that she was mistaken in the name 'Niroatraingsey'. Having now visited that *wat*, and in the company of the same person who was Becker's Foreign Ministry guide, I wish to apologize for my error, which was due to the fact that Wat Niroatraingsey, located outside the Phnom Penh city limits, was not on a list of Phnom Penh *wats* in my possession.
14. In Vickery (1984, p. 293), I reported a story from a refugee in Khao-I-Dang about alleged plans to close Wat Keo Preah Phloeung, which I thought might have caused a rumour about suppression of religion reported by Elizabeth Becker (Becker, 1983). In fact, my source must have been referring to Wat Svay Poper, next door to Keo Preah Phloeung, for the latter was almost completely dismantled during DK, and in no condition to reopen at all. The inference in Vickery (1984) about false rumours remains valid, but the name is wrong, illustrating, incidentally, the ease with which false details slip into oral testimony. See further below on the *wats* in question.
15. See Suksamran (1977, p. 31) on the construction of superfluous *wats* in Thailand as a game of religio-political one-upmanship.
16. On Wat Srah Chok and Wat Saravan in 1981, see Vickery (1984, p. 183).
17. On their economic position, see above, Chapter 9, pp. 134, 135.
18. See Chapter 1, above, 'The Population', and notes 2–4.
19. The first quotation is from John C. Monjo, then Deputy Assistant Secretary for East Asian and Pacific Affairs, before the House Foreign Affairs Committee, Sub-Committee on East Asian and Pacific Affairs, 15 September 1983; and the second is by McBeth (1985, p. 39).
20. Published in *SPK* [French version cited], 17 November 1984.
21. See their names in Chapter 8, above, p. 109. In the military, Bou Thang and Soeuy Keo are Tampuon and Kachak, north-eastern minorities, respectively.

Chapter 11

1. Text of the 'Treaty of Peace, Friendship and Co-operation between the Socialist Republic of Vietnam and the People's Republic of Kampuchea' in *SWB* (20 February 1979, pp. A3/14–A3/16.

2. PRK Constitution, article 10. See above, Chapter 7.
3. See *Far Eastern Economic Review Asia 1985 Yearbook* (p. 132); and *Far Eastern Economic Review* (25 April 1985, pp. 30–1).
4. See above, Chapter 8.
5. *Far Eastern Economic Review Aisa 1985 Yearbook* (p. 131) PRK publication of Heng Samrin's speech in *Kampuchea* (**251**, 5 July 1984). See Chapter 6, above, p. 75, for another inaccuracy attributable to the *SPK* foreign-language bulletins.

Bibliography

* Indicates works of useful reference which have not been used directly in this book.

Becker, Elizabeth, 1983. 'Indochina Stalemate', parts 2 and 3, 'Cycle of Poverty' and 'New Rulers Obscure Role of Party Under Pol Pot'. *Washington Post*, 28 February–1 March.

Bekaert, Jacques, 1985. 'The Wars in Kampuchea'. *Bangkok Post*, 2 September.

Boua, Chantou (trans.), 1980. People's Republic of Kampuchea, 'Concerning the problems that need to be known, concerning the Solidarity Group for Increasing Production'. mimeo typescript.

Briggs, Lawrence Palmer, 1951. *The Ancient Khmer Empire*. Transactions of the American Philosophical Society, New Series, Vol. XLI, Part 1, Philadelphia, The American Philosophical Society.

Bunchhan Mol/Muul, 1973. *Charit Khmer* ['Khmer mores']. Phnom Penh.

Bunchhan Mol/Muul, 1972. *Kuk niyobay* ['Political prison']. Phnom Penh.

Burchett, Wilfred, 1959. *Mekong Upstream*. Berlin, Seven Seas Publishers.

Burchett, Wilfred, 1969. *Passport: An Autobiography*, Melbourne, Nelson.

Burchett, Wilfred, 1981a. *At the Barricades*, London and Melbourne, Macmillan Australia.

Burchett, Wilfred, 1981b. *The China-Cambodia-Vietnam Triangle*. London, Vanguard Books and Zed Press.

Campbell, Duncan, 1984. 'Secret Laws for Wartime Britain'. *New Statesman*. London, 6 September 1984.

*Carney, Timothy, 1977. *Communist Party Power in Kampuchea (Cambodia): Documents and Discussion*. Ithaca, Cornell University.

Carney, Timothy, 1982. 'Heng Samrin's Armed Forces and a Military Balance in Cambodia', paper presented at the International Conference on Kampuchea, Princeton University, 12–14 November, draft version.

Chanda, Nayan, 1980. 'A Phoenix from the Ashes of Death'. *Far Eastern Economic Review*, 4 April 1980.

Chanda, Nayan, 1981a. 'The Bigger Brother'. *Far Eastern Economic Review*, 5 June 1981.

Chanda, Nayan, 1981b. 'The Survivors Party'. *Far Eastern Economic Review*, 12 June 1981.

*Chandler, David P., 1972. *The Land and People of Cambodia*, Philadelphia, Lippincott.

*Chandler, David P., 1976. 'The Constitution of Democratic Kampuchea (Cambodia): The Semantics of Revolutionary Change'. *Pacific Affairs*, 49/3, Fall 1976, pp. 506–15.

*Chandler, David P., 1982. 'The Assassination of *Résident* Bardez (1925): A Premonition of Revolution in Colonial Cambodia', *Journal of the Siam Society*, Bangkok, pp. 35–49.

Chandler, David P., 1983a. *A History of Cambodia*, Boulder, Colorado, Westview Press.

Chandler, David P., 1983b. 'Revising the Past in Democratic Kampuchea: When was the Birthday of the Party?'. *Pacific Affairs*, 56/2, Summer 1983, pp. 288–300.

*Chandler, David P. & Kiernan, Ben, 1983. *Revolution and its Aftermath in Kampuchea: Eight Essays*. New Haven, Yale University Press.

*Chomsky, Noam & Herman, Edward S., 1979. *After the Cataclysm: Postwar Indo-China and the Reconstruction of Imperial Ideology*. Boston, South End Press.

Chou Norindr, 1982. 'Political institutions of the Lao People's Democratic Republic', in Martin Stuart-Fox *Contemporary Laos*, St Lucia, University of Queensland Press.

Clubb, O. Edmund, 1971. *China and Russia, the 'Great Game'* New York and London, Columbia University Press.

*Coedès, George, 1962. *Angkor*. London, Oxford University Press.

Coedès, George, 1964. *Les états hindouisés d'Indochine et d'Indonésie*. Paris, Éditions E. de Boccard.

Coedès, George, 1968. *The Indianized States of Southeast Asia*, (ed.) Walter F. Vella, trans. Susan Brown Cowing. Kuala Lumpur and Singapore, University of Malaya Press.

Corrèze, Françoise & Forrest, Alain, avec la collaboration de Vu Can, 1984. *Le Cambodge à deux voix*. Paris, Éditions L'Harmattan.

Delahaye, Victor, 1928. *La plaine des joncs et sa mise en valeur*. Rennes, Imprimerie de l'Ouest Éclair.

*Delvert, Jean, 1961. *Le paysan cambodgien*. Paris and the Hague, Mouton.

*Ebihara, May Mayko, 1968. *Svay, a Khmer village in Cambodia*. Columbia University, Ph.D. thesis, 1968.

The Economist Intelligence Unit, 1984–5. *Quarterly Economic Review of Indochina: Vietnam, Laos, Cambodia*. London, The Economist Publications Ltd., No. 4.

Eiland, Michael, 1985. 'Kampuchea in 1984'. *Asian Survey*. Berkeley, University of California, January, pp. 106–13.

Encyclopaedia Brittanica, 1985. 15th edn., Chicago, University of Chicago Press.

Encyclopaedia universalis, 1985. Paris, Encyclopaedia Universalis, France.

Far Eastern Economic Review Asia Yearbook 1985. Hong Kong.

Front d'Union Nationale pour le Salut du Kampuchea, 1979, Phnom Penh.

Front [Front d'Union Nationale pour le Salut du Kampuchea], 1980. *Premier anniversaire de la victoire*, Phnom Penh, January.

Front [Salvation Front Central Committee], 1979. 'Documents of the Second Congress of the Solidarity Front for the Salvation of Kampuchea' [in Khmer]. Phnom Penh, September.

Front [Solidarity Front for the Construction and Defence of the Motherland of Kampuchea], 1982. *Statutes* [in Khmer]. Phnom Penh.

Gough, Kathleen, 1982. 'Interviews in Kampuchea'. *BCAS*, 14/4.

Gour, Claude-Gilles, 1965. *Institutions constitutionelles et politiques du Cambodge*. Paris, Librairie Dalloz.

Great Soviet Encyclopedia, 1973, New York, Macmillan.

*Groslier, B. P., & Arthaud, Jacques, 1966. *Angkor: Art and Civilization*. New York, Praeger.

Grunewald, François, 1983. 'Le Kampuchea contemporain et ses problèmes de developpement agricole'. typescript, Phnom Penh.

Haudricourt, André G., 1953. 'La place du vietnamie dans les langues austroasiatiques'. *Bulletin de la Société de Linguistique*, **49**, Paris.

Heder, Stephen, 1978. 'Origins of the Conflict'. *The Southeast Asia Chronicle*, **64**, September–October.

Heder, Stephen, 1979. 'Kampuchea's Armed Struggle: The Origins of an Independent Revolution', *BCAS*, **11/1**, pp. 2–23.

Heder, Stephen, R., 1980a. 'The Kampuchean–Vietnamese Conflict', *Southeast Asian Affairs 1979*. Singapore, Institute of Southeast Asian Studies.

Heder, Stephen R., 1980b. 'From Pol Pot to Pen Sovan to the Villages', paper presented at the International Conference on Indochina and Problems of Security in Southeast Asia. Bangkok, Chulalongkorn University.

Heder, Stephen R., 1980c. *Kampuchean Occupation and Resistance*, Asian Studies Monographs No. 027. Bangkok, Institute of Asian Studies, Chulalongkorn University.

Hess, Jean, 1901. *L'Affaire Iukanthor*. Paris, Felix Juven.

Hickey, Gerald Cannon, 1982. *Free in the Forest, Ethnohistory of the Vietnamese Central Highlands 1954–1976*. Yale University Press, New Haven and London.

Jacques, Claude, 1979. '"Funan", "Zhenla", the Reality Concealed by these Chinese Views of Indochina', in *Early South-East Asia, Essays in Archaeology, History, and Historical Geography* (ed.) R. B. Smith & W. Watson, New York, Oxford University Press.

Kampuchea Démocratique, 1978. *Livre noir: faits et preuves des actes d'aggression et d'annexion du Vietnam contre le Kampuchea*. Phnom Penh, Ministère des Affaires Étrangères, September 1978.

Khieu Samphan, 1979. *Cambodia's Economy and Industrial Development*, trans. Laura Summers, Ithaca, Cornell University, South-East Asia Program Data Paper No. 111.

Kiernan, Ben [1975–6]. 'The Samlaut Rebellion and its Aftermath, 1967–70: The Origins of Cambodia's Liberation Movement', Parts I–II, in Monash University, Centre of southeast Asian Studies, Working Papers, Nos. 4 and 5, n.d.

Kiernan, Ben. 1980. 'Conflict in the Kampuchean Communist Movement'. *Journal of Contemporary Asia*, **10**, No. 1–2, pp. 7–74.

Kiernan, Ben, 1981. 'The New Political Structure in Kampuchea', *Dyason House Papers*, **8**, No. 2, Melbourne, December.

Kiernan, Ben, 1984. *How Pol Pot Came to Power*. London, Verso.

Kiernan, Ben & Boua Chantou, 1982. *Peasants and Politics in Kampuchea 1941–1981*. London, Zed Press.

*Lancaster, Donald, 1961. *The Emancipation of French Indo-China*. New York, Oxford University Press.

Lawyers' Committee for International Human Rights, Kampuchea Mission November 1984. 'Preliminary Summary of findings and Conclusions'. Typescript, New York.

Les élites khmères, 1965, Phnom Penh Université Bouddhique Preah Sihanouk Raj.

Lydall, Harold, 1984. *Yugoslav Socialism, Theory and Practice*. Oxford, Clarendon Press.

Mc Beth, John, 1985. 'Forced Human Bondage'. *Far Eastern Economic Review*, 22 August, pp. 38–9.

Migozzi, Jacques, 1973. *Cambodge faits et problemes de population*. Paris, Éditions CNRS.

'National Assembly Biographies (trans.)': Brief biographies of all candidates in the 1 May 1981 National Assembly elections, translated into English from a Khmer source. The originals appeared on electoral posters for the elections. I acquired them from Ben Kiernan, who believed the translations had been done by Stephen Heder. Heder confirms that he collected a set of posters on the spot and translated them, although at least two more sets were acquired by foreigners at the time and Heder is not certain that the set in my possession represent his translations.

Norodom Sihanouk, 1962. *Principaux discours, messages, déclarations et allocutions de Son Altesse Royale le Prince Norodom Sihanouk en 1962*. Phnom Penh, Ministère de l'Information.

Norodom Sihanouk, 1963. *Prinipaux discours, messages, allocutions déclarations, conférences de presse, et interviews de Son Altesse Royal le Prince Norodom Sihanouk année 1963*. Phnom Penh, Ministère d l'Information.

*Osborne, Milton, 1969. *The French Presence in Cochinchina and Cambodia: Rule and Response (1859–1905)*. Ithaca, Cornell University Press.

*Osborne, Milton, 1973. *Politics and Power in Cambodia*. Australia, Camberwell.

Osborne, Milton, 1978. 'Peasant Politics in Cambodia: The 1916 Affair'. *Modern Asian Studies*, **12**, No. 2.

*Osborne, Milton, 1979. *Before Kampuchea*. Sydney, Allen & Unwin.

Panaritis, Andrea, 1985. 'Cambodia: the rough Road to Recovery'. *Indochina Issues*, Washington, DC, April.

Pen Sovann, 1981. 'Political Report to the 4th Congress of the PRPK'. Typescript, Phnom Penh, n.d.

Pham Nyguên Long, Thành Dúc, Tân Huyên, 1980. *Campuchia dât nu'o'c yêu thu'o'ng tu'o'i dep bât khuât*. Hanoi, Nhà Xuât Ban Khoa Hoc Xã Hôi, Hanoi.

Picq, Laurence, 1984. *Au delà du ciel, cinq ans chez les Khmers rouges*. Paris, Éditions Bernard Barrault.

Pin Yathay, 1980. *l'Utopié meurtrière*. Paris, Éditions Robert Laffont.

Ponchaud, François, 1976. *Cambodia Year Zero*. London, Penguin.

Ponomaryov, B., Gromyko A., Khvostov, V. (eds), 1969. *History of Soviet Foreign Policy 1917–1945*. Moscow, Progress Publishers.

PRK, 1979a. 'Le Conseil Populaire Révolutionnaire du Kampuchea'. Phnom Penh.

PRK, Ministry of Education, 1979b. *Geography for 4th Grade* [in Khmer]. Phnom Penh.

PRK, Central Committee for Propaganda and Education, 1980. 'Illuminating the Revolutionary Path [in Khmer]'. I, Phnom Penh.

PRK, Ministry of Foreign Affairs, Press Department, 1983. 'Policy of the People's Republic of Kampuchea with Regard to Vietnamese Residents'. Phnom Penh, September 1983.

PRK, Ministry of Justice, 1984. *Collected Law Texts* [in Khmer]. Phnom Penh, 3 vols.

Prud'homme, Rémy, 1969. *L'Économie du Cambodge*. Paris, Presses Universitaires de France.

Quinn-Judge, Paul, 1983. 'The Settlers Show Withdrawal Symptoms'. *Far Eastern Economic Review*, 26 May, pp. 18–19.

Quinn-Judge, Paul, 1984. 'Too few Communists'. *Far Eastern Economic Review*, 16 February.

Quinn-Judge, Paul, 1985a. 'The Meagre Harvest'. *Far Eastern Economic Reviewe*, 24 January, p. 66.

Quinn-Judge, Paul, 1985b. 'Secretive Shakeup'. *Far Eastern Economic Review*, 4 April 1985, pp. 18–19.

Quinn-Judge, Paul, 1985c. 'Hanoi's Bitter Victory'. *Far Eastern Economic Review*, 2 May 1985.

Quinn-Judge, Paul, 1985d. 'Same old Khmer Rouge'. *Far Eastern Economic Review*, 9 May.

Quinn-Judge, Paul, 1985e. 'The Phnom Penh Shuffle' and 'Politburo Profiles'. *Far Eastern Economic Review*, 31 October, pp. 42–3.

*Reddi, V. M., 1971. *A History of the Cambodian Independence Movement 1863–1955*. Tirupati.

République Khmère, Ministère de l'information, 1970. 'Cabinets ministériels khmers du 18 mars 1945 à 18 mars 1970'. Phnom Penh.

Royaume du Cambodge, Ministère du Plan, 1958. *Annuaire statistique retrospectif du Cambodge (1937–1957)*. Phnom Penh, June.

Service d'Information du FUNSK, 1979. 'Front d'Union Nationale pour le Salut du Kampuchea'. Phnom Penh.

Shawcross, William, 1980. *Sideshow*. London, Fontana Paperbacks.

Shawcross, William, 1984a. 'The Burial of Cambodia'. *The New York Review of Books*, 10 May.

Shawcross, William, 1984b. *The Quality of Mercy*. Bangkok, DD Books.

Shorto, H. L., Judith Jacob, E. H. S. Simmonds, 1963. *Bibliographies of Mon-Khmer and Tai Linguistics*, London, Oxford University Press.

Snepp, Frank, 1977. *Decent Interval*. New York, Random House.

SPK, PRK news bulletin, Phnom Penh.

Stuart-Fox, Martin & Bunheang Ung, 1985. *The Murderous Revolution*. Chippendale Australia, Alternative Publishing Cooperative Limited.

Suksamran, Somboon, 1977. *Political Buddhism in Southeast Asia*. London, C. Hurst & Company.

Summary of World Broadcasts. See Biblographical Note.
*Szajkowski, Bogdan, 1982. *The Establishment of Marxist Regimes*. London, Butterworth.
*Szajkowski, Bogdan, 1981 (ed.). *Documents in Communist Affairs—1980*. London, Macmillan.
Tân Huyên and Pham Thành, 1980. *Dât nu'o'c Campuchia*. Hanoi.
Thion, Serge, et Michael Vickery, 1982. 'Cambodge problèmes de la reconstruction'. *Asie du Sud-Est et Monde Insulindien*, Paris, tome XIIII, pp. 1–4.
Thomas, David & Headley, Robert K. Jr., 1970. 'More on Mon-Khmer Subgroupings'. *Lingua*, **25**, 1970, pp. 400–17.
Tichit, L., 1981 *l'Agriculture au Cambodge*. Paris, Agence de Cooperation Culturel et Technique.
Tìm hiêu dât nu'o'c Camuchia anh hùng, 1979. Hanoi, Nhà Xuât Ban Khoa Hoc Xã Hôi.
'Treaty of Peace, Friendship and Cooperation between the Socialist Republic of Vietnam and the People's Republic of Kampuchea', *SWB*, 20 February 1979, pp. A3/14–A3/16.
Ulam, Adam B., 1971. 'Soviet Ideology and Soviet Foreign Policy', in *The Conduct of Soviet Foreign Policy*, (eds), Erik P. Hoffman and Frederic J. Fleuron, Jr. London, Butterworth.
Vickery, Michael, 1977. *Cambodia After Angkor: the Chronicular Evidence for the 14th to 16th Centuries*. Ph.D. thesis, Yale University.
Vickery, Michael, 1982a. 'Democratic Kampuchea: CIA to the Rescue', *Bulletin of Concerned Asian Scholars*, **14**, No. 4, pp. 45–54.
Vickery, Michael, 1982b. 'Looking Back at Cambodia', in Ben Kiernan and Chantou Boua, *Peasants and Politics in Kampuchea 1942–1981*. London, Zed Press.
Vickery, Michael 1984. *Cambodia 1975–1982*. Boston, South End Press.
Vickery, Michael, 1985. 'Where Defense is Still the Priority'. *The Guardian*, 8 January.
Vickery, Michael T., 1986. 'Cambodia's Tenuous Progress'. *Indochina Issues*, **63**, January, Washington, DC. Center for International Policy.
Wain, Barry. *Asian Wall Street Journal*. 8 February 1983.
*Willmott, W. E., 1981. 'Analytical Errors of the Kampuchean communist Party'. *Pacific Affairs*, **45**, no. 2.
Y. Phandara, 1982. *Retour à Phnom Penh*. Paris, Éditions A.-M. Métaillé.
Yukanthor, Princesse P. P., 1955. 'Généalogies des familles princières du Cambodge'. Saigon, *France-Asie*, No. 112, October, pp. 248–58.
Zagoria, Donald S., 1962. *The Sino-Soviet Conflict 1956–1961*. Princeton, Princeton University Press.
Zide, Norman H., 1966. *Studies in Comparative Austroasiatic Linguistics*. The Hague, Mouton.

Newspapers

The Age (Melbourne)
Asian Wall Street Journal (Hong Kong)
Asiaweek (Manila)
Bangkok Post (Bangkok)
République Khmère (1970–5, Paris)
Cambodge (French-language newspaper 1947–51, Phnom Penh)
The Economist Quarterly Economic Review of Indochina (London)
Far Eastern Economic Review (Hong Kong)
Kampuchea (Phnom Penh)
Nagaravatta (Khmer-language newspaper 1936–42, Phnom Penh)
The Nation Review (Bangkok)
Pracheachon (Khmer-language newspaper, organ of the People's Revolutionary Party of Kampuchea, first number dated 12 October 1985. Phnom Penh)
Washington Post (Washington)

Bibliographical note

Two Khmer-language PRK newspapers which have been cited frequently are:

Kampuchea, Khmer-language newspaper, Phnom Penh, organ of the Front. It began publishing as a weekly in 1979, but its numbers were dated only by year until No. 64 of 4 December 1980. Through No. 59, only 'weekly'. With No. 60, 'every Thursday'. From No. 64, 4 December 1980, it began dating issues to the day.

Kong tap padiwat, 'Revolutionary Army', organ of the PRK armed forces. It began as a monthly, with No. 1 published in December 1979. It is dated by month and year until October 1980 when, with Nos. 11–12, it became bi-weekly. Then, from No. 31, 10 August 1981, it began to be dated on each 10th and 25th of the month. In late 1982 it began publishing thrice-monthly, on the 5th, 15th and 25th; and from No. 89, 7 July 1983, it has appeared every Thursday.

Summary of World Broadcasts is a publication of the British Broadcasting Corporation, printed and published by the monitoring service of the BBC. Citations here are from 'Part 3, The Far East'.

Index